Love, *Rita*

ALSO BY BRIDGETT M. DAVIS

The World According to Fannie Davis
Into the Go-Slow
Shifting Through Neutral

Love,
Rita

An American Story of Sisterhood,

Joy, Loss, and Legacy

~

BRIDGETT M. DAVIS

HARPER

An Imprint of HarperCollins*Publishers*

The names of some of the individuals featured in this book have been changed to protect their privacy.

HarperCollins books may be purchased for educational, business, or sales promotional use. For information, please email the Special Markets Department at SPsales@harpercollins.com.

FIRST EDITION

All photographs courtesy of the author.

Designed by Bonni Leon-Berman

Library of Congress Cataloging-in-Publication Data

Names: Davis, Bridgett M. author.
Title: Love, Rita : An American Story of Sisterhood, Joy, Loss, and Legacy / Bridgett Davis.
Description: First edition. | New York : Harper, 2025.
Identifiers: LCCN 2024026570 (print) | LCCN 2024026571 (ebook) | ISBN 9780063322080 (hardcover) | ISBN 9780063322103 (ebook)
Subjects: LCSH: Davis, Bridgett M.—Family. | Davis, Rita R. | Davis family. | African American sisters—Biography. | Authors, American—20th century—Biography. | African American women authors—20th century—Biography. | LCGFT: Biographies.
Classification: LCC PS3604.A9556 Z46 2025 (print) | LCC PS3604.A9556 (ebook) | DDC 813.6 [B]—dc23/eng/20240917
LC record available at https://lccn.loc.gov/2024026570
LC ebook record available at https://lccn.loc.gov/2024026571

24 25 26 27 28 LBC 5 4 3 2 1

For Queen Rita, and in memory of them all

For, while the tale of how we suffer, and how we are delighted, and how we may triumph is never new, it always must be heard. There isn't any other tale to tell, it's the only light we've got in all this darkness.
—*James Baldwin*

Unable are the loved to die / For Love is Immortality.
—*Emily Dickinson*

PREFACE

Rita and I grew up in a household of numbers. Because our mother was a number runner, numbers were many things—the name of the game that she ran, the digits that became lottery-style winners, the dollar amounts of the money she made or paid out, the digit-based interpretation of the people, places, and things we all dreamed about at night . . . Numbers out in the world took on special meaning, as any combination of them could become gifts from the Universe, translated into a bet played, and a win.

Pythagoras, the famous Greek mathematician from 550 BC, is attributed with saying, "The world is built upon the power of numbers." Rita and I believed in that power, and while we weren't active devotees to the ancient science of numerology, we de facto practiced it by paying attention to the numbers in our lives. We understood intuitively that numbers contain energy, and if we let them, they provide insight. One day, she and I sat down with our mother and figured out our own personal numbers—the numbers that followed us around, that revealed themselves as patterns in our lives. Mama's number was nine; my number was seven. And Rita's number was four. She had triple proof of this from birth: she was the fourth child, born in the fourth month, with four letters in her name.

Also, in numerology, every name has a vibratory number—obtained by translating the letters of a person's name into figures, then adding their totals and reducing them to primary numbers. Based on this calculation and her signature, *Rita R. Davis*, my sister's "name number," was also four. Fours continued to follow Rita throughout her life: She had four best friends, and four good years in her beloved downtown apartment with its views of the Detroit River; she retired at age forty. And she lived to be forty-four.

Our relationship as sisters has been shaped by the number four in profound ways: We were four years apart in age, i.e., she was four when I was born, her baby sister. And she was in my life for forty years. The power of Rita's personal number follows me into the writing of this book; I completed my memoir of her when Rita would've been sixty-seven. Six plus seven equals thirteen. One plus three equals four. That would've been a "four" year for her. Also, four years after I committed to writing this book, it's out in the world.

According to *The Complete Illustrated Book of the Psychic Sciences*, which sat on the bookshelf of our childhood home, the number four stands for steadiness, dependability, and endurance. Its solidity is represented by the square, the points of the compass, the seasons of the year, and the ancient elements of fire, water, air, and earth. Four is foundational in the world.

Rita was foundational to me.

I've organized this book around my sister's personal number by dividing the narrative into forty-four chapters, in honor of her years on earth; I've further divided those chapters into four parts, to represent the four phases of her life, or rather, because I love the metaphor of Rita's time on earth as a complex symphony, the four movements of her life.

In an important aside, twenty-two is a master number in numerology, which is powerful on its own but also in its primary form breaks down to the number four. After our first familial loss with the death of our father, and as the subsequent losses of loved ones kept coming, Rita and I were the constant family member in each other's lives for twenty-two years. Across the expanse of those years, Rita wrote twenty-two letters to me. I've saved each one, and those letters have inspired *Love, Rita*.

This is the story of Rita, and of us, told in fours.

Love, *Rita*

PROLOGUE

Rita and I stroll side by side along Fifth Avenue, surrounded by a throng of strangers, thrilled to be in New York and away from Detroit, enjoying this brief respite from everything we know. In a few months, a different kind of adventure awaits. I'm off to attend college in Atlanta; Rita's off to attend graduate school, also in Atlanta. My college and her university are walking distance from each other; our side-by-side futures shimmer before us.

Loss is barely behind us. Our beloved father died a month before, and our mother has treated us to this, our first trip together and our first time in New York, as a balm for our sadness. We are our parents' two youngest children. Our three siblings are twenty-five, twenty-nine, and thirty-one. They are adults, out in their worlds already, for better or worse. Rita and I are on the threshold of adulthood, yet still Daddy's girls. Mama knows that losing our father is hardest on us. And given our mother's intuitive understanding of each of her children, she surely saw this trip as an opportunity for me and Rita to strengthen our own wobbly relationship.

The Big Apple has provided us a whirlwind of distracted fun: We've gone to a disco, the Paradise Garage; we've sat on benches in Washington Square Park and people-watched; we've eaten strange new food in Chinatown; we've shopped and window-shopped—at Macy's, in the Village, on Madison Avenue. It's 1978, and we've seen our first Broadway musical, *The Wiz*, featuring Stephanie Mills as Dorothy and André De Shields as the wizard. (Rita declares as the lights go up, "Girl, I loved everything about that!" and she'll return to New York again and again to indulge her love of Broadway musicals.) We've taken touristy photos: beside the ABC logo on Avenue of the Americas and Fifty-Fourth Street; in the gilded lobby of the War-wick Hotel, where we're staying; beside the *Ain't Misbehavin'* poster at Manhattan Theatre Club moments before seeing our second all-Black musical. In the photos, I'm wearing outfits I've purchased at Winkelman's department store, where I work after school. Rita and I swap tops to expand our fashion choices; in one picture I'm wearing the long, loose hot pink tunic, and in another, she's wearing it. I'm experimenting with my hairstyle—a ponytail sticking up on one side. Rita declares that my "artsy" look fits right in here. Her endorsement will fuel my choice to move to New York a decade later.

When I was thirteen and Rita was already a sophomore in college, this is what I wrote about our relationship:

> Dear Diary,
>   You know, Regina and her sister Roslyn are super close, and even though Roslyn's in college they call each other up any time just to say hello. Well, maybe it's because they're closer in age than Rita and me. But I know every time Rita calls, she always asks for "momma" only. And, I don't even call her! I always thought we would become inseparable sisters. I guess not . . .
> Well, nothing to get upset about, I was merely thinking.

And now here we are, making our way up Fifth Avenue together. We've done *a lot* of walking today, and Rita's stride slows down around St. Patrick's Cathedral. She says we need to call it a day, because her leg is bothering her. "Really?" I snap. "Are you just trying to be like Mama?" Our mother's legs often ached, due to blood clots she suffered regularly. Mama couldn't walk for long periods of time; sometimes she'd say suddenly, "I need to get off my legs," and look for a place to sit. I don't want Rita to remind me more of our mother than my sister right now. I want this to be our bonding moment, want us to be united in that way I've fantasized about for so long.

Rita stops walking. "I can't believe you don't believe me," she says, hurt in her voice.

I stop too, fast-paced New Yorkers whizzing by us. "I just know how you can be sometimes," I say.

"And you can be so selfish!" she snaps.

Our bickering often flares up like this, fueled by our beliefs: I think Mama prefers Rita because she's so much like her, which I envy and resent. At first glance they look alike, share the "gift of gab" and the Zodiac sign of Taurus, have such similar handwriting that in a pinch she could forge our mother's signature. Rita thinks Mama spoils me because I'm the baby, which she envies and resents. She often tries to compensate by telling me what to do. I resist, can't believe how bossy she is. She pushes back, can't believe how hardheaded I am. We play out this dance of incredulity on a regular basis. Today, though, it's harder for me to take. I feel my hopes of a newfound closeness between us dashed on the spot, right here in the heart of New York City. For a moment, neither of us speaks, each fuming in disappointment.

"You just don't get it," Rita finally says, exasperated, now limping slightly. "Because you don't have to." Two years before, she was diagnosed with lupus, a chronic autoimmune disease, and the condition sometimes snatches her energy. I don't understand yet what it means that Rita suffers from lupus, only that when she received the diagnosis the whole family came together to be with her, including our father, long divorced from our mother. I do know that rest seems to help. But she's right that I don't really get it. I don't have to, and I don't want to. I can only handle one family misfortune. Or so I think.

"Fine, we'll just go back to the hotel," I say, with forced exasperation. I throw my arm out to hail a taxi, the way I've seen it done in movies, and eventually, but not right away, it works. We slip into the yellow cab, and as it pulls away from the curb, I am crestfallen. Our time together was going great, and now it isn't.

We return to our room at the Warwick Hotel, with its twin beds. Rita lies down, tired, in need of a nap. I gently pull her high-heeled wedges off her feet and, as she closes her eyes, Rita says to me: "Let's not fight, okay? It always upset Daddy."

This is true, and at the mention of him a double pang of grief and guilt crowds my heart. We have never before called a truce on our bickering, so this is something new. But, of course, we're different now. I nod, relieved that she wants what I want, and she drifts off to sleep. Losing Daddy—the unthinkable—is the big tragedy of our lives. If we honor his wishes, get along, the world will right itself a bit, and we'll be okay. We'll make it through.

I watch Rita closely as she naps atop the hotel room bed. Inexplicably, I place my hand atop her body, follow its outline; my palm rests lightly on the curve of her hip, my hand rising and falling with her breaths, her heartbeat in my fingertips. I feel both protective and silly. She's my big sister. She's steadfast and smart and ubiquitous. She doesn't need my protection. And yet, a feeling comes over me. Of duty. I reject it, wanting to bask in my status as baby of the family. I lift my fingers off her body, pull back. But it turns out, Rita isn't asleep. She opens her dark eyes and looks right into mine. "You have healing hands," she says to me in that hotel room in Midtown Manhattan, on that day so long ago.

Was she right? If so, why couldn't I save her? Why didn't I?

ONE

~

1

Our relationship as sisters began this way: As I lay in my French Provincial baby bed, crying my newborn cry, four-year-old Rita came into the room, looked down on me, and said, "Shut your damn mouth!"

Just then, our mother stepped out of the closet, shocking Rita so badly, she ran out of the room. Mama liked telling this story in a bemused way, as an apt example of how jealous Rita was of me, from the start. And how terrified my sister was of having gotten caught saying "damn" in earshot of our no-nonsense mother. Of course, she'd been usurped as the baby, and of course, Rita didn't like that. Now, parenting experts say jealousy is normal, and you should expect your older child to grieve when a new baby arrives, to mourn what's been lost. Our mother certainly wasn't surprised by Rita's jealousy, but I can't imagine she had much tolerance for it. She would say she "did for" all her children equally, so it was uncalled-for. Besides, Rita never owned up to any jealousy. By the time she was well into her teens, after hearing Mama tell the story yet again to a new listener, Rita found the language to give her account of that early encounter with me. She said: "Obviously, my emotional needs weren't being met."

I used to shake my head and lightly chuckle when she said that. What emotional needs? She was four! But she was serious. Now I look at that moment as a freeze-frame, and what was going on outside the frame, and I suspect Rita was onto something. Mama might've been showering me with extra attention, beyond the fact of my newborn status. There are reasons for that. Rita was born when our parents were struggling so bad, the only place they could afford to live was on a street called Delaware, in a cold-water flat within an overcrowded ramshackle tenement on Detroit's dangerous side of town, with rats and roaches everywhere, fire a constant danger, and coals to heat the furnace a rare luxury. It was bad. And it went on for two years. Rita had no memory of life on Delaware Street, but her body likely remembered it, and the stress of poverty.

Just before I came along, the family's fortunes had improved. Our mother, Fannie, had launched a small, underground numbers business two years before, in 1958, where she took in customers' bets on three-digit numbers, paid out their winnings when they hit, collected their wagered money when they didn't, and profited from the difference. The enterprise was now bringing in steady, modest profits, and being a businesswoman likely did distract our mother from focusing on her four-year-old. Rita, her baby girl, was *also* likely the source of our mother's motivation—to figure out how to make a way out of no way. Success allowed Fannie to, by the time I did come along, bring a child into the world the way she'd always wanted. Now our parents were living in a more spacious flat in a four-family house in a safer, colored working-class neighborhood where she planted flowers out front every spring. In the version of the story that I've always been told, my arrival was eagerly anticipated, with the baby's room decorated just so; our mother had now created a stable life for her family. Hence the French Provincial baby bed.

Yet here's a fact: even though our mother never drank nor smoked nor used drugs—she lived right, as they say—I was born two months premature. And while 411 happens to be a lucky number in the mythology of the numbers, my being only four pounds, eleven ounces is also a low birth weight. Long after our mother went home, I spent weeks in Henry Ford Hospital, inside an incubator, keeping warm as my lungs developed. Newborn intensive care units, or NICUs, hadn't yet been invented. Was I showered with such affection upon my birth because I'd made it, because I'd managed to live, had not died from being born too soon?

This is important to note because Mama had a baby girl that didn't make it; Rita and I had a sister we hadn't known we had, and that we'd lost. I stumbled upon her death certificate on Ancestry.com. She was born at the segregated Riverside Sanitarium and Hospital in Nashville, Tennessee, on February 19, 1955. She lived for one hour and

fifteen minutes. Cremated that day, at the same hospital, she was unnamed. The cause of death was prematurity.

Soon after, my parents, John T. and Fannie, migrated north with
their daughter, Deborah, and son, Anthony. (Their six-year-old
daughter, Selena Dianne, stayed in Nashville with my mother's
sister, who convinced my parents that life up north would be hard
enough with two children; and Selena Dianne would be well-cared
for, joining the family as soon as they got on their feet.) Fourteen
months after losing that baby girl, our parents had Rita. She was
their first child born in Detroit, the harsh place they now called
home, and our mother was just shy of twenty-eight years old, now
caring for three children between the ages of newborn and eight; she
had little time to process her grief, her loss; I can only imagine the
stress on her body.

The fact of our sister's brief life is right there on Rita's birth certificate, and mine, where the question reads: "How many other children
were born alive but are now dead?" and the answer inside the little
box is "1." Not stillborn (there's a separate box for that) but born alive,
now dead.

Mama never talked about the baby she lost. In fact, let her tell it,
spacing her children out had been intentional—we were all four years
apart except for the oldest girls, two years apart. "A child should be in
school before another one comes along," Mama would say, controlling
the narrative. Our older sisters, who were eight and six when their little sister died (our brother was two and a half) never talked about the
loss either, about what that felt like knowing their mother was having
another baby, and then seeing her come home without one. Did they
feel something had been taken from them too?

More revealing is that Rita and I never discussed the lost baby.
Rita always seemed to have intimate knowledge of our family's business, figured out ages and amounts and dates, liked to add things
up, do the math. Rita knew exactly how much Mama had paid for
our family home—$16,700—back in 1961, when Rita was barely five
years old. "I don't even know how I know," she once said to me. She

just knew things. But she and I never talked about the baby girl who lived and died on the same day back in February 1955.

We didn't know, or didn't want to know, or chose not to acknowledge what we knew: Rita was conceived and born in the shadow of another child, in the aftermath of loss. As it was, she almost didn't make it either.

Fannie was newly pregnant when two white men in Mississippi tortured and murdered fourteen-year-old Emmett Till, his battered and deformed face put on view by his mother for the world to see. "I almost had a miscarriage when I saw that photo," Mama told us, about the image published in *Jet* magazine, shock and grief overcoming her as the new fetus was barely taking hold. Did she open to that page in *Jet*, see the image of Mamie Till looking down on her child's brutalized face as he lay in the casket, and instantly have sharp abdominal pains? Some bleeding? Did she rush to the county hospital to get checked out? Was she treated well there, or her symptoms dismissed because she was a poor Negro woman? Was Mama beside herself, terrified of losing another baby so soon? What was that pregnancy like for our young mother, far from her large Nashville clan, in this cold city up north where a better life might not ever work out?

After Mama saw that terrorizing image in *Jet*, I suspect genetic changes to her DNA began right then and there, as scientists now believe happens after a person experiences trauma. I believe she passed along those genetic markers to her unborn child. And I believe our mother's own grandfather's traumatic life of childhood slavery was passed down in his cells to his daughter, *her* mother, born in the nineteenth century and listed in the US census as a "mulatto" girl, with all the implications of violence upon the body that brings.

I imagine what got passed along in our ancestor's eggs. And sperm. Our father experienced his own harrowing tragedy as a young man, losing two younger brothers who were drowned. Surely, he brought that early trauma to the conception.

As Dutch biologist Frans de Waal reminds us: "We are bodies born of other bodies."

Delivered at Trumbull General Hospital, Rita came breech, buttocks first, a difficult birth. Mama said that one was the hardest of all her deliveries, and she half joked that after Rita was born, she never did fully straighten out her back, never walked quite the same again. Breech deliveries are rare, only 3 to 4 percent of all births. In recent decades, the accepted medical wisdom is that when a baby is breech and unlikely to turn, a Cesarean is scheduled, because babies die from vaginal breech deliveries at a rate of up to three and a half times more frequently than those delivered via C-section. It's a complicated, dangerous, and risky birth. Much can go wrong, including a compressed or twisted umbilical cord depriving the baby of oxygen or harming its limbs; if babies don't die, they could end up with spinal cord injuries, broken bones, or seizures. The mother could die. Physicians now know that only those with experience and a clear understanding of vaginal breech births should even attempt to deliver babies this way.

Thanks to research, we also now know that Black babies delivered by white doctors are up to 58 percent more likely to die than those delivered by Black doctors. And that includes vaginal births. Thus, what's delicately called "implicit bias" means a white doctor works less hard to save a Black baby's life because said doctor believes that baby is inherently less human, less valuable than a white baby, and so when the infant dies, said doctor's first thought is, *Too bad*, rather than, *Oh God, no!* The statistic is sobering and hits me viscerally. When I was pregnant with my son in 1999, because of fibroids growing alongside him, he never turned, and so my African American female ob-gyn scheduled a C-section. But three days before our planned date, my water broke, and I rushed to the hospital to meet my doctor. Yet the white male attending physician saw how advanced my labor was and said to me, "We may just have to deliver him naturally." I yelled, "No!" and insisted we wait for my doctor to arrive. I had in my mind the story handed down by my mother of how difficult Rita's breech birth was, and I did not want to chance it. Luckily, my Black woman doctor—who'd been waiting for me elsewhere in the hospital, unaware that I'd arrived—appeared soon after, and we had just enough time to prep me for the C-section before she delivered my healthy baby boy. Back in the 1950s, those white doctors just went for it while those Black mothers went through excruciating pain and fear, as they pushed for dear life and hoped for the best.

Why do some babies never turn in their mother's bellies? Why don't they prepare to be born? No one knows exactly why. Yet research now suggests that third-trimester fetuses in the womb can learn and remember just as well as newborns, and part of what they learn, based on what their mothers go through during pregnancy, is whether the world outside the womb is safe and healthy or dangerous and toxic. Was Rita, with this knowledge already stored in her body, afraid to be born into a dangerous and toxic world? Is that why she never flipped over so she could make her determined way through the birth canal headfirst? Was it a protective response to the wordless story of danger she'd already, in vitro, been fed? Was trauma already stuck in her little body?

Scientists also believe if the fetus's mom experiences trauma or earlier trauma causes a variety of stress hormones to get released in her body, the baby may begin life outside the womb with less of a sense of safety and coherence. I imagine baby Rita knowing intuitively that once she left her watery warm home, an unsafe and incoherent world awaited. And I can imagine why she hesitated.

In the end, Rita pushed through.

Mama would tell her, at a difficult moment in her life, "You can make it. You're a fighter. Lord knows, you fought hard to get here." I think about how hard Mama fought to get Rita here, so soon after losing a different baby girl, and how she herself survived through such a harrowing delivery. Rita and Mama fought *together* to be here, which created its own special connection between them. When you fight to live and win, you feel protective of and territorial over the one you fought with, like what happens between fellow soldiers. You bond over your mutual survival.

And yet, more than once, Rita said to me: "I didn't ask to be born. I didn't ask to come here."

That comment takes on new meaning now that I know the exact conditions of her birth. Yes, she fought to be here, but not before she tried to stay in the safety of Mama's womb, and once she *was* born, into an uncertain and possibly unsafe world, it's like she was saying to our mother, *I still need you so much. Tend to me. Tend to me. Tend to me.*

Now I better understand what Rita brought into the room with her that day when she didn't know our mother was in the room too, what she must've absorbed and understood as she looked down on me, the interloper. I imagine the worst-case scenario playing in her four-year-old mind before she ever opened her mouth to insist that I shut mine.

2

Was the story itself proof of our dynamic as sisters, or was our mother repeatedly telling the story what shaped our dynamic?

All I know is this: hearing Mama recount that anecdote of Rita telling baby me to *shut my damn mouth* made me never want to do anything to intensify or justify her jealousy. And so, in some essential way, that anecdote helped define our relationship. I imagine in that moment, when Rita admonished me, I stopped crying; I did what she demanded. I deferred to my sister.

Maybe that's the precise moment when it all began, when I tried not to make too much noise around her, tried not to steal her thunder. Growing up, I always felt I had been given more than Rita, and that made me feel I should defer to her as compensation, make space for her to shine. Even as I write this, I'm embarrassed that I felt that way, and that I continued to feel that way, but I did. The proof for me was that I *was* the baby, doted on. Plus, I did better in school, had bigger breasts, longer and thicker hair, a straighter nose and smaller lips, no weight problem. I was now the daddy's girl. And later, when we were young adults, I didn't have a chronic illness.

To be honest, I never *felt* her jealousy toward me. I assumed it, because Mama had stated it as fact, but I didn't *experience* it. Rita's jealousy never translated to her wishing less for me, not being happy for me, not wanting the best for me, resenting me. In fact, I never sensed that she wanted what I had, physically or otherwise. She didn't even seem envious of all the time I spent with our father. Rita knew Daddy loved her too, so she wasn't worried about that. She wanted our mother's attention. As much of it as possible. Most of it, in fact.

Obviously, my emotional needs weren't being met was her way of saying she didn't understand why Mama wasn't more focused on her, more of the time. Because Mama's attention—and the attention Rita gave back to her—nourished my sister beyond anyone's understanding. In fact, the definition of "jealousy" that most defines Rita's behavior is "fiercely protective or vigilant of one's rights or possessions." Rita was fiercely protective of our mother. She tolerated sharing Mama, but she was not happy about her doing a whole lot for other people, siblings included. Rita was often jealous of whoever took Mama's attention away from her, and while that was not exclusive to me, it certainly included me. After all, they'd survived together to be here.

~

Within days of the family moving into a four-family flat in that nice, working-class neighborhood, two-year-old Rita, still the baby of the family, met Elaine. Elaine went downstairs to take out the trash, and there was a little girl sitting on the stairs. She had on no undershirt, no shoes, just a diaper. Her hair was wild. Elaine thought to herself, *This little girl is lost. I better take her home with me.*

She asked her name, and the little girl said, "Rita." Elaine dropped the trash bag into the bin, picked up Rita, and carried her up the stairs into her home. She screamed as loud as she could, "Grandma! Grandma! I found a baby! I found a baby!"

Her grandmother came into the kitchen, took one look at Rita in Elaine's arms, and laughed. "That baby is not lost. That's Fannie's baby."

"Who's Fannie?" asked Elaine.

"The woman who just moved in downstairs with her family."

Elaine still wasn't convinced. "No, this baby is lost, because there was nobody out there with her."

"She was just sitting there playing, Elaine."

"Well, can we keep her?"

Her grandmother proposed another idea. "Why don't you go and ask Miss Fannie if the child can stay upstairs and play with you?"

Elaine went to meet Miss Fannie and did just that.

"How old are you?" our mother asked.

"I'm ten," said Elaine. "And I'm a good babysitter."

"Well, I know where to find you," said our mother, twinkle in her eye as she gave Elaine permission to "babysit" two-year-old Rita.

"Every day I looked forward to going downstairs, picking up Rita," recalls Elaine. "Getting her dressed, taking her to the store, taking her with me to the Laundromat, playing games, or just spending time with her."

So began a lifetime love. "I'd always wanted a little sister," explains Elaine. "I had prayed and asked God for one, but it hadn't happened. Then Rita came into my life. I really believe she was an answer to my prayer."

Rita had real big sisters. Selena Dianne was nine, but Rita didn't know her yet; she was still living in Nashville with our aunt Florence, soon to make the migration north to be with the rest of the family. Our brother, Anthony, was six and didn't play with Rita because he had boys in the neighborhood for that. Our sister Deborah Jeanne was turning twelve, and she much preferred books over a toddler.

There was no big sister just fourteen months older than Rita, who would've been a ready-made playmate, a bestie. Did she feel the absence of her phantom sister? Was she lonely for her without knowing she was? And did she sense herself a replacement child, born in the shadow of the lost baby girl, bearing the brunt of our parents' unprocessed grief?

When ten-year-old Elaine swooped in, filling a vacuum in Rita's life and her own, the two created a bond that stayed strong, and stayed necessary. Meanwhile, Selena Dianne, whom we all referred to by her middle name, rejoined the family, and she and Elaine—the same age—became fast friends. For the next two years, Elaine doted on Rita even as her bond with Dianne deepened; she became our designated cousin largely in charge of keeping Rita entertained. And then I was born, but twelve-year-old Elaine's attention didn't shift from Rita. "Just like a baby sister, she wanted to go with me everywhere I went," recalls Elaine. "And so, I took her."

That fall, when I was three months old, Mama enrolled Rita in a kindergarten class, even though she was still four years old, something allowed back then. That decision was the first step toward setting Rita on a trajectory of being the youngest in her grade; today, most school districts require children to be five or turning five before they begin kindergarten. Education experts came to know more about a child's maturity and its importance in a school setting. The thinking now is that younger children in kindergarten can be at a disadvantage physically, emotionally, socially, and intellectually. But I can understand why our mother made that choice back then, her hands full running a numbers operation while raising five children between the ages of infant and thirteen.

Before Rita could complete her kindergarten year, and as I was turning one, our mother moved the family into a four-bedroom redbrick New England–style Colonial in northwest Detroit. Mama had hit the number for good money, used the proceeds for a down payment, and promptly entered into a risky arrangement to buy the house "on contract" from a white man named Mr. Prince. Buying directly from a seller was Mama's only option, and not just because she was an off-the-books wage earner; nearly all Blacks were kept from traditional mortgages vis-à-vis redlining, which deemed anywhere Blacks lived or tried to live as "high-risk," allowing banks and other lenders to refuse loans to Black homebuyers. This practice was ensured and enforced by federal housing policy "that could well have been culled from the Nuremberg laws," as one urban studies expert, Charles Abrams, noted as far back as 1955. Despite those race-based hurdles and the predatory, high-interest contract she had to sign, our mother pulled it off, and as she crossed the threshold of our new home, she stepped us into the middle class.

A good thing though it was for the family, moving is a big change in a child's life. I wonder, did Rita abruptly leave her kindergarten class before it ended that June? Or did our father drive her every day back to the old neighborhood to finish out the school year? Did she instead transfer for the last two months to Winterhalter Elementary, near our new house, becoming the new girl at school? Did she have a best friend in her old kindergarten class that she had to suddenly leave behind? What about our cousin Elaine? Did she miss her? And did the family celebrate her fifth birthday, just two weeks after we all moved into our new home? Did Rita get to have a party?

~

Rita met her childhood best friend, Linda, in second grade. Linda remembers it this way: Rita was always impeccably dressed, her clothes "fashionable and crisp," as she put it. (I can imagine our mother dressing six-year-old Rita in shiny patent leather shoes, cute jumpers, lace ankle socks.) "She was sharp every day," recalls Linda, and they bonded over being the two well-dressed Negro girls at school. Both would get their classwork done quickly, and then "run our mouths," says Linda; people called them both Chatty Cathy, like the popular doll that talked in a tumble of phrases whenever you pulled her string. The teacher's response to the girls' chattiness was to give them more classwork.

One day on the playground, Linda pointed to a white teacher's aide and said, "Ooh, look, Rita! That woman got skinny legs!" Maybe Rita laughed? Anyway, the aide heard Linda's comment, and reprimanded them both in front of everyone on the playground; they were sent to the principal's office. Their mothers had to come up to the school—Linda's mother having to miss time at work. Both moms insisted that these were just little girls—seven or eight at most—so why the harsh discipline? It made no sense. Sixty-plus years later, Linda is still upset by this. "That was terrible, the way they punished us," she says. "And I didn't even say anything *to* that woman! I was talking to Rita!"

Now we have data showing that despite *not* being more disruptive, Black girls in school receive more severe penalties than white girls for the same behavior. Back then, in early '60s, before white flight, the girls were minority students at the school, and thus deemed de facto troublemakers. Linda recalls that Rita's umbrage over the playground incident came from the fact that she was punished just for being there. "Why am I in trouble?" she kept asking. "I didn't even say anything!" From the time I can remember, Rita hated to see anyone unfairly blamed or mistreated, and I wonder, did that incident prompt her visceral reaction to such wrongdoing? She and Linda bonded over this injustice they'd experienced together and started going to each other's houses after school. But as the years passed, they mostly did their visiting over the phone. "My mother could not understand what we would talk about," says Linda. "Because Rita and I could talk for two hours, hang up, call each other back, talk some more. Like we were grown women."

People often used that word to describe Rita when she was still a child. Folks said she looked "so grown." It's true that she had her face early; she was one of those people who always looked like themselves, from the start. And even though she wasn't that much older, because she liked to boss me around when we were young, I certainly came to feel she acted *grown-ish*. But back then, Rita was clearly a little girl, always younger than everyone else in her grade. Could that explain why Linda remembers Rita in those years as a crybaby? "Rita cried about everything," recalls Linda. "It would get on my nerves! I would say, 'Quit your crying!' She was very sensitive."

I think about what could've made Rita so sensitive, as Linda described her. I do know this: despite the nice house we lived in, our family's hold on the middle class was tenuous at best. Mama had just become her own numbers boss; she needed her business to grow and succeed, so that we could keep our family home. Our father was working the assembly line at General Motors, but it wasn't steady employment, as he'd get laid off indiscriminately, and his health wasn't good. Adding to the pressure was that shaky land contract Mama had signed, allowing the seller to take back the house if she missed just one payment.

Meanwhile, everything about the numbers was high-risk: Mama had to worry about "busting out" if too many customers hit for too much money; she had to worry about getting robbed or our home burglarized by those who knew about her cash business; and most of all, she had to worry about getting caught by authorities. That year, the city's famous Gotham Hotel, known to be a numbers headquarters, was raided in an over-the-top ambush that involved Detroit police and US Treasury agents. Forty-one people were arrested. I'm sure Rita didn't know about the bust per se as a second grader, but that had to be unnerving for our mother, who couldn't afford to get arrested, nor leave the numbers alone. I was only a two-year-old, oblivious. But Rita was old enough to pick up on and absorb that anxiousness moving through the air. And the Gotham bust reinforced our mother's insistence that none of her children reveal the family secret. That's an especially big burden on a six-year-old. But Rita carried the secret in her belly throughout her childhood, telling no one what happened inside our walls—not even her best friend, Linda.

Many years later, when they reignited their friendship as young adults, the first thing Linda noticed about Rita was that she no longer resembled that weepy girl of their childhood, that she'd become tougher. Linda asked her, "What happened?"

"I learned that you've got to stop doing all that crying," said Rita. "People don't care."

3

The earliest memories I have of Rita are when I'm five and she's nine; they come to me in flashes. In one, we're walking the four blocks together to Winterhalter Elementary, where I'm in kindergarten and she's already in fourth grade. Sometimes she shares her Now and Later candy with me on the way to school; she knows that the apple flavor is my favorite. In another, Mama insists that Rita "take your little sister with you" when she goes outside to play. Rita drags me along grudgingly, pulling me by the hand as she makes her way up the street, around the corner to Buena Vista. I watch from the sidelines as she plays jacks and Hula-Hoops and jumps rope with her neighborhood friends. Once, returning home before the streetlights come on, she holds my hand in hers and stands still, looking up at the late-day sky, marveling. "Wow," she says. "Can you believe there's a sun on every block?" I think it's a wondrous discovery, and we count suns together as we run the few blocks home.

In another flash of memory, Rita consults me before wearing a certain outfit to school. "Does this look good together?" she asks as we stand before our twin closets in our bedroom. "Does this blue match this red?" I'm super proud that Rita is taking fashion advice from me, her little sister. Years later, despite our different body types, we realize we're the same size in tops; we pool our money to buy expensive silk blouses and blossomy tunics and plush sweaters to share, swapping and wearing them with our own separate skirts or jeans—as we did on that first trip to New York. When one of us receives a compliment while wearing a shared top, the other says, "It's mine too."

No photos exist of Rita before the age that I first remember her. In fact, there are zero baby photos of any of us five siblings. I do have in my possession a few treasured black-and-white photos of us as children: one of Dianne holding my mother's hand as a little girl; another of Anthony, as a toddler, sitting in the middle of the floor of our grandparents' front room; another of Deborah dressed up for

Easter, age five. And I have a handful of color photos of me: in one, I'm about three, sitting on my heels in a dining room chair; in another, I'm graduating kindergarten, a mortarboard I made from construction paper atop my head.

But for Rita, there aren't *any* little-girl pictures. It's as though she came along at such a rough moment in our parents' newly migrated, impoverished lives that the lack of documentation is deliberate, a way to block out a painful memory. But that absence of any image of her as a small child also has the odd effect of reinforcing the idea that she never got to be one, was robbed of her little-girl-ness, the lack of photographic proof itself proof. What does remain are a handful of random photos of Rita as an older girl of unspecific age; in one taken on Christmas morning, she sits in a chair, Anthony behind her on the couch clowning for the camera. Her hair is long and free, and her legs are on display, already shapely. She's maybe ten, her face serious as she looks at the camera. Most of the other photos I have of Rita from that time period oddly show her wearing a plaid skirt. When I study these images closely, I can tell they are two different plaid skirts from three different days, different times. One is taken at a party, and captures her dancing, doing the jerk in her plaid skirt with a white turtleneck and rust-colored sweater—dressed for a day of school while a cousin captured in the frame wears a party dress. Her attire seems so practical and no-nonsense, the way I remember her back then. I wonder: Did I help her choose her outfit that day?

~

When I think about why Rita and I weren't closer growing up, I always blame our four-year gap in age for essentially putting us in two completely different social universes. But what I hadn't thought about until now is that Rita started her period when she was nine. By the time I was consciously aware of her as my sister, by the time she was captured in those random photos as a child, she was already bleeding monthly—saddled with a teenager's responsibility in the fourth grade.

Once Rita told our mother that she had blood in her panties, Mama turned to our seventeen-year-old cousin Elaine to help Rita navigate it all. Elaine can still recall the enormous responsibility she felt as she drove Rita to the store to purchase Kotex, and showed her how to use the pads, how to prepare herself so no one would see a lump in her pants at school. "Kids will tear your nerves up asking questions," Elaine recalls Fannie telling her, so she encouraged Elaine to show Rita how to go undetected by buying her tight black shorts to wear on top of her underpants. "If you have an accident, you won't have to worry about it getting on your clothes," Elaine explained to Rita. But she also warned her: "Always wear dark clothes during that time of the month."

Elaine also bought Rita a small bottle of feminine hygiene spray and a little makeup bag to hide the spray and pads inside, and told her to keep that in her book bag, so nobody would know she had her period. She bought Rita a calendar and explained to her that every twenty-eight days her period would come and taught her to keep track so "you'll be prepared, and it won't sneak up on you, when you might be somewhere and get embarrassed." She taught her how to dispose of her pads by wrapping them up in newspaper to avoid any odor. "She paid attention to all that, and I never had to have a conversation like, 'You need to get these soiled pads out of here,'" says Elaine, pride still in her voice. To prepare her for menstrual cramps, Elaine got Rita a heating pad and some Midol. "These will help you 'cause if your stomach is hurting so bad, you may feel like screaming, and that's okay," Elaine explained. And if Rita ever didn't want to go to school, because of the cramps, "Just tell your mother and she'll understand," Elaine advised her.

"Rita was very shy about it all," Elaine recalls. "I can imagine being in elementary school and so little and so young, that she really didn't want to hear all that." Elaine didn't start her own period until she was almost fifteen, so she had great compassion for Rita. Once she told her all that she must do during that time of the month, Elaine explained what it all meant. She told her: "It's like you're a young lady even though you're a little girl." Rita listened, recalls Elaine. "And she asked questions too." She wanted to know what that meant, being "a young lady." So Elaine talked to her about sex—sort of. "I had to say, 'You cannot play with boys anymore, especially when it's that season for you.'" Elaine added, "Do not play those hide-and-seek games anymore. You don't want to get tricked in some kind of way and end up having a baby."

How did nine-year-old Rita handle all that? "She was just quiet and concerned and reflective," says Elaine, looking back. "She handled it, took it in stride; you never saw stains on her pants, and she was always fresh and clean. No problems with boys. Really, she did very well, and when I think about it, she was always mature, even as a little girl."

My question is: Did maturity come first for Rita, or the necessity for it?

Entering puberty so early, having to worry about all the issues around menstruation, and having no girlfriends in her grade-school class to talk about it with, must have been lonely and isolating for her. We now have language for how menstruating affects Black women: *period trauma*. Studies show that Black girls are three times more likely than white girls to begin menstruating before age eleven. But those studies cannot answer why that is, why Black girls are robbed early of that particular girlhood innocence. Researchers, looking for some genetic marker—alongside signs of poverty, poor diet, and violence—don't consider the obvious: that for a Black girl like Rita, who began life with inherited societal trauma, compounded by lived-in stress from both home and school, that very stress and trauma wreaked havoc on her body, in the form of too-soon puberty.

For years, Rita suffered terrible premenstrual and menstrual headaches. Would a school nurse have taken her cramps and discomfort and pain seriously back then, when the word about Black girls was that most of them were "fast," too mature for their own good? Would she have been unconsciously judged for even being on her period at such a young age? Rita was the opposite of "fast," innocent really, yet older boys did like her because, as Elaine puts it, "Rita was attractive *and* mature. She spoke well, could handle a conversation. That's what made people think she was older."

My own daughter started her period at age nine, and when a "friend," a white woman, found this out, she told my visiting daughter to "sit over there" away from her nine-year-old twin boys, just in case my daughter "had any ideas." Again, she was *nine*, but to this white woman's eyes, she was a sexualized Black girl lusting after her boys.

Rita hated starting her period in fourth grade, with those awkward and bulky Kotex napkins between her legs, held in place by those tight shorts as she walked to school, ran on the playground, played tag. She kept that time of the month a secret, embarrassed by it. I was no support, a five-year-old and clueless. In my fantasy, I imagine her with the lost baby girl, close in age to Rita like an Irish twin, also menstruating. I see the two sisters going through their menses together, rubbing each other's crampy tummies and sharing a bathroom stall at school as they change their bloody pads.

Funny that I can't remember Rita and me together during the city's 1967 racial uprising, which news media and the world forever dubbed "the Detroit riots" and Black folks named "The Great Rebellion." After police busted an after-hours joint and arrested everyone inside, shoving and hitting them, a growing crowd of Black folks—filled with pent-up anger over constant police brutality—gathered outside; clashes ensued and quickly escalated, and that led to five days of chaos, violence, burning, and looting. Thousands of officers, National Guardsmen, and federal troops converged on the city to squash the protest. Armored tanks rolled down our block, and our father stood guard over our home each night, frightened the house might be set on fire by angry, frustrated rioters. Forty-three people died that week, most of them Black. I was turning seven and paralyzed with fear the whole time, but Rita was eleven, old enough to be both fearful *and* aware of our teenage brother out in those riotous streets as he rebelled with youthful rage. Because she was already an anxious, alert child, I can imagine Rita's fear laced with that knowledge—a frightening combination.

What I do remember is that once public school resumed that fall, Rita was quickly double promoted—skipping seventh grade and becoming an eighth grader. As the story goes, she finished her work early and talked a lot during class and therefore must be bored, so the solution was to give her "more challenging" work. Maybe her teachers decided she looked more mature than other seventh graders? Whatever the thinking, she suddenly found herself two years younger than her thirteen-year-old classmates. Today skipping a grade is frowned upon; parents and education experts are concerned that it creates loss of friendships, difficulty fitting in, and problems with emotional and physical maturity. But they did that kind of thing with Black students a lot back then. It was effectively a sly form of *social* promotion—advancing some students to the next grade regardless of how much they've learned just to get the "troublemakers" out of a teacher's class—masked as a reward. That's why, I suspect, Rita worked so hard to be a B student throughout junior high and high school—she'd been forced to skip an entire year of learning!—and perhaps why our mother adopted the motto within Rita's earshot that "If a child of mine earns a C she worked hard for, that means more to me than an easy A."

This created a wider gulf between me and Rita. You have even less in common with your little sister who's in second grade while you're in eighth. And yet, Winterhalter was an elementary school that went up to eighth grade, so while we didn't walk there together anymore—her classes now began earlier than mine—I did sometimes cross paths with her in the building. One day, I decided to wear the same thing to school that she'd worn, a cream-colored pleated knit dress with gold buttons on the bodice; our mother had bought one for each of us. I made a point of finding Rita in the lunch line and standing beside her. I'd like to say I did it as a way to bond with her, but I more likely did it to annoy her. And she was annoyed, mortified really, because her junior high friends laughed and teased her about her and her baby sister's matching dresses. Is that why she later made it clear that no one—me included—could ever again pick out clothes for her? Is that why Mama would say over the years, before taking a chance and buying her something, "She may return it. You never know what Rita will like. She's got her own taste"?

Speaking of her taste, in one of my favorite photos of Rita—undated, as nearly all our family photos are—she's standing in the walkway of our home, captured in her liminal, in-between-girl-and-woman space, both innocent and knowing. She's wearing a pink shell and matching pink jeans with a white sweater thrown over her shoulders, its sleeves hanging loosely at her sides. She has her hair up, with side bangs, and pink oval sunglasses sitting atop her head. She is petite and poses for the picture like a fashion model, one leg slightly bent. Behind her is the wide, empty street where we lived, making clear why the avenue was appropriately named Broadstreet. Also in the frame are the houses that stood across from ours, substantial brick structures, each wide and multistoried and majestic. A white car sits parked in front of one house, a late-'60s, sleek American model showcasing what gave Detroit its "Motor City" moniker. The street scene captured within the frame is still, peaceful. I've always loved this photo in part because Rita looks so '60s chic, but also because she has a quality about her that I seldom saw back then—at ease, without anxiousness, a body resting in motion. As she looks at the camera from the curvy path leading up to and away from our home, I try to imagine which scenario is most likely: Is she headed somewhere special, yet turns back to pose for the photo? Or is she returning from that special somewhere as she pauses to have her picture taken? Is she going toward the sill of the front door, its threshold, or has she just crossed it? Either way, she is facing home, her haven. When I look at that photo now across time and distance, I instinctively want to protect Rita—looking *grown-ish*, yet still so young.

~

In those latter years of the '60s, our household dynamic was largely nurturing, amidst bustling activity and escalating dysfunction. Mama's numbers operation required its own daily busyness, with customers constantly calling or coming by to place their three-digit bets and collect winnings. Phones and doorbells were forever ringing. Meanwhile our teenage brother and twentysomething sisters each had friends making steady treks down to our remodeled basement on weekend nights to hang out and party, as *the* place to be. Our mother's myriad friends also loved to drop in, and someone was always needing a place to crash, or visiting from out of town. Rita called our house Grand Central Station, and not in a positive way. Also, by then Deborah had begun experimenting with and soon became addicted to heroin. Anthony also got addicted to heroin. And Dianne had gotten involved with a drinking, irresponsible man our father despised. Daddy and Dianne argued bitterly about her boyfriend George; with Daddy saying, "I know all about no-good niggers like him," and Dianne lashing out at our father rather than listening to him.

In addition to all this, our parents had for a few years been living separate lives in the same household—one up, one down. I suspect that the divide in my and Rita's loyalties to our individual parents can be traced to that up-down living. It's as though, in such an arrangement, a daughter is forced to choose. Rita chose the upstairs-living parent, Mama, while I chose the downstairs-living parent, Daddy. Why this was had everything to do with my being the baby and our father's last symbol of togetherness with our mother, the love of his life; and it had everything to do with the bond between Rita and Mama that formed when Rita was being born into the world, and together they fought to be here.

Despite the separate living, I do remember specific occasions in those years when our father spent the night upstairs; he'd sleep curled up on the floor outside my and Rita's bedroom door, keeping guard over us; he didn't trust the teenage boys who'd have sleepovers down the hall in Anthony's room. By then, boys did crush on Rita, and men's eyes lingered on her too long. She was so-called developed for her age, with a pear-shaped body, round hips, and big, pretty legs. Yet she was an innocent, an eleven-year-old girl in eighth grade.

Every child is born into a different family, of course, and every child grows up differently in the same family. In those coming-up years, I was just young enough to be inured from much of the volatility. I could spend my days in the den with Daddy and live in my head, fantasizing about make-believe worlds, a dry run for becoming a writer. Rita wasn't so lucky. Already an anxious child, she naturally grew into an anxious adolescent. She was often nervous, stressed out, as she absorbed the family chaos even as she herself was going through the turbulence of puberty. From my child's point of view, she was worrying about "grown folks' business," but she couldn't help it. Whatever worried our mother worried Rita. And Mama was in a worry-inducing business. The daily question was always: Did anyone hit, and for how much? That question lingered over our days, until each evening, when the winning numbers were announced. I've come to describe that nightly experience as a tense silence moving through our home like a nervous prayer. Rita took on that daily stress, waiting to learn whether it had been a good day for Fannie, or a bad one. She was deeply invested in our mother's emotional and physical well-being. If Mama had a headache, or was upset, or slept a lot, Rita fretted. It's clear to me now that she suffered from anxiety, but we had no language nor luxury back then for such conditions. Rita was simply a "worrier," a child who took on too much.

In the midst of it all, she graduated from Winterhalter and began high school at age twelve. But I don't know what school she attended for ninth grade. Was it the nearby Mackenzie High, where our older siblings attended? Was it Mumford High, nearly four miles from our current home, the school she'd eventually graduate from? Did our father drive her to school for those first weeks? I don't know how or even where she experienced that huge rite of passage. I do look back and wonder: Who was looking out for her, checking up on young Rita throughout all the household chaos? How could her emotional needs have possibly been met?

5

Daddy moved out of the house in fall 1968. Rita and I never talked about our parents' separation, and soon after, their divorce; we never talked about what that meant for us, the two youngest girls. We just dealt with it. The biggest change with Daddy's absence was that I rejoined Rita every night to sleep in our double bed together, in our bedroom that we shared but that I'd never been in because I'd spent every night since age four downstairs in the den, curled atop Daddy's back. But after he was gone, and I shared a bed with Rita, I vividly remember a game she and I would play: Lifting our pajama tops, we'd take turns writing words on each other's backs with our index fingers. The trick was to try to guess what the other was writing, just from how she formed the letters on your skin. I recall that it was hard for me to guess those words, but once, Rita wrote the letters *S-I-S-T-E-R* across my narrow back, forming the letters in small strokes. The squiggly shape of the *S* tickled, and I giggled. I can still conjure her light touch on my back, and how good it felt when I guessed the right word.

This was many years before Rita's body sounded the alarm over the deep and persistent trauma that lived inside her, what Native Americans call a "soul wound." Back then, Rita figured out inventive ways to offset her anxiety: She "popped" gum constantly. She memorized her favorite Psalms. She talked a lot. And she wrote letters to God.

The letters were like a personal diary, but to a higher power. In these handwritten pleas, she asked God to heal a family friend's sick baby "in the name of Jesus Christ my Savior," and another friend's sick grandmother; she asked Him to "Please don't let 543 come out tonight," referencing a specific three-digit number that too many of our mother's customers had played, knowing that if it was the winning number, Mama would owe out a lot of money. "And please take away Mama's headaches," she wrote. She signed these letters, "Your loving servant, Rita."

In what I believe is her first letter to God, penned just a couple months after our father moved out and shortly after our sister Deborah overdosed and was gratefully revived, she simply wrote:

January 7, 1969

Dear God,
Please stop me from worrying.

Thank you,
Rita

She stuffed all these letters into the giant family Bible until her thirteenth birthday, when her godmother, Lula, gave her a Holy Bible of her own. It was a thick, white, zippered King James version produced for Sears, Roebuck & Co. and proclaimed itself "translated out of the Original Tongues and with the Former Translations diligently compared." In the back, among other reference materials, were a glossary of Biblical terms, a dictionary, a fact book, as well as maps of Palestine, Galilee, and Jerusalem. Color illustrations were interspersed throughout.

Lula, who was our mother's best friend, inscribed it:

To Rita with Love,
From God-Mother Lula
April 29, 1969

I hope you stay as sweet as you are, & always keep in touch with God, as you have started to do. He will never turn his back on you. His divine Love is the best you can have.
"Lula"

Her godmother gifted the Bible to Rita barely three weeks after our mother semisecretly remarried. While Rita and my other siblings intentionally kept this fact from our father, I was never told *not* to tell him that Mama had married someone else; I didn't feel any pressure. Honestly, I was only nine, and didn't tell Daddy because I didn't want to hurt his feelings. But Rita was so close to Mama that she *was* expected to keep the news from our father; clearly her loyalties lay with our mother. But I'm sure that was hard for Rita, because she was in some ways still a daddy's girl too.

Anyway, Rita treasured that Bible, and maybe she relied on it to help her get through those interminable months when she was thirteen and expected to hold yet another big secret in her belly. For many years, she kept that Bible on her nightstand, and whenever she passed by, she'd pick it up, bring it to her lips, and kiss it. The Bible's cover became worn in one circular spot from all those kisses. Later, as a woman who wore red-hued lipsticks, she'd leave a bright imprint of her full lips on that faded spot. I have her Bible now, and I can see traces of red where the sacred memory of her lips still lingers, decades later.

Back then, I marveled at Rita's love of God, her faith. We were not a go-to-church-regularly family, and in my earliest years I don't recall attending church at all. Perhaps on Easter? Nor do I recall our parents insisting that we be good Christians. Yet God was a given in our household. I sometimes placed my palm on Rita's Bible when no one was looking. I was intimidated by the book itself, both scared and curious about something I knew was big and important yet evaded my understanding. That's why a tinge of guilt hovered around me when I was in the presence of a Holy Bible. Yet Rita forged a healthy relationship with her personal Bible from the start, both revering it and refusing to be precious with it.

Trauma therapist Resmaa Menakem says African Americans have found ways over the years to be resilient by developing their own intuitive balms, "a variety of body-centered responses to help settle their bodies" and blunt the effects of trauma, of their soul wounds. He notes that many Black folks have used humming, singing, chanting prayer, rocking their bodies back and forth, or "getting happy" in church. Rita likely developed some of her resiliency, settled her own body, not only by popping gum and memorizing Psalms and writing letters to God. Kissing her Bible repeatedly was surely its own intuitive balm.

I wonder how she found her way to Him, how she managed to develop that one-on-one rapport, that intimacy, so young and all on her own. How did she already know she'd need God in her life?

~

Mama married our stepfather, Burt, in April 1969 and eventually moved us two youngest girls to a new house, to join her in a new life. But we didn't move for six long months, during which Rita and I still didn't tell our father what we knew—each of us for different reasons. In that time, Rita finished ninth grade, and started tenth, either in a high school a few miles from home, or one she knew she'd be leaving soon. She was really on edge, ready to get out of the limbo we were in; it was such a complicated time for her. I know because she wrote about these things in a letter to God:

Sept. 26, 1969

Dear God,
I know you are saying that I am changing. I curse and smoke. But I have stopped because I know it isn't right. Bless all my friends and enemies and forgive me for my wrong. Please let us hurry up and move in the new house.

Thank you,
Rita

So much about that letter makes me sad. Just thirteen years old, and secretly smoking. Angry enough to be cursing. Feeling shame for both, begging for forgiveness. Speaking of enemies. And really wanting to get out of that house on Broadstreet, where our brother and oldest sister were struggling with their heroin addictions. Also, the month before, our twenty-year-old sister Dianne had married her boyfriend, George, at the City-County Building, in a rushed decision that concerned her friends, as well as our parents. They all knew that George drank too much. No surprise that Rita was desperate to move, to escape. She was hoping that our new home life would bring some relief.

Even after we moved to live with our mother and new stepfather, neither Rita nor I told Daddy that Mama had remarried, still holding on to the secret for no good reason. Of course, Daddy was bound to find out. And he did, when he came to visit us at the new place and saw another man's clothes in the closet. I vividly remember how upset both Rita and I were by how hurt Daddy was, how worried we were about him, and Dianne trying to reassure us that he'd be okay.

I can't imagine high school was much fun for Rita. She didn't yet have a best friend at Mumford. That would come later. And as it turned out, even though things were supposed to be better in the new home, she still found a reason for writing to God: now her letters were focused on the stress and havoc that our new brother-in-law brought to all our lives. A few months after he and Dianne married, Rita wrote:

Feb. 5, 1970

Dear God,
I come to you again asking you to do me a big favor. Which is please let my mother win this suit against the man who hit my mother's car when George was driving, I have faith in you that she will win. This will be a everyday prayer. I ask this in the name of Jesus Christ my Savior, I'm asking.

Thank you,
Rita

And barely two months later, she wrote:

April 2, 1970

Dear God,
Please do me a favor and that is please let George be super safe
while driving my mother's car. He been drinking a lot. I ask this
in the name of Jesus Christ my Savior.

It stings to read these letters today, to know that she planned to
make that man's irresponsible drunk driving the focus of her "everyday prayer," that she felt the need to be concerned about our mother's
vehicular lawsuit that *he'd* caused, that his drinking worried her so.

No wonder one of Rita's favorite sayings as an adult was, "Kids
deserve to be kids."

6

She met her best friend from high school in an eleventh-grade civics class. Rita complimented Jill on her shoes, and also told her how smart she was; then Jill told Rita how smart *she* was. "And the rest was history," recalls Jill. "No reservations, no leeriness, just mutual acceptance."

Back then, Jill was going through a lot—with a depressed mother, an authoritarian father, and three younger brothers and a sister she had to babysit all the time. Our home was a reprieve. "The only freedom I had was when I'd come over to Rita's house after school," she recalls. Rita and Jill became tight, and our mom became Jill's de facto godmother. She came over a lot, and eventually, not right away but at some point, she was brought into the family's inner circle of confidence. Rita told Jill that our mother ran numbers. "It didn't feel like a gigantic revelation to me," Jill now says. "I was like, 'Oh, okay, no big deal.'"

But it was a big deal. That was our big family secret. Years would go by before I shared the same revelation with my own high school friend Stephanie. By the time Jill came into her life when she was fourteen, Rita understood that she needed to share our family secret with *someone*—something I wish I'd understood about myself back then—and she intuitively understood that that someone was Jill. In fact, when she began driving and our mother would send Rita to customers' homes to collect money they owed, Jill often rode alongside her in the car. "We'd go over to this neighborhood I'd never been to, but I understood it was where your family started out," says Jill. "The thing is, Rita had such a natural rapport with all those people! She knew how to laugh and talk with them, and you know, she could give great compliments. 'I really like your sofa,' or 'Your lawn looks good,' things like that. I was amazed that these folks were giving her money and seemed happy to do it! And she could really count that money too! I loved watching her count it . . . You know, the way Rita was with them, it felt almost festive."

Jill also could see that Rita, like our mother, was a giving person. Her generosity was something Jill was not used to at all, and it touched her heart. "There used to be a hamburger shop up on Wyoming," Jill recalls. "We'd go in there, and if Rita had a hamburger, I had half of it. It reminds me of what Ray Charles said about Quincy Jones: 'If I got a dime, Q's got a nickel.' That's the way Rita was."

Jill thinks about it now. "We were like sisters. Chosen sisters. We never brought that up, but we were."

Meanwhile, Rita wrote a long letter to God on New Year's Day 1971, showing that she had a lot on her mind. She made a list, projecting good outcomes for her loved ones that highlighted what she saw as going terribly wrong for some of them; this included an ominous request to Him about our brother-in-law:

Dear God,
Please help me and do a favor for me and my family.

1. I, Rita Davis, will not worry, have positive thinking and have faith in you.
2. My mother Fannie Robinson will be in good health and not worrying about things she have no control over . . .
3. Anthony Davis my brother will marry Renita and straighten up and get off the dope
4. My father will be in good health, get a job and be very happy with his children
5. Deborah Davis my sister will get a job, get off dope make my mother proud of her
6. Dianne/Selena Dickens will buy a home, George will continue to be nice to Dianne
7. Burtran Robinson my stepfather will stop suffering from his knees
8. Lula Isom my godmother will be in good health
9. My aunts Two-Tank, Alice, Big Sis, Florence, June, be in good health
10. My uncles Gene, John, Bob will be in good health

Jesus thanks a lot for letting me leave my prayers to the throne of grace.

This can be a year of happiness. If everyone tries.

Thank you,
Rita

Rita didn't include me in her list because she knew she didn't have to worry about me. I was thriving at Hampton Elementary, hanging out after school with my best friend Diane, reading Trixie Belden mystery books together, and spending most weekends with Daddy. I got good at losing myself in my own imagination or a book, oblivious as possible to our household dramas. I did *not* want to be a worrier like Rita.

Despite the concerns she penned to God at the start of the year, Rita did have some fun in '71. A highlight came that summer, when she got invited to her childhood friend Linda's Sweet Sixteen party at Top of the Pontch, located on the highest floor of Detroit's upscale Pontchartrain Hotel. This was her first formal affair, and Mama had the local designer Latrelle Powers create a custom gown for Rita, as if it were her own coming-out party. Latrelle was Detroit's top designer, having designed clothes for several Motown artists. The gown she made for Rita was floor-length, in soft pink raw silk, with a high collar made of silvery trim; it had a matching long, collarless coat whose sleeves were trimmed in the same silver. Mama's hairdresser friend did Rita's hair, attaching a "fall"—a hairpiece that cascaded into long curls down her neck. She wore bangs and a pink bow in her hair. The whole day was festive and filled with excitement and anticipation. Rita was going to a big, dressy party! With an escort! A professional photographer (or maybe an acquaintance with a "real" camera) came to take pictures. One photo captures Rita earlier that day, posing dramatically with one hand in the air, fingers spread like a dancer's, the other hand sitting elegantly on her thigh; her hair is already done up, save for her bangs still in a pink sponge roller. I can recall that day, how she and I danced around the house, getting down as Rita got ready. On the den's hi-fi, she played "Want Ads" by the group Honey Cone, and together we sang along to those exuberant lyrics: "Wanted! Young man single and free! Experience in love preferred but will accept a young trainee!" Yet it was James Brown's new single, "Soul Power," that we blasted on repeat. Daddy once said that the Godfather of Soul was "the only man alive who can release a song with just two or three words and make it a hit." Sure enough, JB belted out those two words over and over in his raspy, powerful voice, as we sang along with him:

> Know we need it, soul power!
> We got to have it, soul power!

I most remember how giddy Rita was, how freely she danced to the song, and how wonderful and rare it felt to watch my sister acting silly. I connect that moment to a shift in her, fifteen and entering her senior year of high school, open to whatever might come next. And when I now think about the driving repetition of James Brown's music, his two- and three-word lyrics, I see them as funk-infused mantras, a way to help us Black folks settle our bodies, develop some resiliency, blunt the effects of white resentment on our lives. We loved him so because every time James Brown chanted those words, he affirmed us. Poet Gregory Orr has said that popular music is a kind of lyric poetry, and not unlike poetry, the songs that you love deeply help you to live.

I relish the memory of that summer day in 1971, when James Brown's lyric poetry gave Rita new life, when his words healed her soul wound with some soul power.

Ironic that years later, in the '80s, James Brown met Rita in Atlanta and wanted to date her. She knew enough to decline. By then, it was no secret that James Brown was an abusive, violent man. He was arrested and charged with spousal abuse several times, which included savagely beating and attempting to kill his third wife. He spent two years in prison for holding others hostage at gunpoint. Rita liked his *music*, but that was it.

~

On her sixteenth birthday, Rita stepped out of our home's side door to find parked in the driveway a brand-new white Ford Mustang Mach I. Atop the car's roof sat a gigantic red bow. (I still wonder where our mother found that enormous ribbon.) She was both surprised and excited. She jumped into the car and drove straight to Jill's house on Santa Barbara, barely a mile away. When she arrived at Jill's, the bow was still on the roof.

Rita's new car was stylish and sporty, with black stripes running along its sides, what Mama called a "youthful" look. The Mach I was considered one of Ford's "performance vehicles," but none of us thought of that car that way. Rita never, ever drove fast. She was such a cautious driver that she avoided the freeway for years, and for the longest, she refused to make left turns against oncoming traffic. Wherever she was going, she'd figure out a way to get there by right turns alone.

I adored that car, with its white leather bucket seats and compact size—so much cooler than my parents' sedan models. I learned how to drive in the Mach I. When I was fourteen, Rita would let me take the wheel and practice in the parking lot of the church across the street. The gearshift was located between the seats, something I'd never seen in a car, and I loved that it mimicked a stick shift but had all the ease of an automatic. I snuck and drove Rita's car to joyride with my friends and our cousin Jewell long before I had a driver's license. Did Rita know? By the time I took the driving test to get my learner's permit, the instructor kept saying he was *very impressed* by my confidence behind the wheel, *very impressed.* Rita's Mustang launched my love affair with driving.

Beyond her generosity, Mama had good reason to gift Rita that car as soon as she was old enough to drive: Not long before, Rita had been abducted by a man as she was walking home from school one day. He gripped her arm and pulled her along several blocks, threatening her not to scream. Somehow, she managed to talk him into letting her stop at a gas station as they passed by, and miraculously she used its pay phone to call home. The men at our house rushed to where she was; I was terrified that they'd get there too late, that she'd be gone.

But she was there, and the men rescued her. "I can't believe he let you make that call" is all I could manage to say to her afterward. "I just kept talking and talking to him," she told me. "And somehow I talked myself out of that situation."

I was and still am in awe of her ingenuity, her presence of mind. I also think about what that did to her, the terror that coursed through her body, and also how that must've made her feel about herself, as a teen girl vulnerable to potential danger just by walking down the street—her naturally developing body making her a target. Surely, that awareness, and that pressure to be extra vigilant, added to Rita's existing anxiety.

Jill remembers Rita telling her about the man snatching her off the street but doesn't recall that they dwelled on it for long; situations like that were just part of what you had to watch out for and learn to deal with, sadly. "There were a lot of creepy places around Mumford," Jill recalls. "On those side streets, they would wait for girls to walk by—mostly older men lurking, parked in their cars and trucks. I was walking home from school one day and this man was there, and as I walked by, I saw he was playing with himself."

Black girls and women have always been at a disproportionate risk of sexual violence. According to the National Center on Violence Against Women in the Black Community, one in four Black girls will be sexually abused before the age of eighteen, and 40 to 60 percent of Black women report being subjected to "coercive sexual contact" by the time they're eighteen.

My memories of Rita's Mumford High days before and after the abduction are more impressionistic than fully formed recollections. Flashes come to mind: a major research paper she wrote on the work of Langston Hughes, endless index cards filled with notes spread across the dining room table; her flash cards for Spanish class; a dance routine she performed for school that Elaine helped her choreograph, done to the recitation of the 23rd Psalm. I can see her practicing in our spacious blue living room, walking with long strides, hands gesturing to each side, then placing a hand over her heart as Elaine spoke the words from the well-known Psalm, which she knew by heart:

"Yea, though I walk through the valley of the shadow of death, I will fear no evil: for thou art with me; thy rod and thy staff they comfort me." I remember the senior-class trip Rita took to the Bahamas, and the blurry photo of her posing on a beach with a short Bahamian man dressed in native costume, feathers sticking up from his hat as palm trees swayed in the background.

Another memory, a fun one, asserts itself: We're in the kitchen, eating freshly fried catfish. A song that's been climbing the R&B charts comes on the radio. Like me, she's not much of a singer, but even still Rita belts out the catchy lyrics: "A clean up woman is a woman who gets all the love we girls leave behind!" Then, with a brilliant comedic stroke, Rita grabs the broom and glides it across the floor as she sings along: "The clean up woman, she'll sweep him off his feet. She's the one who'll take him in when you dump him in the street!" I can't stop laughing as she sweeps that broom around like a dance partner, watching my sister the way I love her best. Whenever I'm in my car driving and I hear "Clean Up Woman" play on SiriusXM's Classic Soul channel, I can't stop smiling.

She graduated from Mumford High just two months after turning sixteen. Her graduation picture, the cap-and-gown image framed and once displayed on a shelf in our family den, is sepia-toned; at the time, I wished she'd taken her photo in color, because the brown hue looked to my eyes old-timey, made *her* seem old-fashioned. At twelve, I had strong opinions about these things. Yet not only were sepia graduation pictures still popular in the '70s, that choice actually suited Rita. There was a quality about her not unlike a sepia-toned image, warm and timeless and understated. She had a radical evolution, moving away from the low-key look, folks later describing her style as "flashy"—a moniker she fully embraced. But back then she was so modest, sitting for her cap-and-gown photos wearing not a trace of makeup, not even lip gloss. That too would change.

In a photo from the graduation ceremony, she smiles for the camera, her cap sitting on the back of her head, mushroom-style hair framing her face. It's the first snapshot I know of that captures her magnetic smile. In the picture, she's surrounded by graduating classmates, the girls like her in pretty light blue cap and gowns, the boys in maroon regalia, Mumford's school colors. The photo is a stand-in for my own memory because I couldn't attend her ceremony alongside the rest of our family. Turns out, my sixth-grade graduation was the same day, so my sister Dianne and her husband, George, attended mine as stand-ins for my parents. Mama let me know she understood my day was special too: in between helping Rita with her class-ring selection, senior trip details, those graduation photos, and her myriad senior-year outfits, Mama took me shopping for my graduation-day attire. I don't remember what store we went to, maybe Hudson's, but what I chose is vivid: a navy-and-white-checkered, pleated-skirt suit, the jacket with wide white lapels. I loved my skirt set because it reminded me of Lois Lane, and I already thought of myself as becoming an ace reporter. I wanted to wear white clogs with my outfit, but Mama vetoed that and instead bought me delicate ankle-strap patent leather shoes with wedge heels. Those heels made me feel so grown-up!

I don't think I was jealous, but I *was* sad that my parents wouldn't be in attendance; even though I never bragged about my school achievements, this felt like a great way to show them and fully absorb their pride: as part of the ceremony, I was selected to give out the "Honor Awards for Scholarship" (which included me), and the poem I'd written for the class of '72 was included in the guests' mimeo-graphed program. I recited its rhyming verse at the end of the cere-mony, what school officials called our "farewell assembly." What I'll always remember is our beloved twenty-three-year-old sister Dianne in the audience, clapping and clapping after I read that poem, and how suddenly I felt okay about our parents being at Rita's graduation ceremony rather than mine.

7

Rita likely chose Fisk University in Nashville because that's where our mother wanted her to go, or rather because Mama planted the idea in her head. I don't think she applied to any other college. And Fisk *was* a perfect choice. Since both our parents grew up in Nashville, we had a plethora of cousins and aunts and uncles there, kin who chose not to migrate north. Hence, Rita had a community of extended family to watch over her. This meant everything to our mother, who was sending her young, inexperienced, sheltered, and sensitive teen daughter off to college. Mama knew how attached Rita was to her. Going out of state only made sense if she chose a place that felt familial. And that's what Nashville was. Mama and Daddy were sending their daughter back to our ancestral home.

Also, Fisk was a special place with a storied past in Black culture. Founded in 1866, months after the Civil War and three years after Emancipation, Fisk School began in former Union Army barracks; its early students, all formerly enslaved, ranged in age from seven to seventy. The following year, in 1867, the institution was incorporated as Fisk University, making it the country's oldest private African American university. Fisk's one building for housing the university was built with walls two feet thick, with a tower on the roof, to keep an eye out for Ku Klux Klan members hungry to burn down a place trying to educate the colored. Fisk's website states: "Probably no single institution has played so central a role as Fisk in the shaping of black learning and culture in America," and it's no hyperbole. Its most famous alumnus is W. E. B. Du Bois, class of 1888. Fisk also boasts as alumni historian John Hope Franklin (the skylit modern library is named after him), poet Nikki Giovanni, dancer and choreographer Judith Jamison of Alvin Ailey fame, and Congressman John Lewis. The faculty were equally renowned: Du Bois returned to his alma mater to teach; Harlem Renaissance writers Arna Bontemps, Sterling Brown, and James Weldon Johnson all taught at Fisk; abolitionist and journalist Ida B. Wells-Barnett and famed artist Aaron Douglass also taught there. The esteemed poet Robert Hayden (the first African American appointed poetry consultant, now called poet laureate, to the Library of Congress) taught at Fisk for over twenty years. And Booker T. Washington sat on the board of trustees, married a Fisk graduate, and sent his children to Fisk.

Not just a native daughter but a history buff who also loved W. E. B. Du Bois's writings, our mother knew all too well the significance of Fisk University, as did most Black folks. And so, for Mama, ease of mind mingled with hometown pride over Rita's attending Fisk. Black colleges, too, were already a tradition in our extended family. Three of our Nashville cousins—Ava, Buddy, and Anthony—all attended Tennessee State University. I recently learned that our father also briefly attended Tennessee State University. The rich legacy of Black college attendance runs deep in our family, and continues to this day, as my daughter now attends Spelman College, my alma mater.

Meanwhile, many of Rita's friends were choosing historically white colleges and universities, which were in their early days of affirmative action, door-opening to Blacks, after an initial forced acceptance in the 1950s and '60s. Rita's high school bestie Jill chose to attend Oakland University, and later Mercy College, both Detroit-based. Rita's childhood bestie Linda went to the University of Michigan. Understandably, many Black parents back then sent their children to what we now call PWIs, predominantly white institutions, because they believed making it in the world meant learning early how to deal with and tapping into the networks of white folks. Yet Black students paid a clear price for being part of that stressful vanguard, being "othered," always in the minority. Doors opened to them, but attitudes didn't change. They faced daily hostile living and classroom environments.

Unrest popped up regularly on white college campuses during that time, as Black students agitated for change. From '65 to '72, in what was later coined the Black Student Movement, college students staged multiple simultaneous protests across the country. Linda remembers participating in a few. And Black colleges and universities—known by 1965 as HBCUs—were experiencing their own internal unrest.

These institutions, almost all begun by white philanthropists and missionaries, were conservative places that stressed respectability and no rabble-rousing. But the Black Power movement had influenced students to agitate for their Black colleges and universities to keep up with the times and become more progressive. Students staged sit-ins, demanding a more Black-oriented curriculum, including at Fisk.

By the time Rita arrived in fall '72, campus protests had died down. In their wake, Rita found at Fisk an unapologetic Black space, a safe haven that affirmed her, and a place where she didn't have to prove or explain herself to white people. That would come later.

~

Preparation for Rita's departure was intense. Mama bought a foot-locker that sat in our living room propped open for weeks, and it slowly filled with things Rita would need at school, soon stuffed with linens and towels and toiletries and more. I was jealous of the attention she was getting, but also intrigued by it all. Rita was the first in our family to go away to college. Anthony, struggling with his addiction, dropped out of high school before later getting a GED; Dianne attended Macomb Community College for a semester before quitting; and Deborah had left Wayne State University in her senior year. "I gave them all the *option* to go to college," Mama used to say. "What they chose to do with that opportunity was on them." Our mother knew Rita would make her proud by taking full advantage of that opportunity and getting a college degree.

Several of us came to Detroit Metro Airport as part of Rita's send-off. Elaine and I were there to travel with her, as emissaries. Our mother also came, along with Anthony and his new wife, Renita. Her departure was such a big deal that we posed for photos at the airport. The snapshots remind me that people still dressed up to get on air-planes back then: Rita wore a stylish pink-and-brown paisley dress, and I wore a red-and-blue knit top over the skirt from my sixth-grade graduation suit. In a slightly blurry photo, Anthony has his arm around Renita, her own arms folded across her chest; they are both twenty years old, still hopeful for their young marriage. And in a wondrous time capsule, Elaine and Rita stand before the departure gate, each with her fist raised in the Black Power salute. Although Elaine wears a curly Afro, Rita's hair is straightened; she never did opt to wear an Afro. Even though neither she nor Elaine was "radical," heightened Black consciousness had gone mainstream. In the four years since Tommie Smith and John Carlos raised their fists into the air at the Summer Olympics, we all comfortably called ourselves Black as opposed to Negro.

Rita left for Fisk at a brand-new, post-civil-rights moment when pride in our culture was gaining traction. In movie theaters, we had options for which Black films we wanted to see, in whatever genre: the love story *Lady Sings the Blues* or the neo-noir *Superfly*? The horror flick *Blacula* or the comedy *Buck and the Preacher*? The crime drama *Black Caesar* or the mystery thriller *Melinda*? Everyone I knew went to see Cicely Tyson in the Depression-era period drama *Sounder*. Also, that year Shirley Chisholm convincingly campaigned for president, and Andrew Young and Barbara Jordan became our first Black congressional members from the South since Reconstruction. Muhammed Ali, soon to regain his heavyweight title, graced the September 1972 cover of *Ebony* magazine with his pretty wife and baby son. Also, songs of empowerment dominated the airwaves that summer, including one of Rita's favorites, the Staple Singers' gospel-infused hit "I'll Take You There." Despite what was happening in the country—including Watergate and Vietnam—we were an optimistic Black family that late August day. Rita was headed off to college!

When I think about it now, Mavis Staples could've been singing directly to Rita, her deep, lusty voice tumbling out from radios and 8-track players and turntables, with its promising invitation to freedom: "I know a place," she shared in confidence. "Ain't nobody cryin' . . . I'll take you there . . . !" Rita was on her way to a special new freedom, and I felt sheer excitement over getting to accompany her, to witness this big adventure taking place in my sister's life.

That trip marked an important milestone in my own life: my final day in Nashville, I bought a diary using spending money our mother had given me—the words ONE YEAR DIARY and an image of an owl on its cover; the diary was turquoise and came with the requisite lock and key. On August 27, I wrote:

> This is my first time writting [*sic*] to you. I just bought you today for $3.50. At first I thought that was too much, but I decided it wasn't since you are going to be my closest friend and I will tell you my deepest, darkest secrets.

And then I wrote:

> Today is Sunday, and on Thursday, I left going to Tenn. with my sister and my "pretend" cousin. Rita, my sister, is going to go to school in Tenn.

That entry marked the beginning of a fifty-plus-year ongoing ritual of keeping diaries and journals, and in my first-ever entry, I wrote about the most exciting trip I'd experienced in my young life: accompanying Rita on her new journey to become a college student.

Our Nashville cousins met us at the airport. Once we arrived at Fisk, I walked around in awe. Not only was it the first college campus I'd ever set foot on, it was filled with nothing but Black students, walking up pathways and sitting on grassy knolls and lounging on building steps. There they were, in their head wraps and platform shoes and hip-huggers, as though they'd walked off *Soul Train*, that new show that glued us all to the TV on Saturday afternoons. Some, with their perfectly round Afros, looked like real-life versions of the models used in those commercials that sang out, "Watu Wazuri, beautiful people, use Afro Sheen!" I lived in a majority Black city, and still I'd never seen anything like *this*, certainly not at newly integrated Hampton Elementary. As I strolled along one of those paths, my hair down and falling to my shoulders, two male students passed by; one turned to the other and said, "Damn, the freshmen are looking younger and younger every year!" Beaming, I suddenly *wanted* to be a college freshman, at a place like Fisk. But I had to get through junior high and high school first.

The buildings on campus looked to my twelve-year-old eyes like something out of a fairy tale. I adored Memorial Chapel, this castle-like structure made of stone with its giant red-and-white belfry. I liked that it was really old, as a castle should be. I learned later that Fisk's campus chapel was *old-old*, erected in the last decade of the nineteenth century. My most vivid memory of that campus tour is standing before another old, majestic structure sitting at the top of a small hill—Jubilee Hall. It was so imposing, this four-story, red-brick, many-windowed, massive building with porticos and columns, gabled dormers, and a belfry inside a rising steeple that stretched into the sky. I'd read the entire Brothers Grimm collected fairy tales, and as I gazed upward, I thought of Rapunzel in her locked-away tower. Jubilee Hall, it turns out, is Fisk's crown jewel, its first permanent building, erected in 1876, and once housed the entire university. It got its name from Fisk's famed Jubilee Singers, as money those students raised while on tour singing "slave songs"—what were in fact freedom songs we now call Negro spirituals—financed its construction. Since its creation was literally made possible by singing voices, architectural enthusiasts now refer to Jubilee Hall, with its Gothic Revival style, as a perfect embodiment of "frozen music."

To this day, each October 6, Fisk pauses to observe Jubilee Day, the anniversary of the singers' departure from campus as they began their tour, just eight years after slavery's end. Having recently celebrated 150 years, the contemporary Jubilee Singers perform each year on that date at a convocation inside Memorial Chapel, to honor their legacy; they conclude the day's ceremonies with a pilgrimage to the burial sites of the original singers, where the sacred songs they made famous, like "This Little Light of Mine" and "Swing Low, Sweet Chariot," are sung. I wonder, did Rita ever attend this ceremony? The thought of her honoring and connecting with Black ancestral history on her own college campus, on hallowed ground as it were, moves me.

~

Back at Rita's freshman dorm, Scribner Hall, Elaine had lots of advice for her cousin's new life as a college student. Elaine was twenty-four and had herself just graduated from college. She'd gone to West Virginia State, which *had* been a historically Black public college—one of the few that offered aviation and trained many Tuskegee Airmen—until federal desegregation laws passed in 1954 transformed it into a school for "all" students. How that played out by the time Elaine arrived in 1968 was white students using it as a commuter college during the day. "But as soon as the sun went down, it was all African American," recalls Elaine. "In the evening, you'd walk through the student union, and you'd know you were at a Black school." Rita had visited Elaine at West Virginia State a few times, which had given her a brief taste of college life.

Now, Elaine offered Rita guidance on how best to decorate her side of the dorm room, and which outfits to wear during freshman week. I remember that Elaine instructed her to shave under her arms before she wore her yellow halter top around campus. I could sense Rita's growing irritation as I watched her from my perch atop her bed.

"I tried to help as much as she would let me fuss over her," says Elaine. "But she wasn't tickled pink; she was reserved, with a kind of attitude like, 'Well, I'll be all right, and this will be all right, but this is not really my heart's desire.'" The way Elaine sees it in retrospect, Rita was not one of those girls so excited to leave home that they had their bags packed before they got out of high school. "She was a family-type girl, and wasn't really trying to get away from home," says Elaine. "So, she wasn't exuberant."

I'm sure Rita's behavior baffled Elaine, who couldn't wait to be away from home when *she* left for college. Now it's obvious to me that at barely sixteen, Rita's leaving us was a big, scary thing. She wasn't fully ready to be away, yet she must've felt all that expectation emanating from Elaine, so genuinely excited for her. Rita and I talked about this years later, and she said to me, "Girl, Elaine worked my nerves. I was relieved when y'all left."

Elaine and I definitely overstayed our drop-off. We were in town for four long days; before we left, we went to visit kin in Nashville.

First, we visited our mother's sister Ella, whom we all called Big Sis, at her boardinghouse/home on First Avenue South. In a group photo taken on the wide porch of Big Sis's house, against its bright redbrick exterior, our cousin Bill wears a rakish brimmed hat, and Rita wears wide-legged jeans and a fashionable smock top. We also visited our first cousins Ava and Anthony and Buddy and Junior. Then we went across town to visit our father's sisters—first Aunt Bea, and then Aunt Katherine, her husband, John, and our cousin Ennis in their home on Osage Avenue. Already, Rita's presence in Nashville was strengthening the connective thread between our down-south and up-north families. Hers was a brief reverse migration, and that linkage did wonders for deepening the bonds within our extended families.

When she needed a home-cooked meal, Rita went to the Goodlettsville home of our mother's big sister, Alice, knowing dinner would end with our aunt's signature 7UP pound cake. In fact, Rita's roommate from freshman year, her homegirl Pat Rencher, remembers our aunt Alice dropping off a plate of food to the dorm. "And it was delicious!" she recalls. When Rita needed straightforward advice, she went to Aunt Bea, who you could talk to about *anything*, and when she needed sympathy and pampering, she turned to Aunt Katherine. When she needed extra money, she could go to any one of them. And when she got hungry, she could walk from campus to the new eatery Ed's Fish House, and get herself a free meal, since the place was owned by extended family. Pat remembers going there herself and getting "the best fish sandwiches for seventy-five cents!" (Ed's celebrated its fiftieth anniversary in 2022 as one of the city's oldest Black businesses, now run by my cousin Anthony's grandson.)

Throughout her Fisk years, Rita really got to know our Southern relatives, developed a genuine relationship with each cousin, each uncle, each aunt. I didn't understand the value of that at the time, but I do now, and I long for what Rita had, and what I missed out on during my own college days: being embraced in a familial hug of protection; she was steeped in the Black tradition described by scholar Farah Jasmine Griffin as "Nurtured in love and governed by an ethic of care." Those Nashville bonds stayed with Rita. Most importantly, she became the young family griot, staying in touch, keeping the rest of us abreast of what was happening with our family down south. Because she was the one who'd pick up the phone and call them, I never had to. I simply learned from Rita what was going on with everyone. She was my connective link.

8

The first letter I ever received from Rita came two weeks after she'd begun college, and after I'd already written to her. She wrote me back in her pretty, flourished handwriting, small fat circles dotting her *i*'s like snowflakes. She spelled my name with just one *t*, as I didn't add another one until high school:

September 15, 1972

Dear Bridget,
Just a short letter to let you know your letter made me cry. No, I didn't cry long. I think I cried because I miss home and the letter made me feel at home.

The reason I'm writing is when you said you leave for school at 8:00 in the morning, I hope you're walking to school with someone (Not by your self).

Well, Bridget I'm going to close for now.

Love,
Rita

P.S. Tell everyone I said hello. Tell Deborah I got her letter. Tell Daddy I said hello. Tell Mama I said to study hard (smile).

Bridget write me back to let me know who you're walking to school with. It can be just a short letter.

Also Bridget I'm glad my Spanish notes helped you.

Later.

I can imagine from her letter what I wrote to her in mine—sharing my daily rituals and wanting her to know I appreciated what she'd left behind for me (her Spanish notes!). And there she was, beautifully playing the role of big sister, insisting that I *not* walk to school alone each morning. Even from afar, Rita was the family worrier. And she missed home, missed me. Reading that letter now, I think, *These two sisters are really close.* But in my memory, we weren't, not quite, not yet.

Rita wrote our mother a month later, to prepare her for some not-so-good news. Her letter was written on the pretty, bright green stationery that Elaine had insisted she buy when we escorted her to college:

Hi Mama,
Just a few lines to let you know I'm thinking about you.

Mama, please don't be mad when you receive some of my mid-term grades, because I know for sure I got a D in art, but this isn't my final grade. I have been studying.

I wrote N., B., Mrs. G., and DD.

Mama, please send my card to fly home to Aunt Alice, because next week I'll be making my reservations for Thanksgiving. I can't wait to come home. Make a list of things you want me to do for you when I come home. Stay off your legs as much as possible.

Love,
Rita

PS: Call me some time: 1615-859-2776

Any time after 9:00.

When Rita came home for Thanksgiving and later for winter break, it was clear that she'd blossomed since being away at school, that getting out from "up under" our mother, gaining some independence, had been good for her. She seemed freer, lighter. She'd regale us with funny and engaging tales of life at Fisk, as Mama and I gathered beside her at the kitchen table. I loved how through her stories, I got to experience this new world of college. And she had so many stories! I marveled at how Rita could make me feel I was there, experiencing it all alongside her; she'd act out a scenario, even mimic folks' voices,

turning them into fascinating characters. I envied her for that ability. Some people become writers because they are themselves natural
storytellers; others do so because they've grown up listening to great
storytellers. That was me: I wanted to become a writer as much from
years of listening to Rita tell juicy stories as anything else.

I remember her telling us that some of her classmates were much
older men, already in their twenties, because they'd been to Vietnam.
I was touched by that. Also, she told us how some girls dressed up and
wore full makeup to classes, even if all the getting ready made them
late. That, I found funny. Pat Rencher, Rita's freshman roommate, confirms this phenomenon, recalling that some girls were still upholding
the "Fisk Tradition" by dressing with decorum, wearing skirt sets and
simple sheath dresses; meanwhile, others wore the latest fashions, like
the popular Nik Nik polyester shirts in bold prints, paired with pants.
But by sophomore year, "It was all jeans and bandanas on the head,"
says Pat. Everything in the early '70s was changing.

Also, based on Rita's accounts, Fisk's musical tradition begun with
the original Jubilee Singers hadn't changed, and had in fact carried on
into a new century, across the decades. Music remained an integral
part of Fisk's identity, and that translated to campus life—including
Fridays in the cafeteria, when a DJ played music and students sometimes got up and danced. Apparently, the university naturally attracted musicians to its student body. One man in particular Rita told
us about was Bobby Hebb, a quasi-famous freshman already in his
thirties. He was a singer/songwriter who'd written the 1960s jazzy
soul standard "Sunny," which went on to sell over a million copies,
becoming one of the most played, performed, and covered songs of
all time with its simple yet emotional lyrics: "Sunny, yesterday my
life was filled with rain. Sunny, you smiled at me and really eased
the pain . . ." More than five hundred singers and musicians have
recorded the song, including Ella Fitzgerald, Marvin Gaye, Stevie
Wonder, José Feliciano, James Brown, Johnny Mathis, Shirley Bassey,
and Cher. (Billie Eilish sang "Sunny" online in 2020 to help raise
money for coronavirus relief.) Hebb also cowrote Lou Rawls's hit "A
Natural Man," which became like an anthem for our father, with its

great line, "I don't want no gold watch for working fifty years from nine to five while the boss is guzzling champagne and I'm belting beer in some dive." I was awed to think that a man whose songs I'd heard on the radio, that Daddy sang along to, was a classmate of Rita's. Also, many major R&B and soul artists came to the college to perform. Pat remembers Earth, Wind & Fire, Herbie Hancock, and Chaka Khan all coming to perform. Rita's yearbook shows that Hugh Masekela, Stanley Turrentine, and Parliament-Funkadelic also gave concerts on Fisk's campus. Could college *be* more exciting?

I most vividly recall Rita telling us about a girl in her freshman dorm named Hazel Payne, who sat on the floor outside her room playing her guitar. "She's always there, so we just walk around her," said Rita. "She's from California, so, you know." I remember having a light bulb moment: College could be a place where you got to do something creative? I hadn't understood that before. Rita's major was business administration, which seemed the kind of pursuit college was meant for; I hadn't known there were other options. While we enjoyed music and went to local theater productions, ours was a practical, non-artsy household. No one played an instrument, or tried to get discovered at Motown, or took dance classes. There was no piano in the living room. But I tucked away this new discovery, held the image in my mind's eye of this girl sitting cross-legged outside her dorm room, plucking away at her guitar. That image helped spur me a few years later in high school to choose the performing arts curriculum.

Hazel Payne didn't return for sophomore year, and Rita figured it was likely because she spent more time playing her guitar than going to class. We later learned that Hazel had joined a rising R&B group called A Taste of Honey. The summer I entered college and Rita entered grad school, A Taste of Honey had a major hit with "Boogie Oogie Oogie," which became *the* disco anthem of the era. Hazel played electric guitar while her colead, Janice-Marie, played bass guitar. And right there in the middle of the song was Hazel's distinctive, whining guitar solo. Who'd ever seen a Black woman—let alone two!— playing guitar in a band, male musicians relegated to the background? And these women were beautiful. A Taste of Honey became the first

Black performers to win a Grammy for Best New Artist. Rita and I stayed up late one night to watch *Burt Sugarman's The Midnight Special* on Channel 4 (which didn't come on in Detroit until one a.m., *after* Johnny Carson's *The Tonight Show*), where the duo performed their hit song. Janice-Marie sang lead, belting out that catchy chorus: "Get on up, on the floor, 'cause we're gonna boogie oogie oogie till you just can't boogie no more," while Hazel jammed on her guitar, sporting a sandy-colored Afro surrounding her face like a halo. "Her hair was long and straight back at Fisk," Rita noted.

~

One of Rita's classmates and closest friends, Pierre, told me that Rita was a dynamic presence on campus from the start. "She had that little Mustang she drove around," he recalls. "And she could eat out every day. She was really something, this big city girl who had it going on!" And Pierre sheepishly admits that the young men on campus used to secretly call her "Booty Mama." When I look back at photos of her at the time, hers wasn't a Kim Kardashian behind, not even a Tracee Ellis Ross behind, and yet it was a distinctive part of her physique. Pierre stresses that it was truly a term of endearment; all of the guys thought Rita was really attractive. Yet what he remembers most distinctly is her intelligence, which he first witnessed in a class they had together. "The professor would have us read something, and then Rita and I would have our own opinions on that," he recalls. That would often lead to rich, ongoing debates and spirited discussions between them. "I haven't had any other friend like that, from that standpoint," notes Pierre. "We had a real intellectual connection."

Another distinction is that she never ever smoked marijuana. "Rita wouldn't do nothing like that!" says Pierre. Didn't matter that it was the early '70s, and marijuana abounded among college students; Rita didn't even experiment with getting high, given what she'd witnessed with our siblings' heroin addictions. Back then, the prevalent belief was that weed was a gateway drug. Besides Rita was not an escapist personality. She believed in staying alert, aware, and grounded in reality. She didn't drink either, for much the same reasons. In that way she really was like our mother. Besides, she was already a dynamic person. As Pierre puts it, "She was high enough on her own. She'd start laughing and giggling and moving her head like a sistah!" I smile when he says this, picturing her just that way, in the midst of making a point about something.

Rita wrote her second letter to me during spring of her freshman year, as she was approaching her seventeenth birthday, and I was approaching my thirteenth:

March 1, 1973

Hi Bridget,

I guess you thought I had forgotten about you, but as you know you're a hard person to forget.

Well, what have you been doing? How many new outfits have you gotten since I've been gone? (smile) Last question. How are the <u>dogs</u>?

Let me tell you this about M.; she really goes to class this semester. She told me her parents were really mad about her grades. However, she's not coming back to Fisk in September. As for Eric he is sharp as usual in his high heels.

Did Mama tell you that Robert Walker has been writing me every week? I wonder why is he writing, is it because he likes me or does Robert just want some mail? Why don't you answer the question when you write back.

Bridget, I'm going to close for now, because I'm writing you at lunch time.

Love Ya,
Rita

You're a hard person to forget. I love that. And, oh, I wish I knew what I wrote her back about Robert Walker, the nerdy boy who used to come by the house, sit quietly beside her on the living room sofa.

A total gentleman. Did he take her to the prom? I can't recall. Many years later she once said to me, "I should've married Robert Walker." Wish too that I could recall who this Eric was in his high heels— someone she'd regaled us with stories about, I'm sure.

When Rita returned home that summer after her first year, I'd really missed her, and what I'd missed most was her energy around the house, the excitement she brought with her little daily dramas. Rita was a sharer. And she knew how to report on any mundane encounter—an exchange at the supermarket, an encounter at the bank—and make it sound engaging, suspenseful even. She was also nosey in the best way, gossipy in the best way, not to criticize or judge or take glee in others' misfortune; rather, because she cared about people. I now realize her way of sharing had the added benefit of keeping us all implicated and invested in one another's lives. I was introspective, moody, quiet, naturally secretive, a good listener, but not a good sharer. Rita was the opposite. In her absence, we all felt the void. With her back home and filled with more college-life sagas to recount, I hung on to her tales as though they were dramas on the radio.

That's when Rita announced in no uncertain terms—as though her year at an HBCU had been one of research on the subject—that I would fit right in at Spelman. She explained to me that Spelman was a Black college for women in Atlanta. She said something about the girls who went there being "like you." I intuitively understood what she meant, knew that she was saying Spelman women were set apart, were the kind who might've gone—like me—to their hometown's magnet high schools rather than their neighborhood schools— like her—or private schools even, young women academically strong, known for sophistication and "high-class" ways. I knew she was complimenting me, even as I also knew she was saying Spelman would not be the right fit for *her*, thank you very much. But it would be the right fit for *me*. I understand it now as a difference between Diana Ross and Gladys Knight. When the two artists were both at Motown, Ross was its star, while Knight was signed to its subsidiary, what author and scholar Mark Anthony Neal calls its "Blackity-Black" soul label; Diana had the pretty, crossover voice, and Gladys had the raspy, gospel-tinged one. I had just seen her in *Lady Sings the Blues*, and I really loved Diana Ross; Gladys Knight was riding high with her hit song "Neither One of Us (Wants to Be the First to Say Goodbye)," and Rita really loved *her*. You knew Diana Ross was a glamorous, mega-watt star—Miss Ross to you!—rarefied and one step removed, which you understood and accepted, but you felt you *knew* Gladys Knight, the Empress of Soul, as down-to-earth and friendly, someone to give you good advice, help you keep it real. Diana would've gone to Spelman. Gladys would've gone to Fisk.

So, before I entered ninth grade I knew where I was going to college.

9

Rita's first boyfriend, her college sweetheart, was Cordell Montgomery from Birmingham, Alabama. They likely became a couple sometime during the start of sophomore year. Pierre was his best friend, and eventually they were roommates, living together in an off-campus apartment. "They hooked up quickly," Pierre recalls. "And it was clear, he had a good woman."

Rita talked *a lot* about Cordell. I didn't mind; I was glad she had a boyfriend. She hadn't really dated anyone in high school—in fact, I never saw her being what I thought of as a typical high school teen—and this seemed like a typical college-girl thing to do. In my mind, up until she left for college, Rita had been a mini Fannie, ever concerned with grown folks' business. Plus, it was good to see her living her own life, rather than worrying about Mama's. Elaine, our cousin Ava, and Rita's bestie Jill all recall hearing about Cordell. He met our extended family in Nashville too, often having dinner at our aunt Alice's home. "Oh, Cordell was eating like a king down there!" recalls Pierre, with a laugh.

I must've met Cordell during one of my visits to Rita at school during her sophomore year. I liked him well enough, although he had these eyes that were big and piercing, and a way of staring at me that I found unnerving. But he and Rita seemed to be in love, and that was nice to witness. My most vivid memory of Cordell comes from a photograph. Those who know, know that Black colleges have a plethora of pageants and balls attached to social events; the biggest is homecoming weekend, which includes the homecoming game and the ball and the attendant homecoming court. At Fisk, it's called the Royal Court and includes Miss Freshman, Miss Sophomore, Miss Junior, Miss Senior, and most importantly, Miss Fisk. But there are plenty of other titles to be crowned, especially those associated with fraternities. Pledgees of each fraternity vote for a court of young ladies to represent them at the crossing-over ceremony. Omega Psi Phi's pledgees are called Lampados, and at Fisk each year they select a court. That fall, Rita was crowned Ms. Lampado of 1973—their queen.

In the photo taken of her during the ceremony, Rita's arm is slipped through Cordell's and her hand lightly atop his, as they walk down the aisle in Memorial Chapel. She's wearing a purple dress with a flouncy, sculpted collar, pinned with a white corsage. Her hair is in an upsweep, with a curled side bang, and she's wearing expertly applied makeup—eyelashes and eyeliner, soft-colored lipstick. She's looking down, as if watching her steps, smiling, face radiant. Cordell wears a coordinating lilac tie and a brown suit. He's also looking down, but not smiling; in fact, he looks oddly serious, stern even. It unnerved me when I first saw the picture, and it does now, anew.

When Rita recounted the whole experience of being crowned Miss Lampado, I knew I was glimpsing a different Black world, still foreign to me; I also knew I was witnessing another Rita, someone whose life clearly reached well beyond Detroit, whose new college world seemed more sophisticated and glamorous. And she was at the center of it, regal in her way. Some years later friends started calling her the moniker that stuck for life: Queen Rita.

While Rita was experiencing life with her first boyfriend, I almost had my first real date, with a guy I met at work. I'd really wanted an after-school job, but I was only fourteen, and most places avoided hiring anyone that young, given the child-law restrictions in place. Deborah, who knew ever more clever ways to use the system for your own benefit, had told me how to get an ID that would make me older. She didn't show me how to get a fake ID; she was too smart for that. She told me to go down to the DMV with all of Rita's information, tell the clerk that I'd lost my license and needed a replacement, and then hand her the necessary proof of address. "We all look alike to them," Deborah assured me. So I took mail addressed to Rita, went down to the DMV office, did everything Deborah told me to do, and had my picture snapped with Rita's name. I couldn't believe it when the driver's license came in the mail with my face on it. Apparently, in the '70s, government paperwork and procedures were far more lax. (Lest we forget, we went through the entire decade with seat belts in our cars but weren't required by law to use them until the '80s.) I presented my/Rita's ID when I applied for that first job, at Red Barn near Northland Mall—a fast-food restaurant chain that specialized in the usual burgers, fish sandwiches, "country-style" fried chicken, and its real novelty, the first-ever self-service salad bar. All of Red Barn's buildings were distinctive, designed to resemble a barn; my uniform consisted of a short dress, red in my memory, with a matching pinafore to mimic a farm girl's look. I met this cute guy at work; he saw my name tag said RITA, so I couldn't correct him. I don't remember how he got my home address—was I dumb enough to give it to him?—but one day, he showed up at our house. He rang the bell. Rita, home on break, answered the door. "Hi," he said, "I'm here to see Rita." "I'm Rita," she said. By now, I was already standing behind her, watching with humiliation. When he saw me, he said, "But that's Rita. I met her at Red Barn." Rita quickly caught on and, only slightly bemused, left us alone for some awkward moments. I still remember his incredulous expression when I told him the truth; I never heard from the poor guy again. And Rita let me know she did *not* appreciate my impersonating her, using her identity for myself.

It's amazing how easily I got used to people calling me by her name at work, and surprising how much I liked it. But after only three weeks on that job at Red Barn, I quit.

~

That summer Rita was home after sophomore year, I spent a June Saturday with my junior high friends at Cedar Point amusement park in Sandusky, Ohio. Cedar Point is just over a two-hour drive from Detroit, and it was a big deal that I was allowed to travel there, essentially on my own. I don't remember how we all got there—perhaps we took the long bus ride. Anyway, I'd been gone all day, riding the rides, eating amusement park food, hanging out with my best friend Regina, filled with the exhilaration of freedom. Our mother was in the hospital, recovering from a blood clot, and our stepfather had given me permission to go. Rita was at the house, and she'd been waiting to hear from me. But I did not call home to check in. Once it had gotten dark, and I wasn't home yet, she grew increasingly worried. Her concern was valid, of course, more so because it was a dangerous time: Detroit had just been dubbed "Murder Capital, U.S.A.," the city's crime rate that year including tens of thousands of robberies and thousands of reported forcible rapes. And, of course, Rita knew firsthand what could happen "out there in the streets."

On this day, when I finally walked through the door, she was stressed out and angry. She let me have it, admonishing me nonstop. I did not want to hear her mouth. Mama had made it clear that my older sisters didn't ever have to babysit me, and likewise I didn't have to take orders from them; this wasn't like my cousin Lisa's household where her big sister Leslie had to care for her like a mother and so got to punish her like one. I did *not* want to be scolded by Rita; she wasn't even *that* much older than me, barely eighteen.

But this was different, and Rita wouldn't let it go. At one point, as I stood in the doorway of our mother's bedroom, brushing my hair, Rita sat on the edge of the bed, much like Mama often did, and kept at it: Didn't I understand how dangerous it was out there? What was my problem? Why couldn't I stop and think about somebody other than myself for a change? The more she fussed, the more infuriated I got. Finally, I yelled back at her, "You're not my mother!" using my hand holding the brush for emphasis as I slashed the air to make my point: *You're. Not. My. Mother.*

As I said the word "mother," I flung the brush at her. It moved with velocity, hitting Rita forcefully, right below the eye. We were both stunned. Suddenly, Rita rose from the bed and ran after me, and I instinctively turned and ran for my life along the hallway, through the kitchen, down the basement steps, Rita on my heels. I just managed to rush into the basement and slam closed its metal door, locking it a second before she caught up to me.

I have no idea what would've happened had she caught me. We argued a lot back then, but we never, ever physically fought. In fact, it was a cardinal rule in our home that we never put a hand on each other. Our mother didn't believe that brothers and sisters fighting was normal sibling rivalry. Arguing, sure, but not fighting. She told us to save that energy for all those folks out *there*, in the world, who could do you real harm. Even now, my friends with siblings and those with children cannot believe that my sisters and brother and I never passed a lick between us.

Except for this day. I used to tell this story by saying I hadn't intended to hit Rita, that I was simply pointing the brush at her for emphasis when it "flew" from my hand; but I recently read a diary entry I wrote at the time, and it says, "I really can't explain this right, but I'm trying . . . we were discussing it, and I ended up hitting her with a brush . . . I know that was wrong."

I stayed down in the basement behind that locked door for as long as I could, in terror of both Rita and the consequences. First, our sister Dianne arrived. She said I was in big trouble. Rita chimed in. "I spoke to Mama," she reported, "and she says she *should* have me bring you to the hospital and give you a whupping right there!"

I was beside myself with fear and guilt, and an adolescent's dread of being misunderstood. I tried to explain, crying through my defense. Finally, Dianne, always a softy toward me, told me to just call Fannie and explain. If I felt Rita had been really hard on me, I should tell that to her. And I certainly did feel that way. "Everything she did when she was my age was okay, but whatever I do now is just horrible," I lamented in my diary. ". . . I don't know what to do. All I know is I feel bad." I simply couldn't bring myself to call our mother. Instead, I spent hours curled up in a ball under a blanket, stretched out on the carpeted living room floor, whimpering as my two Yorkshire terriers, Tiffany and Mickey, curled up beside me.

The next morning, Rita had a black eye, a doozy as they say. Every time I saw her, I cringed. Our stepfather, Burt, proceeded to chastise me, something he'd never done before, and even though he wasn't that harsh, I cried even more. It was also Father's Day, so Rita and I spent the entire day at Daddy's place, Rita sporting her shiner as a symbol of my transgression. Our father admonished me too. This was another humiliation. He spanked me only once in my life, when I was four—three slaps on my bottom as I lay across his lap, for running across the alley without permission, slaps that wounded me for years. Now Daddy was quite upset. Rita could've lost an eye, he pointed out. Mostly, he just seemed so sad that we couldn't get along. There should be no greater love than ours, he said. Look at his own two sisters, our aunt Katherine and aunt Bea. They were so close, they still talked to each other every day, and only called one another "sister."

I knew our mother would wield the harshest blow. I expected my first whupping ever from her, which I believed I deserved; I *hated* knowing I'd disappointed her, the worst punishment of all. That evening, she called me from her hospital room.

"Why didn't you call and tell me what happened yesterday?" she asked.

"Because I was too upset," I answered.

Mama surprised me. She said she'd been waiting to hear my side of the story. She listened to what I had to say and, unlike everyone else, did not scold me. Instead, she said, "I was upset too when you didn't call home all day, because if anything had happened to you, I would've had a heart attack." She told me that hitting Rita with the brush was absolutely wrong. "After all," said Mama, "she was just worried about you." I was so relieved, grateful to our mom for not further shaming me, and for caring about my feelings. I gushed in my diary: "I have a beautiful mother! . . . I think I understand things better now since all of this happened . . . All I know is I love my mother and the next time she'll be the first I talk to instead of the last."

And yet the biggest surprise came from Rita. She didn't stay angry at me. Not when she woke up with the black eye, not as her eye went from black to purple to normal again, and not in the days or weeks or months that followed. Not once did she throw it up in my face, ever. The brush incident did not become an origin story to explain why we "just don't get along," the way it had for a friend who once fought so badly with her sister that she broke her leg, which she could never live down and her sister could never get over. Rita chose to forgive her baby sister, right away. She kept her heart open to me.

10

Turns out, that same summer was a life-altering one for Rita's boyfriend, Cordell. I only learned in recent years what happened: as their friend Pierre tells it, he and Cordell and another friend were on a trip to Atlanta, and Cordell tried a psychedelic drug, likely mescaline, which caused him to experience a psychotic break, one that he never recovered from. Cordell returned to school in the fall, apparently still using drugs and with a clear mental illness—possibly an underlying condition triggered by the drug use. That was when his relationship with Rita turned dark. He became highly paranoid, and obsessive toward her. He was, according to Pierre, convinced that "everyone on the yard" was involved with her, including his frat brothers. Cordell thought Pierre and Rita were involved too, even though they were just good friends. One day, as Pierre recalls, when Cordell saw him and Rita talking together in a hallway, he abruptly turned and walked away; Cordell never spoke to his best friend again.

I can't imagine how hard that was for Rita, witnessing her boyfriend's mental deterioration and delusions. He apparently did receive some mental health treatment and was labeled as "psychotic"—a catchall diagnosis used by psychiatrists and medical doctors back in the 1970s. At the time, Rita shared with Mama and the rest of us that Cordell was experiencing some mental health challenges. Did she share with anyone the extent of his struggles? I'm not sure, but I *am* sure that she waited several years, long after their involvement, to confess to me something Cordell had confessed to *her*: one day when they were together in his campus apartment, his mind told him to drag her to the bathroom, put her face under the tub's running water, and drown her. I was stunned to hear this, of course, and worried about her retroactively, the way you do when someone you love confesses a close call with death. As Rita told me that story, I knew she had no doubt Cordell could've carried out that act. I knew she knew that once again—just like with that potential abduction on a Detroit street—she'd narrowly escaped a terrible fate.

Greg Johnson, Cordell's Omega Psi Phi line brother and classmate, has this take on their relationship: "Cordell was in love with your sister!" he tells me. "When they broke up, he was devastated." He adds that Cordell talked about Rita for decades afterward. "It was not good," admits Greg. "His fixation on her."

Asking questions about a loved one's life can uncover what you never knew and change what you thought you knew. All these many years, I believed that Rita had broken up with Cordell after his mental collapse, that she'd protected herself by getting away from him. But that wasn't true. I'd created a fiction in my mind, a protective fantasy. In reality, she stayed with him, difficult as it had to be, for the rest of her time at Fisk. This was confirmed by Pierre.

I believe that being so heavily involved with Cordell, and later dealing with all his struggles, are what kept Rita from having a close girlfriend at college, as she'd had in elementary and high school. She likely had so little time to develop a tight friendship with anyone. And here's another truth I recently learned: Cordell was physically abusive toward her. A college friend of Rita's shared with me a text that Cordell sent to a mutual friend, all of them having been at Fisk together. It reads: "I have to apologize for treating Rita like a jerk in school . . . whacking her around when she was a teenager . . . embarrassing her in front of her friends." Rita's high school bestie Jill says Rita did share that fact with her, a confidence that she kept. "I knew some things, and so I didn't like Cordell," she admits. "He was obsessed with her, and she was nervous."

That hurts.

I recently made a far more most disturbing discovery: Twenty-three years after he thought about drowning Rita in the bathtub, Cordell stabbed his girlfriend to death, a woman named Joy, and left her body face down in the bathtub with the knife still lodged in her skull. He stabbed her six times in the neck, back, and head. Afterward, he walked into a Birmingham jail and turned himself in. In a videotaped statement he gave to police shortly after the murder, Cordell said he'd been thinking about killing Joy "for twenty-three years," when in fact he'd only known her for a short time. It's not a stretch to imagine who he was actually thinking about killing for all those same years.

First tried and convicted to life in prison, Cordell's new attorneys appealed and got the conviction overturned. They argued successfully that he was mentally insane with "perhaps the most serious disorder" at the time of the murder, and not experiencing a "lucid interval," because he'd stopped taking his antipsychotic meds; therefore, they argued, he was not responsible for his acts. Known as Montgomery v. State, the case was decided by the Alabama Court of Criminal Appeals on April 28, 2000 (the day before Rita's forty-fourth birthday), in a 4–1 decision. Cordell's conviction was reversed and he now resides at a residential mental health treatment center in Birmingham.

Among Rita's belongings is a photo Cordell sent her of himself—much older, dressed in black, his hands rigid as he poses unsmiling for the camera; he signed the front of the photo, in small, tight handwriting, "Love, Cordell." A couple years ago, Cordell's frat brother gave me his number; I called him and left a voice message, asking if he'd be willing to talk to me about Rita. He didn't call me back, but he did text: "Bridget . . . how's it going kidelle," he wrote. "I can't begin to tell you how happy it is to hear from you. . . . Not a day goes by that I don't remember . . . I can't tell you anything cause Rita real protective of me when it comes to girls . . . sisters included. By the way I can get away with saying anything I want cause I have a schizophrenic label."

When I asked again if we could talk, he texted back, "Suffice it to say I was the love of her life when it comes to boys and she was the love of my life when it came to girls . . . and it's still that way. I didn't formally marry her cause I didn't have the wherewithal to generate the wealth for career, house and kid . . . as I say I have schizophrenia." Cordell then texted me a memory of Rita: "She never left her purse on the floor." True. She believed the old wives' tale that placing your pocketbook on any surface below waist level shows a lack of respect for your money. She used to say, "A purse on the floor is money out the door."

Obviously, Rita and I never talked about Cordell murdering that poor woman named Joy. If she did know, it's odd that we didn't discuss it, which makes me doubt that she knew. Who might have told her? I only know because his frat brother told me, and I subsequently learned that the entire brief of Cordell's appeal, which apparently became a precedent for similar cases, is easy to access on the internet. That's how I came to know the details. On the rare occasions when his name came up, Rita spoke about Cordell with genuine compassion. "You have no idea what it's like to not be in your right mind," she'd say. It was one of her own biggest fears, losing her right mind. She'd certainly seen the effects of such a thing up close and personal.

~

Rita met a new man when she was nineteen, following her junior year at Fisk. Given what I now know about her struggles with Cordell, I imagine it was a relief to date someone while home who was vastly different from her college boyfriend. Elijah was thirty-one, and along with his brother ran E&E Fish Market on Fenkell and Dexter; our mother was one of their best customers, coming in on Fridays and buying $30 to $40 worth of fish. While home for the summer, Rita joined our mother at the fish market one day and Elijah noticed her right away. "She was so attractive," he recalls. "I just said 'hi' to her, treated her real nice."

Elijah also had another job, as a city bus driver. One day when Rita and I were standing on the front lawn of our home on West Seven Mile Road, Elijah pulled up in his eastbound bus and parked it at the curb. He opened the automatic door and leaned out, said hi. Rita walked up to the bus, and the two chatted as I and the bus full of passengers looked on. When their brief conversation ended, Rita walked back as Elijah closed those automatic doors and steered the bus back into traffic. I marveled at what had to be the coolest gesture a guy who likes you could make. Rita was impressed too; she was smiling coyly.

"I knew the house because sometimes your mom just called down, ordered fish, and we'd bring it out to her," explained Elijah. When he was driving by and saw us outside, he says, "I couldn't help myself. I stopped."

The next time Rita appeared at the fish market, Elijah asked her out on a date. They dated that whole summer. "Oh, she was beautiful," he says. "She always had a smile on her face." He laughs. "Though, now, if she didn't have a smile on her face, watch out!"

During their summer romance, he and Rita did a lot of things together, he recalls, like going to the movies and out to dinner; they also went to hear live music at Watts Club Mozambique, where the Hammond organ player Charles Earland often performed. "Whenever he was in town, we'd go and sit right up front," recalls Elijah. They also got to see the jazz guitarist Grant Green perform at the same club. They had a lot of fun, and Elijah was clearly smitten. "Rita was really sweet," he says. "We spent all our time having a good time." He pauses. "We had this thing between us that I ain't gonna say more about . . ."

I liked Elijah a lot. I liked him for Rita because he was so fun-loving, easygoing, and genuinely kind. Clearly, he was really into Rita, and she seemed to be into him. Our mother liked Elijah too; I know she admired his work ethic. At the end of the summer, she asked him to drive Rita back to school in the new car Mama had bought her—a yellow Pontiac Firebird. Elijah recalls that once in Nashville, they stayed for a few days at our aunt Alice's home. Rita was annoyed our aunt wouldn't let them share a bedroom. "We're grown!" she said to Elijah. He responded, "But we ain't that grown." He says he told her to be patient and try to understand that staying in separate beds was just a matter of respect for your elders. They slipped off to stay at a hotel one night.

What I remember most about that time, as Rita made her way through her last year of college and I made my way through my first year of high school, were fraught days for our family. Anthony, now twenty-three, had "gotten in trouble with the law" by participating in an armed holdup, desperate to pay for his yearslong drug addiction. He got caught, and by fall of '75, he was awaiting his trial.

When he was later sentenced, Anthony got five years. That was a tough reality for us all to accept, hardest of all on our mother. She looked to Rita's graduating from Fisk as the bright spot; and it *was* a well-timed milestone, with Rita being the first of Fannie's children to get a college degree. But the oddest thing is that I don't remember the actual commencement ceremony. Her college buddy Pierre recently sent me a photo he snapped of Rita that May, in front of New Residence Hall on Fisk's campus, as their graduation approached. She's holding a couple boxed files in her arms and smiling softly. Dressed in a light green halter top and jeans, she looks relaxed and so young, and hopeful. This image is the closest I can get to conjuring that season in her life; I simply don't recall the details of her actual graduation: that the ceremony took place outdoors; that all the graduates clustered beneath large, old swaying oak trees before marching to their seats; that the day before, the Jubilee Singers performed their commencement concert of Negro spirituals in Memorial Chapel; that this day marked Fisk's 102nd commencement, and Rita was one of three hundred graduating seniors. I don't recall that Andrew Young—on the verge of winning a third term to the House of Representatives—was the commencement speaker. Apparently, during the ceremony, an alumnus spoke about Fisk's financial woes. But I've since learned these facts. I don't recall anything from that day.

Is it possible that because I had an elaborate sixteenth birthday party in the same month (which Rita said I planned like a wedding), my big May event blotted out her big May event? I don't recall what Rita wore to her graduation, and no photos seem to remain. Yet I vividly remember what she wore to my Sweet Sixteen party: the lightest pale yellow three-piece pantsuit with a golden satin, pointed-collar blouse. I loved her fashion choice for the party, thought she looked sharp, like a modern '70s woman, straight out of the pages of *Essence*. Still, why don't I remember *any* part of my sister's college graduation? Maybe because memories are possessive, and the one about her that consumes me is this: shortly after her big May event, and mine, we learned that Rita had lupus.

TWO

~

11

I didn't know what symptoms initially sent Rita to the doctor. At the time, it seemed her health issues came out of nowhere; I wasn't aware of her being sick at all before. I now understand that she was likely feeling fatigue, and achiness in her bones and joints, maybe some swelling of her limbs, or headaches—"invisible suffering," they call it today. Because these symptoms lingered, our mother, who believed in going to the doctor, likely took Rita to see Dr. Carey, the family doctor. Rita didn't have the red butterfly rash that tends to spread across some sufferers' nose and cheeks; nor did she have the facial lesions that led a physician in the thirteenth century to name lupus the "wolf disease"—the word "*lupus*" is Latin for "wolf"—because the face marks resembled wolf bites. Those particular sufferers have a type of lupus called "discoid"—the kind that the singer Seal suffers from. Rita definitely didn't have that.

But she had *something*. How many doctors did she see before she made her way to a rheumatologist, the one who named her condition? I don't know, but I suspect Dr. Carey, who was Black, took her complaints seriously and sent her to a specialist. I distinctly remember Mama saying, "We were lucky to find out what it is," to learn exactly what condition Rita was suffering from. I naïvely thought our good fortune in Rita's accurate diagnosis was connected to our *overall* good fortune. I thought that because Mama could afford quality medical care, she was able to get her daughter to the right place, right away; I thought we were lucky to be *that* kind of Black family, with resources and access. Rita would get the treatment she needed, and everything would be okay. Because when you have an illness, and you get to the right doctor, in time, he heals you, right?

I now know that Mama was relieved not *just* because lupus was—and still is—a frustrating and complicated disease to diagnose given that, as the medical profession puts it, no two cases "present" exactly alike. Even now, patients are notoriously misdiagnosed. A major study done a few years ago by the Lupus Foundation of America puts that number at a shocking 46 percent of adults with lupus who were initially told they had something else wrong with them. And more than half of those sufferers were told there was *nothing* wrong with them, that the symptoms were psychological.

For me, the most harrowing example of misdiagnosis is the story of African American singer Toni Braxton, a six-time Grammy winner who has sold over sixty million records worldwide. Braxton was told, after suffering a heart attack, that she needed a heart transplant; this was just two weeks before doctors realized she had lupus, and instead needed to be treated for *that* disease, which was attacking her heart. Braxton suspects she suffered from lupus for two decades before she got an accurate diagnosis at age forty-one.

Our mother was also relieved because of what she knew. She knew that separate and apart from having a misunderstood illness, Rita was up against a greater hurdle than most. The "luck" that Mama spoke about was that once she was referred to a specialist, Rita's symptoms were not simply dismissed; she wasn't told it was *all in her head*; the doctor didn't guesstimate her condition without running any tests; she wasn't diagnosed with a virus and told to *go home and take some aspirin*; she wasn't admonished to *take better care of yourself, avoid smoking, and lose weight*; wasn't accused of overexaggerating her pain in hopes of getting prescribed drugs. The "luck" Mama spoke about was that Rita, already victim to the general bias against sufferers of lupus, had dodged a bullet—the devastating shot of disdain routinely fired at Black folks, Black women especially, by white doctors.

For two decades, we've had proof in the form of statistics and copious research that quantifies these lived experiences of implicit bias in the health-care system. I think about that word, "implicit," which according to the dictionary means "something understood although not directly expressed." It's just *understood* that Black people will face bias from medical personnel. It's not even news; it's just a Tuesday. Maybe that's why so little has been done about the uneven access, poor quality, and at times nonexistent care experienced by African Americans in the twenty years since studies began proving this reality. The statistic that stands out—the one that still hits me hard—is that Black women with the highest education, income, and wealth still have worse outcomes in the health-care system than *poor* white women. Basically, the moment a physician sees your Black-woman skin, you're already in trouble. Unconscious assumptions walk into the examining room with the doctor, who then makes inadequate and/or inaccurate treatment decisions, and by the time he says, "You can get dressed," and closes the door behind him, your health care has been compromised, your health itself jeopardized.

Of course, Black folks don't need the findings from research, because we are armed with a pileup of anecdotes—handed down and firsthand—that keep us wary of "routine" office visits, hospital stays, and emergency rooms alike. Black men and women generally know the risk of seeing a doctor, that it could go either way. (Not unlike calling the cops.) One of the most egregious cases of maltreatment is what happened to someone I've come to know, professor and author Emily Bernard. As a twenty-six-year-old African American graduate student at Yale, Emily was in a coffee shop one day when a white man pulled out a knife and began randomly stabbing people, including her. Bleeding profusely from her gut, she was rushed to the hospital. The surgeon on call walked over to her lying on a gurney and did not look at her or say a word as he plunged his fingers into her gaping wound. The pain was excruciating, and she instinctively grabbed his hand. Only then did the doctor look at her, and say icily, "Don't. Touch. My. Hand." Bernard writes in her essay collection *Black Is the Body* that "His eyes were Aryan blue and as cold as his voice." He refused to answer any of her questions, showed no regard for her trauma, her pain, her body—her humanity. She writes that whenever she tells the story of the night she got stabbed, she always says that the person who did the most injury to her, "who left the deepest wounds," was not the man who stabbed her, but rather, the ER surgeon.

Certainly, our mother knew from her own experience that maltreatment by doctors is routine and damn near ubiquitous when you're Black. She'd had plenty of encounters with the health-care system, having given birth to six children—one that died seventy-five minutes after delivery—and having suffered her entire adult life from deep vein thrombosis, which caused those recurring blood clots. And our father understood the same. He'd suffered from high blood pressure since before my memory of him, subjected to years of dismissive or inadequate medical treatment. Rita's experience of being listened to and taken seriously and accurately diagnosed was worth celebrating exactly *because* hers was an exception to the rule. Rita's rheumatologist was a white man named Samuel Indenbaum, who graduated from Wayne State University's medical school the year Rita was born. She really liked Dr. Indenbaum, and he seemed to like her. That was a big deal, because she'd go on to have a twenty-four-year relationship with this doctor, entrusting him with her care and treatment.

When I think of how relieved we all were about the diagnosis, none of us—except perhaps our mother and father, each suffering from their own chronic conditions—knew at first how debilitating lupus could be, that it was a progressive disease without cure, causing chronic inflammation and potentially severe complications, including damage to a person's vital organs. When Dr. Indenbaum explained to Rita that she had a common form of the disease called systemic lupus erythematosus—or "systemic" lupus—I assured myself, and kept assuring myself, that it was the "milder" type of lupus because it wasn't the rarer type. I don't know where I got this idea; it turns out, systemic lupus, or SLE as it's known, is the *most* dangerous type because it can severely affect so many different parts of the body.

I now know that lupus affects Black women at *two to three times the rate* it affects white women. The Lupus Foundation of America tells us that one in 250 African American women will develop lupus in her lifetime. And Black women not only are at a higher risk of suffering from the disease but tend to present at an earlier age and suffer higher rates of serious health complications. In other words, Black women like Rita are affected earlier and attacked by the disease more aggressively, thus spending a longer time trying to manage the condition, all resulting in a shorter life expectancy. As a 2006 study published in the journal *Annals of the Rheumatic Diseases* found, African Americans with lupus *also* have *a two- to threefold higher mortality risk than whites.*

I wish I could say these facts surprise me, but honestly, who is really surprised these days by statistics like that?

Why *does* lupus disproportionately affect Black women, and why is it more deadly? I could also ask why Black maternal death and infant mortality are so much higher than that of white women and babies, no matter those Black women's economic status and "lifestyle"; I could ask why Black women start their periods earlier, suffer three times more from uterine fibroids, and are *half as likely* to be diagnosed with endometriosis because their chronic pelvic pain is assumed to be from a sexually transmitted disease, a "bad period," or an overreaction—i.e., all in their heads. I could even ask why Black women born in Michigan the year Rita was born could expect to live *seven years fewer* than white women born in the same year in the same state. We know why, don't we?

When I think of tens of thousands of Black women with systemic lupus, I think of tens of thousands of encounters with systemic racism—some direct, some indirect, all causing lingering effects.

Yes, research has proven this correlation. A 2019 article's title says it all: "Racial Discrimination, Disease Activity, and Organ Damage: The Black Women's Experiences Living with Lupus." The authors of the research, published in the *Journal of Epidemiology*, put it this way: "Our findings suggest that experiences of racial discrimination is a unique source of *stress* that exerts negative health impact . . . [and] contributes to racial disparities in SLE outcomes." The authors make sure to note that these findings are true no matter the Black woman's socioeconomic status or unique "health-related characteristics."

Stress makes lupus worse, and experiencing racism is uniquely stressful.

But why *Rita*? Why was she the one among 250? Experts say lupus is either genetic or caused by nebulous "environmental factors" that we now know can include being Black in America. Genetics is certainly a possibility. Rita came to believe that our mother had undiagnosed lupus. But even if that is the case, why did our mother's genes morph in just such a way as to cause an autoimmune disease? And why did Rita inherit those compromised genes? What I want to understand is, why Rita *in particular*? Why not another sister? Why not me?

A few years ago, an acquaintance who suffers from alopecia, another autoimmune disease, asked me: "Did your sister have a trigger event?" I answered, "Yes, many."

I was thinking about all that Rita went through across the first twenty years of her life. I think about the stress of her difficult breech birth in a county hospital, how she almost didn't make it; I think about the stress of her first years of life, when our family was made poor and desperate by needing to escape Jim Crow and migrate north; I think of her stressful encounters in elementary school (younger than her classmates, admonished by teachers at a tender age); I think of her anxious pubescent years spent worried about our mother's risky business *and* her general well-being, even as she fretted over family crises. I think of her trauma from being accosted by a strange man and dragged along the street while still in high school; and I think of her dating a young man in college whose schizophrenia led him to be obsessed and paranoid and entertain thoughts of killing her, a mentally ill man from whom she had to escape.

I'm thinking about Rita's lived experience.

I'm thinking of a corollary experience too: that during Rita's childhood and teenage years, she was doted on and loved and affirmed and well cared for; that she had close friendships and nourishing rituals of self-care that included writing letters to God and kissing her Bible. Maybe that helped her escape the fate of other Black girls diagnosed so much earlier—like rapper Snoop Dogg's daughter, Cori, who first showed signs of lupus at age six; and Valerie Horn, one of the longest-living Black lupus patients. Valerie first experienced symptoms at age fourteen and went through a battery of painful procedures throughout her teens (kidney biopsy, bone marrow tests, lymph node tissue extraction) and a misdiagnosis of arthritis before learning she had lupus.

I also suspect that college life at an HBCU, with its penumbra of protection, helped keep Rita's lupus at bay. Absent of the 1970s racial animus and tokenism and othering on white college campuses, perhaps Fisk University—coupled with her ancestral home of Nashville— allowed Rita to stay healthy for a little while longer.

12

After college, and following her diagnosis, Rita stayed in Nashville. Armed with her fresh degree in business administration, she soon was hired at Truckstops of America—one of the first truck stop chains in the country. As a branch accounting clerk, she handled daily financial records for eight regional locations. In my teenage arrogance, I remember thinking, *A, I could never live in Nashville, and B, I could never work for a place that had "truck stops" in its title.* The truth is, I could never have done what Rita was doing, as I was and remain abysmal at math, at working with numbers. But in my mind, I was destined for more exciting, creative things. In eleventh grade, I switched my curriculum from chem-bio, dropping my dream of becoming a psychiatrist, to performing arts. I was beginning to think of myself as a writer. I'd already written my first short story, which our mother told me she liked. I was also on the *Cass Technician* school newspaper staff, which made me feel I was really on my way to an adventurous career as an ace reporter.

Shortly after Rita started her new job that August, I flew to Nashville to visit her for a week. According to my diary, I chose to go for two reasons. I wrote, "I wanna see Rita, and I wanna go SOMEWHERE this summer." I forgot to take my diary with me on that trip, and so the pages across those days are blank, leaving no record of what we did together. But I'm sure we had a good time, especially since we were out from under the competitive presence of our mother's orbit. With just the two of us hanging out together, Rita had no need to jealously command Mama's attention, and I had no need to jealously resent her for it. I was simply an excited high schooler visiting her twenty-year-old sister for a week of summer vacation, getting a glimpse of her life as a brand-new grown-up.

Rita worked at Truckstops for just over a year, which gave her a bit more time around our Nashville kin, and more of a chance to absorb their neighborly Southern ways. Rita's friend Pierre believes she stayed involved with Cordell during that time, even though she'd dated Elijah back in Detroit. Cordell hadn't graduated but was still enrolled at Fisk and, according to a classmate's younger brother, still struggling with drug use and mental challenges. Interestingly, Rita and I didn't exchange any letters during her sixteen months of living and working in Nashville. Anyway, I'd like to believe that without the crucible of a college setting, she was able to eventually extricate herself from Cordell. But I already knew how hard that could be.

During that time, I was in a relationship that I needed to extricate myself from, yet I had not. My high school boyfriend—I'll call him Nigel—was physically and verbally abusive. I can recall every one of his cruel acts during the three-plus years I stayed with him: Nigel yanking my hair in front of everyone in the cafeteria at Cass Tech; Nigel walking by as I stand in front of my locker at school, and violently wiping the lipstick off my mouth; Nigel throwing hot coffee at my chest in the break room where we both work, me clad in a white angora sweater; Nigel stomping on my stockinged feet with his shoes while we're out on the dance floor; Nigel sitting on top of me with his full, massive weight, in the driver's seat of my car, trapping me inside as his Morehouse brother says, "I'm going to let you two work that out," ignoring my pleas for help; Nigel calling me a bitch in front of my girlfriends on a street in Atlanta, prompting me to burst into tears of humiliation . . . After each one, Nigel always saying the same thing: "You made me do it."

Rita was home on a visit when my dear friend since fourth grade, Diane, told her what she'd recently witnessed. We'd all been at a backyard party together, and suddenly—were we arguing?—Nigel pushed me hard, causing me to fall down—once again, in front of everyone. Humiliated, I tried to play it off, saying to Diane that I'd "stumbled." Diane didn't say anything to me, as I recall, but she did report the incident to Rita, and Rita promptly told our mother. Mama sat me down to talk to me, and I'll never forget how nervous she was—upset really—as she explained that no good could come from having a boyfriend who'd dare put his hands on you. "That's the worst type of man there is," she told me. "That's no man at all." The whole time, Mama kept her hands busy by untangling some jewelry in her lap. I felt then—and I still do—that the worst part of Nigel's abuse was how it upset our mother. And as soon as I got the chance, I told Rita that I was *never, ever* speaking to Diane again.

"Hey, you listen to me!" Rita said, her words landing hard. "Diane is your *best* friend, you hear me?! That's a friend for life. Don't you *ever* forget that."

She was right, of course. I never said anything to Diane about the incident, and we are still close friends today. But what struck me in the moment was how forceful Rita was, and how, clearly, she was stepping up as my big sister, telling me what I needed to hear whether I liked it or not. This didn't feel like the old childhood days of her "fussing" at me; this was something else with more weight, more urgency. Now, knowing Cordell had dared put his hands on *her*, I understand better why she was so emphatic. It's sad to think that we were both going through traumatic relationships, being mistreated by our boyfriends, and never talked about it with each other.

~

Just before New Year's of 1978, as I began my second semester of senior year, Rita moved back home. Still only twenty-one, she hadn't yet figured out what she wanted to do next with her life. And so, living in Motor City, she did what many Detroiters did: she got a job in the auto industry. Rita became a test driver at General Motors' proving ground in Milford, Michigan. To me, that job sounded thrilling and exotic. I loved driving, so the idea that you could make a living by driving cars fast around a track seemed to my young mind a dream job. Plus, she worked the overnight shift, which meant she left as Johnny Carson's *Tonight Show* was coming on, rushing to get to work before midnight, like a reverse Cinderella, and returning home just as the rest of us were heading to school and work. This added to the allure. Her official title was "light vehicle tester," and her role was to assist engineers in evaluating the performance of 1980 automobiles for the Environmental Protection Agency. GM's proving ground is a sprawling four-thousand-acre facility; its roads stretch for 132 miles and are meant to mirror the conditions you'd find on public roadways.

Ever fascinated, I once asked Rita to describe a typical day at work, and she said it went like this: After she clocked in, she picked up her schedule. On a given day, she might be assigned a diesel Cadillac to drive for two hundred miles on the fast track. This run wasn't her favorite assignment because diesel Caddys were "loud and clunky," she said. Still, she popped a cassette of one of her favorite R&B artists into the car's stereo player, eased the Caddy onto the simulated road, and started clocking her miles.

Turns out, Rita liked driving alone for long distances. "It's something about driving a car, listening to the music," she told me years later. "When you're alone, you've got a lot of time to think." In the three-plus hours it took her to drive those two hundred miles—she'd better *not* finish sooner because that meant she was going faster than the sixty-five-miles-per-hour speed limit, a no-no—she could make her way through all the songs on the latest albums by Peabo Bryson, Rufus featuring Chaka Khan, Teena Marie, *and* the Emotions. She also liked that she could see the sun rise up over the road before her. What most of the other test drivers loved was the fast track itself, which was essentially a massive expressway, with seven lanes divided by fresh white road lines. Manicured lawns and planted trees had been placed along the embankments to give the whole experience the feel of a real highway. Although it wasn't officially allowed, some guys raced around the fast track on the outside lanes in GM sports cars like Camaros and Grands Prix. That was not her thing.

After she'd clocked her required miles, Rita turned the car into the little island in the center of the track and gassed up. Then she did her final assignment: sending the Caddy through the corrosion booth, which was like a sadistic car wash, where concentrated salt and water spewed out and pummeled the luxury car in an "accelerated corrosion life testing"—essentially defacing a thing of beauty to see how much abuse it could take.

Once done, Rita went to the employee lounge and napped for a couple hours before clocking out by seven a.m. to go home. And then

---

she turned around and did it again the next night. She was one of very few women test-driving cars, a job folks coveted. Given the choice of assembly line work or being outdoors, alone in a fast car, driving hundreds of miles without traffic or risk of accident, and without supervisors, who wouldn't prefer the latter? "Getting paid for tearing up the road" is how Rita put it. Not that the proving ground was without its microaggressions of sexism and racism. Rita told me she wasn't allowed to change her own oil because as a woman she'd "mess it up." And more than once, as she was filling up her gas tank in cold weather, the men wouldn't loan her their gloves.

Still, that was a special time for her, which included a fling with a young guy who also worked at the proving ground. Rita later told me, smiling like a Cheshire cat, that on some of those nights she left to go "to work," she was really going to spend time with him. Mama was none the wiser. And neither was I. I vividly remember her back then, young and having fun. She was in good health, but already there was one key way in which lupus affected her life: Rita was never able to take birth control pills, because the potential side effects included blood clots, already a risk for lupus sufferers. Now I'm imagining how hard that had to be as a young woman coming of age in the 1970s, to not have the liberation of reliable birth control. That had to bring its own level of stress.

13

Rita had been at her proving ground job for a couple months when our father checked himself into the hospital, making it on his own to the emergency room. Clearly, his high blood pressure—which was already causing spots in front of his eyes, dizziness, and severe headaches—had gotten worse. He was soon transferred from the VA hospital in Allen Park to the one in Ann Arbor. Even though I'd never known our father to be in the hospital—unlike our mother—I assumed he'd get better and come home. I didn't understand the dangers of his illness because I'd only known our father as a man with high blood pressure, and he seemed to be managing it. I understood only enough about his chronic condition to know it prevented him from working.

I wonder what Rita, newly suffering a chronic condition, understood. Did she assume as I did that he'd keep on managing his, keep on living with it? Did she know yet the term "progressive disease" and the fate that it implies? She certainly tried to talk to me about her concerns while our father was still in the hospital, fighting for his life. On this one day, she and I were together in our bedroom, a suitcase opened on my bed as she sat atop hers. I was packing for my upcoming senior trip to Toronto. Rita watched me placing clothes into the suitcase. "Will you still go on your trip if Daddy doesn't get better?" she asked me.

"He will," I answered back, too quickly.

"But what if he doesn't?"

"He will," I repeated.

She left it alone, but I'm sure she knew enough to know his prognosis wasn't good. And I'm sure looking back that she'd wanted to share her fears with me, but I wouldn't let her. I couldn't.

Today research shows that the prevalence of high blood pressure in African Americans is among the highest in the world. Now we know that more than 40 percent of Black people suffer from it, and that, like Daddy, we tend to develop it earlier in life and with more severity. Only now do I see how similar those facts are to Black women disproportionately suffering from lupus. Did Daddy understand more than we did when Rita was diagnosed—what that would mean for her life? Perhaps that's why he rushed to her side when he learned the news.

We also didn't know how little was being done to treat our father's high blood pressure—was anyone calling it "hypertension" back then?—nor what could've been done. During his hospital stay, one day a doctor offhandedly looked at Daddy's swollen feet and said to me, "That's a sign of heart disease. He should've been treated for that. Why wasn't he?" We didn't know that high blood pressure often leads to cardiovascular disease, as well as strokes. But the implication was that we *should've* known, and like doctors and nurses who at the height of the pandemic began to give up on very sick coronavirus patients who'd chosen not to get vaccinated, I can imagine those medical professionals giving up on our father for supposedly not doing what he could to take care of himself. It was his fault, they reasoned, so why bother?

While apparently up until the 1960s doctors viewed high blood pressure as an untreatable condition of aging, by the early '70s there *was* some effort to treat it, often with diuretics. But our father wasn't, to my knowledge, taking any medication to treat his condition. Today it's standard procedure to prescribe an antihypertensive medication. Even if he was, startlingly, research shows that Black men taking medication for their high blood pressure have worse outcomes than whites. It's not stopping their strokes. Little has been done to understand why. Lots of attention *has* been given to salt, and how HBP sufferers should avoid it. This news made its way to Daddy late in his journey with the disease, and he began trying to reduce his use of table salt. Researchers have even found a gene that they say could make Blacks more sensitive to salt, with as little as half a teaspoon of extra salt intake raising blood pressure significantly. The implication is that Blacks really just need to change their diets to mitigate the severity of hypertension. In fact, I will never forget the brazen insensitivity of a white nurse telling seventeen-year-old me that my father was "a very sick man" and admonishing me for not encouraging him to lose weight. This fat-shaming was standard at the time and persists to this day. Obesity is used to blame the victims of high blood pressure (as well as diabetes and countless other diseases). A whole acronym has emerged to address these food-based causes: DASH—Dietary Approaches to Stop Hypertension—i.e., shorthand for avoiding bad diets and irresponsible eating.

But research has revealed that dietary changes also have *not* led to high blood pressure control in African American men. One 2014 study in particular from the *American Journal of Medical Sciences*, titled "Racial Differences in Hypertension: Implications for High Blood Pressure Management," looks specifically at that fact, the article noting that researchers don't know *why* diet doesn't help—because evidence from clinical trials and studies "is often inadequate and insufficient" when it comes to African Americans. Treatments that work on white lives don't always work the same on Black lives. After years of researchers blaming salt sensitivity and body mass and inexplicable "resistant hypertension," the article's author admits that "there are numerous other factors with significant racial differences that could affect the disparities in hypertension including social determinants, access to care, fetal/early life origins, and differential treatment response."

To translate the above: implicit bias in the medical field, compounded by Black mothers' lack of prenatal and neonatal care, alongside early life racialized traumas, coupled with medical treatments for HBP designed for white bodies, all lead to poor outcomes for Blacks suffering from hypertension. And in a more recent study, the National Institutes of Health showed that once researchers ruled out other causes by controlling data for obesity, exercise, use of substances, and socioeconomic status, among others, "a higher perceived exposure to discrimination was linked to a 34% higher risk of developing hypertension."

Thanks to Dr. Arline T. Geronimus, a professor in the School of Public Health at the University of Michigan, we now have an apt term for what my and Rita's father and millions of Black men and women like him have faced, one that no longer requires reading between the lines or hedging with words like "higher perceived exposure" to bias. That apt term is one word: "weathering." As Dr. Geronimus defines it in her book of the same name: "Weathering is a process that encompasses the physiological effects of living in marginalized communities that bear the brunt of racial, ethnic, religious and class discrimination. . . . [It] is a stress-related biological process that leaves identifiable groups of Americans vulnerable to dying or suffering chronic disease and disability long before they are chronologically old."

Weathering as a concept is mind-blowing, because it eviscerates the long-touted claim that Black folks suffer disproportionately poorer health outcomes than whites because of "lifestyle and personal choices," that old chestnut called "environmental factors," and poverty. Dr. Geronimus makes clear how ubiquitous its effects are: "Weathering afflicts human bodies—all the way down to the cellular level—as they grow, develop, and age in a racist, classist society," she writes.

Experiencing racial discrimination makes hypertension more likely, and much worse.

~

Once he was actually in the hospital, our father's health further declined. On one of my visits, Daddy told me he'd had two ministrokes *since being there*. Research done shows that once a patient experiences a stroke while already admitted to the hospital, he or she is less likely to receive immediate attention than a stroke patient who enters through the ER. That fact is coupled with the preponderance of data confirming that Black patients are treated more poorly in hospitals than white patients, thanks once again to those same not-so-implicit biases.

And why *was* our father transferred to a VA hospital forty-five miles away from Detroit? Had he been closer might we all have been at the hospital daily, for more hours each day? We didn't question it at the time because we all thought he'd receive better care at the "white" VA hospital in Ann Arbor as opposed to the one inside Detroit. Black folks already largely believed that VA hospitals had higher quality than other hospitals, and so Black vets would de facto get the same care as white vets. This is why we felt Daddy's being a veteran gave him a slight advantage. He served in the army during World War II, although he barely spoke to us about his service. Recently, via Ancestry.com, I found his draft registration card from 1944. This was two years before he and our mother married. As is so often the case, that dry document provided all kinds of new information. I learned he was eighteen when he registered. On the form, under "telephone," it said "none"; under "person who will always know your address" was listed his older sister, Mrs. Beatrice Caruthers, with whom he lived at the time, and who'd essentially raised him. His place of employment was listed as Melrose Bowling Center. He was drafted and served in that final year of the war, becoming one of 1.5 million Black men serving in the armed forces back then. The only thing I know about his time in the army is that he worked in the kitchen on base. I used to think this explained his short-order-cook skills. He could whip up a few basic yet delicious meals—eggs, burgers, home fries—with confidence. And when our brother was born in 1952, on his birth certificate Daddy's occupation is listed as "cook." I doubt he was one of the official military cooks who'd received culinary training; more likely he was on basic kitchen patrol duty. It's likely our father didn't see combat, given that was typical of the Black soldiers back then, often kept behind the front lines to do all the menial work. While Black men *did* serve valiantly in battle during WWII, with over seven hundred dying in combat, segregation and racism kept those fighting Black men the exceptions that proved the rule. And the fact that Daddy barely spoke about his army experience suggests it was likely filled with humiliations and unjust treatment that were the norm in a segregated military, and certainly worth putting behind him. Never mind what our father experienced in the eighteen years *before* he got drafted into the army.

14

How does a parent's early life affect their children's lives? I learned details of Daddy's coming-of-age days while still a young girl. Often after he and I had eaten dinner together—our two favorite meals were fried liver and smothered onions, and pork chops with gravy—he'd share details of his harsh teenage years; a vivid memory is Daddy describing himself hoboing his way around, jumping on and off trains. He also told me a bit about his mother, Hattie, who was too "easy" with men and suffered from "the drinking disease," how one day he walked in on her having relations with a man on the floor. His birth certificate provides some of the only known details about his mother, Hattie: Daddy was born in 1926, when his mother was twenty-four. She already had a nine-year-old daughter, Beatrice, born when Hattie was fifteen. Under question number five, "Legitimate?," is scrawled the word "No." In fact, the entire section for information about the father is blacked out. Hattie's occupation is listed as "labour," and under question number eighteen, "Number of children born to this mother including present birth," the answer is "3"; yet to question number nineteen, "Number of children of this mother *now* living," the answer is "2," which makes clear that, like our mother, our father's mother lost a baby. The full name Hattie gave our father, her first boy, was John Thomas Matthews Davis, all Biblical names. I doubt she wanted the *s* at the end of "Matthews," but historically Blacks' birth certificates are rife with careless error, given that white registrars/hospital employees filled out the paperwork and often just spelled the names the way they wanted. (My own name was spelled wrong on mine, left uncorrected until I was nearly eighteen.) Our father dropped the second middle name, keeping "Thomas," and soon everyone called him John T.—except his sisters, who only called him "brother." The official signature on his birth certificate is that of a midwife, as there is no "Dr." in front of the person's name. Under the heading of "Color," his mother's race is listed as "Col," for "colored."

I have no idea when Hattie, our paternal grandmother, died. And I've never seen a picture of her. Our father likely didn't know his own father, even though he was apparently named after him, and so I cannot fathom the miracle of how he lovingly fathered his own son, Anthony, as well as me and Rita and his two oldest girls. I don't know how he learned to love us so fully and fiercely, but I do know that he reserved that love for his family alone. "Hell, I don't really give a damn about nobody else," he used to say. "Why would I?" When our brother, Anthony, was sent to prison, Mama said she slept better at night knowing where he was; Daddy said he served every day with him. And when our parents learned of Rita's diagnosis, I know our mother worried about her, but knowing Daddy, I know it broke his heart. Rita inherited that same deep love and anguish for family from our father. She certainly had her favorite people, friends she really cared about and would do many things for. But she reserved her true devotion and energy for her own family. And, like our father, she largely distrusted outsiders, folks she suspected were only coming around to take advantage. We all used to tease her about how she and Daddy were so alike in that way—with a healthy dose of suspicion.

Did she also inherit his trauma?

Maybe Daddy clung to that fierce and protective love of his family—and a distrust of outsiders—because of the great losses he suffered so early. When his two younger brothers died, they were about five and eight at the time, the details of their deaths almost unfathomable. According to Daddy, a ne'er-do-well drifter from Alabama got with his mother, and soon took out life insurance policies on the two boys. Daddy and his sisters always believed that monstrous man drowned their little brothers in a quarry, in order to receive the insurance money; after their so-called accidental drownings, the man skipped town.

Rita tried to talk to our aunt Bea about what happened, as they'd become close during Rita's time in Nashville. Aunt Bea had basically raised her two youngest brothers, and she told Rita she still couldn't talk about it, decades later. She did say, "I still owe them a spanking for going near that quarry; I told them to stay away from there."

And as Rita repeated that story to me, we both understood the toll it had taken on our beloved aunt Bea. Daddy also lived with deep sorrow and regret that he hadn't somehow protected and saved his little brothers, as the oldest boy—the big brother they looked up to. He felt he'd failed them. But he was, of course, not there when it happened, and was himself a teenager, already adrift. Our mother's parents, who treated Mama's childhood sweetheart like a son, anchored his life. Our grandfather Pap adored John T.; he taught his son-in-law how to paint and plaster, the trade that provided Pap with a robust livelihood.

I wonder what life would've been like for our father had he been able to make a living in Detroit as a painter and plasterer. But, of course, that's not why he left everything he knew in Nashville to migrate north. He came like millions before him to get a good-paying hourly job in one of the auto factories. And that's what he did. Daddy was a heat treater at GM's Pontiac Motor Division. Our family migrated initially to Pontiac from Nashville and lived there a year before moving to Detroit, but Daddy remained employed at the Pontiac plant, in a job that was dangerous, difficult, and low-rung—melting metals using high temperatures and inhaling toxic fumes. The thirty-mile commute from Detroit itself presented a challenge, particularly in those early days when he didn't yet have a car.

After several years at GM, our father was injured at work—an inevitability given the job he was forced to do. He filed a case with Michigan's Bureau of Workmen's Compensation, and then waited and waited for a decision. It took over *seven years* before he was finally awarded a onetime payment of $1,000 in 1971. The award required expenses be deducted for attorney's fees and medical costs, so Daddy, by then nearly forty-five, received a total of $710. Cross-out lines were drawn through the space on the award letter where it stated the defendant was required to make weekly payments of compensation to the plaintiff. There'd be none. This decree was declared the bureau's final decision. Our father "won" his case, but GM prevailed, and the "hearing referee" made clear what he believed our father's work life and injured body was worth in monetary terms: not much. Studies have been done on this too—how Blacks suffer disproportionately more on-the-job injuries, yet face discrimination in the form of delays, more required medical exams, and smaller award amounts than white plaintiffs receiving workmen's compensation. Shortly after filing that workmen's comp suit, Daddy had to stop working altogether, due to the severity of his hypertension. He'd weathered so much across the first three decades of his life: born, like Rita, after his mom had lost a child; living under the stigma of illegitimacy and a "loose" mother; surviving the South's punitive and demeaning Jim Crow laws; traumatized as a teen from multiple sibling loss; serving in a racist army; losing his newborn baby; migrating, which brought northern poverty coupled with on-the-job discrimination; and later suffering through dismissive treatment by biased doctors—all while, humming beneath the surface, lay the ever-present possibility of his arrest or even death from encounters with police.

Poet Elizabeth Alexander, in her moving memoir about her husband and his early death from a heart attack at age fifty, writes that a cardiologist told her he believed "unequivocally" that escaping war from Eritrea affected her husband Ficre's heart. I think the same way about Daddy. As his arteries carried blood from his heart to the rest of his body, that blood began pressing too hard against his arteries' walls, and so each time our father's heart beat, and each time his heart rested between those beats, the pressure grew and grew—until the pressure became too much. Life in America damaged Daddy's heart.

Did our father ever stand a chance?

As journalist and author Linda Villarosa has powerfully described it in her book *Under the Skin*, we now know that lived experience—which for Black Americans often means an accumulation of demeaning, racialized encounters big and small, as it did for our father—creates a fight-or-flight response in the body; the brain responds to this stress by releasing a flood of hormones to help the body respond to the challenge. Doing this long-term leads to wear and tear on the cardiovascular, metabolic, and immune systems, making the body vulnerable to illness and early death, i.e., weathering. So often, for a host of reasons, the person suffering is left to fend for himself, scrambling for ways to self-manage his condition.

Daddy definitely sought ways to cope. He suffered constant, excruciating headaches. As a child, I'd often massage his temples with my
small hands, trail my fingers over his closed eyelids, or place a cool
washcloth across his forehead to help bring relief. He claimed it made
him feel better. For a while, he tried using Stanback powdered aspirin,
chased back with big swigs of Pepsi-Cola, to mitigate the pain. But
over time the headaches got worse, and he turned to a pharmaceutical
drug as a way to gain relief. He started taking Demerol, an opioid
analgesic that's often prescribed by doctors for severe pain.

When I was around seven or eight, I witnessed our father inject
Demerol into his veins. He kept his paraphernalia in a crinkled brown
paper bag hidden underneath the floor-model Magnavox TV in our
den. One day, he directed me to "feel up under there" and grab the bag
from its hiding place, hand it to him. I watched him pull out the vial,
the syringe, the rubber band; I watched as he tied the band around
his arm, filled the syringe with a carefully measured amount of dark
liquid, and injected himself. Right away, I could see his body relax,
the tension across his face disappear, and his mood lift. He laughed at
my jokes, chuckled during the TV sitcoms we watched together, and
soon enough, Daddy drifted off to sleep, snoring lightly. In my child's
mind, that injection was a magical elixir.

Michael Jackson was prescribed Demerol after he was badly burned
in an accident while filming a Pepsi-Cola commercial in 1984 (my father loved both a young Michael Jackson and Pepsi-Cola). The drug
is similar to morphine. It makes your brain respond differently to how
your body feels, and to the pain. It makes you feel good. I suspect
Daddy got the liquid Demerol from our family doctor, Dr. Carey, who
appreciated the severity of our father's condition. As a young adult,
I once thought that Dr. Carey bore some of the blame for Daddy's
addiction, until I got older and understood how most doctors tend
to keep pain medication *away* from Black patients, not believing in
or assuming they can endure their suffering, and I have gratitude for
handsome Dr. Carey and his compassion toward our father, true to his
Hippocratic Oath on behalf of another Black man.

I believe Daddy let me witness him shooting up because he *wanted* me to know, wanted me to understand who he was, what he'd gone through, what he'd come through, and where it had taken him—as a survivor. He wanted his youngest child to bear witness. And I did. I also never shared with anyone what I'd seen Daddy do with that needle—including Rita.

In those final days, I was given our father's wallet by the hospital staff; inside I found an ID card for the Narcotics Treatment Institute, dated November 26, 1973, with his photo and signature. He would've been forty-seven at the time. Below his name—DAVIS, JOHN T.—it read, "The person identified by this card is under medical treatment and must receive daily medication." He was receiving methadone at a clinic every day, trying to overcome his yearslong dependence on a wondrous and wicked painkiller that provided relief. I can understand why he kept this fact a secret, because best believe back then there was no outpouring of compassion toward opioid users the way there is today—and certainly not ones who looked like our father.

When I think about how weathered our father's body was, how he suffered such a debilitating disease that robbed him of a livelihood and a normal life, I marvel at what he *did* accomplish.

~

Rita answered the phone on that day when I called home from a pay phone in the employees' lounge at Winkelman's, the clothing store where I worked at Northland Center mall, asking how Daddy was doing. "About the same," she lied. "When will you be home?" she asked, her voice calm. I snapped at her, saying obviously I'd be home after my shift ended at nine. As soon as I pulled up to our house that night and saw all the cars parked in front and in the driveway, I knew something was wrong. But I did not assume the obvious. When I opened the door, everyone was standing there, waiting for me. Our sister Dianne said, "He didn't make it, Bridgett. He didn't make it." Daddy was just shy of his fifty-second birthday.

I understand now what an act of protective love that was for Rita to lie to me when I called to get an update on our father's condition. Just as she'd wanted to make sure I was walking to school with a friend when I was still at Hampton Junior High, she wanted to make sure I drove myself home safely before learning such devastating news. His death certificate reveals that our father died at 7:50 p.m. that evening, which means Rita had *just* learned the news herself when I called home. How hard did she have to work to hold it together, just so I wouldn't detect a hint of grief, of sadness, in her voice?

A letter written to our father from his only son, Anthony, arrived after his death. We placed the letter, unopened, inside the pocket of Daddy's suit jacket, and buried it with him. That had been Rita's idea.

We learned from our father's death certificate that he died from respiratory arrest due to a "brain stem infarction," which means he stopped breathing after suffering a stroke that occurs when a blockage obstructs blood flow to the brain stem. People do survive brain stem strokes, but recovery has everything to do with how quickly the stroke is detected and treated. Daddy also had pneumonia, listed as one "other significant condition" at the time of his death. Again, our father got worse once he was in the hospital.

Rita and I talked about this, or indirectly so. Years later, we asked ourselves whether the outcome would've been different if we'd kept vigil daily—despite his being placed at a hospital nearly an hour's drive away; we asked ourselves whether Daddy might've gotten better care if we'd been better advocates for him. Yet, the truth is that back in 1978 we just trusted the doctors, and hoped for the best; we told ourselves, "At least he's in the hospital," because when you're Black, getting a loved one to the hospital is itself a feat, not a given. Sometimes ambulances don't come soon enough, sometimes hospitals don't admit you, sometimes you wait too long to go, sometimes fear of the bill or denigration keeps you away. Voluminous studies now track healthcare workers' racial bias—from nurses to doctors to technicians—but back then Rita and I simply chose to believe that our father would be cared for and would get better. We were young and naïve.

After the unimaginable happened, we lost our naïveté; nothing was ever the same for me, or Rita, or us.

15

The widely accepted belief in our family was that I was the closest to our father, and so my grief over losing him was the hardest. It's true that the first few years of my life were spent sleeping curled atop Daddy's back, and that he was in many ways my primary parent during my early years. He doted on me, I spent much of my free time with him, and everyone understood that we were close. Even after they divorced and we moved away when I was nine and Rita was thirteen, I spent many weekends with Daddy up until I became a teenager. I was a full-on daddy's girl. When he died, my mother and siblings were secretly worried about me. Sometime later, Rita admitted to me: "I just kept thinking to myself, *If I'm feeling this bad over Daddy, I can't imagine how bad Bridgett is feeling.*"

When Rita and I went on our spring trip to New York so soon after our father's death, a lot was going on for each of us, and between us. We weren't just feeling our way through a closer bond as sisters; as we walked along Fifth Avenue that day and Rita's leg began to ache, that was the first time I witnessed her having a flare-up. Since her diagnosis nearly two years before, she'd been mostly away from home, working in Nashville. I hadn't known yet what living with lupus looked like. In fact, I suspect that Rita's lupus had been in remission up until that point. And then Daddy died. Despite the fun we were having, we were carrying our heavy hearts around Manhattan. Also, losing a loved one is highly stressful, and stress triggers lupus flare-ups, activating the immune system into overdrive to attack its own healthy cells. Rita's leg ached not because we'd walked too much, but because she was grieving, and grief can land hard on the body. If Rita hadn't experienced Daddy's dying at that nascent stage of her condition, might that have slowed the disease's progression? If our father had lived, would Rita have stayed in remission longer, been healthier for more years? Instead, so began her life of lupus and loss.

That winter when our father suffered the multiple strokes that would lead to his death, I'd already been accepted to Spelman College, and Rita had already decided to apply to graduate schools; she chose Atlanta University's MBA program. With us both headed toward higher education, Rita and I were clearly distinct from our three older siblings: Our brother Anthony's incarceration sat like a boulder on the chest of our family, slightly blocking our air passages; who can breathe fully when someone you love is locked up? The fact of it was an unspoken yet palpable affront and disappointment to our mother, which itself was hard for Rita and me to witness. Our sister Deborah was still struggling with her addiction, which had morphed over the years into her using various drugs in an attempt to chase her high. And our sister Dianne was nearly a decade into her marriage to George, still a raging alcoholic. He generated constant crises—either blacking out, or having car accidents, or losing another job; they struggled financially. Throughout all her husband's transgressions, Dianne vociferously defended him to us, which was also hard to witness.

Rita and I were Mama's two non-problematic children, doing what we were supposed to do: getting our education, staying away from drugs and out of trouble with the law, not married to the wrong men. And as young women, we weren't getting pregnant and becoming unwed mothers; that was our shared commonality within the family cosmos. It felt good to be at a similar place in life as Rita, for the first time ever. Even though hers was graduate and mine was undergrad, we were both headed to the same new Southern city to attend school, escaping Detroit and our family misfortunes.

Rita was still working at the proving ground when she wrote her third letter to me, at Spelman, where I was attending a pre-freshman summer program; the envelope was stamped "special delivery," and inside was a money order:

7–6–78

Hi Bridgett,
Just a few lines to say "hello."
I'm planning another trip to New York. Are you going?

Did Mama tell you I'm on afternoons? Please start praying that I get laid off on July 15th.

I took the dogs to the beauty shop. They really looked cute. They had the nerve to come in the house with an attitude when they came back. (Didn't want to be bothered with us).

Take Care,
Rita

P.S. Buy me a cute top. Don't forget.

Mama sent the money. I just signed my name, little sis.

I'm not sure what was magical about the date July 15—she'd qualify for unemployment? Who knows, but I suspect once she knew her life was about to change, she got sick of driving new cars in circles, headed nowhere.

When I returned home after the pre-freshman program, I arrived back to a familiar household dynamic: Mama and Rita tight as ever, in their own bonded world, with folks saying how much they looked alike, and me just on the outside of that. *And* I'd lost my status as a daddy's girl. Rita and I bickered a lot, the promise we'd made to each other in that hotel room in Manhattan months before too easily broken. Also, I wasn't really speaking to our mother, for reasons I don't even recall. When I left home for my official start of college that August, and Mama asked if I wanted her to accompany me, I said no thanks. Given the contrast between the fanfare that accompanied Rita's departure—with family members coming to the airport to send her off, and Elaine and me traveling with her to Fisk—I'm sure I was intent on distinguishing myself as more independent than she. (It was an easy stance to take since I'd already spent a month on my new college's campus.) In hindsight, the simpler truth is that I was devastated that one parent was gone, and I took my hurt feelings out on the remaining one. Now experts call this "displacement grief," where we're really angry at the Universe/God, but we take that anger out on the people we most care about. That was me.

Right after I left, a group of extended family—Mama, Rita, our cousin Jewell and her parents, and another aunt—all went to Las Vegas for several days. I knew that Rita would've opted to skip *her* first week of college if it meant taking a trip to Vegas with Mama, but I chose not to go, deciding that I didn't want to miss out on freshman week. Yet my journal reveals that I didn't have much fun. "Freshman week is exhausting," I wrote. "The party was basically boring. I was ready to go so soon!" And then to reassure myself I wrote, "It's going to be okay—I'll like it. I think I've conditioned my mind in such a way that it would be impossible for me not to like it."

What I hadn't anticipated was how lonely I'd be during those first days of college, and that my nights would be filled with fitful dreams about our father. I soon regretted missing out on a restorative family trip of fun and love and togetherness. As an aside—or maybe to underscore the point—Rita came back with a lovely headshot of herself, taken by a photographer at a club on the Vegas strip. That photo remains one of my favorites, as it captures her looking so relaxed, her smile sweet, eyes optimistic.

~

"Rita got here today," I wrote in my journal at the start of our semesters. "I liked seeing her. All the conflicts I was experiencing with her and Momma while I was home—why? Nothing is more important than family and nothing else comes first."

Barely a week after I wrote those words, our mother was carjacked on the street near our home, and when she got out of the car, the carjacker pulled out a gun, hit her over the head with it, then jumped into her car and took off. Rita and I were awash in relief and gratitude that she'd survived. We flew home together, holding hands on the plane. My plan was to tightly hug our mother as soon as I laid eyes on her, and then have a real conversation with her about the thing that was on my heart: "I want to talk to her about Rita and me," I wrote in my journal. "We can't seem to get along and I don't really know why. The relationship is so strained. I can't say certain things to her without her getting offended and the same goes for me. It's hard on both of us and I don't know what to do!"

I had plans for *how* I'd engage with our mother:

> . . . I want to do all this talking with her while Rita's not there.
> I don't feel like competing for her attention. I'm going to tell her
> how I've envied the relationship she and Rita had for so, so long
> that it's hard for me to stop. I think I'll feel a lot better once I do
> this. I just hope I can say it all the way I want to. I hope it makes
> her—and me!—feel a lot better!

I'm amazed now that I was able to articulate the central conflict in my and Rita's relationship, and that I was willing to admit my envy. No question our mother already knew and understood what was going on with me and Rita; my confession would've simply been confirmation. Once we were home, I don't recall whether I actually *had* that conversation with our mother, but I did write in my journal, "Rita's with me, Momma's fine and the world is right."

I'd made the decision upon starting college that I wanted to be called Brih-jet, rather than have my name pronounced like Brigitte Bardot or Bridget Fonda. Our aunt Gladys always said my name in that more lyrical way, with the emphasis on the second syllable, and I liked how it sounded. So I changed the pronunciation and began introducing myself that way. Rita, unlike everyone else in our family, got on board immediately, and from that day forward only called me Brih-jet. "You get to say your name however *you* want," she told me. I felt so seen by that, and grateful to my sister for supporting me.

~

One of those early days of college, I snap a picture of Rita sitting on my dorm room bed in Abby Hall. She's wearing a red tank top trimmed in white and smiling gently at the camera, her body at ease. My room décor surrounds her, with its newspaper-style bulletin board and flowery comforter, collection of books lined along the windowsill.

I cling to this photo as proof that Rita and I did in fact spend some special time together during our Atlanta days, because I have fewer memories of us back then than I want to admit, and because she and I would never live in the same city again—apart from a few months that I'd later spend in Detroit, before moving elsewhere.

My favorite memory of us back in 1978 begins on a November day: I've just returned to my dorm room, and I find a note on the bed that my roommate Del has left.

> Bridgette, your sister called (REAL SISTER!). She wants to
> know if you would like to usher for the Richard Pryor show! (See
> if you can get me in).

I loved that my *real* sister had called, not my college Big Sis, and I loved that she lived nearby. It made me feel special among my classmates.

Rita and I did end up ushering for that Richard Pryor show, and it remains one of my all-time favorite concerts. Not only did I have a crush on Pryor (I carried a photo of him in my wallet as a young teen), Rita and I both loved the singer Patti LaBelle, who was that night's special guest. And seeing Pryor perform live was an incomparable experience. He looked really good dressed in a beautiful cream-colored suit with an off-white silk shirt, and he was *so* brilliant and so funny, at the height of his powers. That night he told iconic jokes about heavy stuff—his heart attack, his arrest after shooting up his own car, and my favorite: his grandmother ordering him to go outside and get a switch from a tree branch, for her to "beat yo' ass with." (Turns out, that same tour produced the first-ever stand-up comedy special released as a film, Pryor's iconic *Live in Concert*.) Rita and I couldn't stop laughing as we stood together in the aisles, co-ushering.

Before the show began, we listened to this amazing R&B singer whose powerful soprano tumbled out from the speakers of the venue; both Rita and I wondered, *Who is that?* We didn't recognize her voice, but as we used to say, she could *blow*. Months later, Rita showed up at my dorm room to gift me a copy of that singer's debut album, *Wild and Peaceful*. Her name was Teena Marie, and because the album cover didn't have her picture on it, everyone—including all the disc jockeys playing her music on Black radio—assumed she was Black. Only when she appeared on *Soul Train* with Rick James later that year, performing "I'm a Sucker for Your Love," did we all discover that Teena Marie was in fact a white girl. (And the first one to appear on *Soul Train*.) She was the same age as Rita, who would forever love Teena Marie's music. When I play my favorite song from that album, "Déjà Vu," and she sings, "I'm young and I'm old, I'm rich and I'm poor, I feel I've been on this earth many times before . . ." I think of Rita, who had a wise spirit about her that made folks believe *she'd* been here before. Teena Marie's voice forever reminds me of that night at the Pryor concert, its magic and euphoria, a better sisters' memory than our New York trip—so fraught with fresh grief—and a way better memory than our growing-up days. For the first time, we genuinely had something in common: fatherless daughters now bonding as inseparable sisters, just as I'd longed for in the privacy of my diary as a thirteen-year-old. We were both young adults, Rita and I, choosing each other, having fun together. Getting along.

16

In many ways, graduate school went well for Rita, right from the start. Because she'd waited a couple years after college, she was finally the same age as most of her classmates, a new experience for the girl who graduated high school at sixteen. Also, our cousin Elaine, ever her guardian angel, had set things up beautifully for Rita before she arrived on campus. Elaine had herself attended Atlanta University and had been working in the registrar's office for a few years; although she'd left the job a year before Rita arrived, she made sure the key administrator in that office, Johnnie Robinson, knew about Rita's pending arrival. "I told her, 'My young cousin is coming to school here,'" recalls Elaine, "'and I want you to look out for her.'" Johnnie met Rita and they quickly became close. In fact, Rita soon started doing work-study in the registrar's office, alongside Johnnie.

Rita loved having older women in her life, beyond our mother and aunts. She was more a friend to her godmother, Lula, than a goddaughter, for instance. And so having Johnnie as a good friend made sense. She found her, as a woman with more life experience, genuinely fascinating, someone to learn from. Rita had an ease around older women that escaped me. And clearly Johnnie loved Rita. "All she would talk about was Rita, Rita, Rita," recalls Clayvon Croom, a classmate. "'My girl, Rita,' she'd say." In fact, all the women working in the office apparently adored her. "She'd come in there with her fly clothes, looking cute, and with that warm spirit," says Elaine. "She could make every friend feel special, like they were her best friend. You know how she was."

I do. It's what I envied and admired about Rita, in equal doses. She was so much chattier and more outgoing than I, and more personable, warm. I think because she had a special quality, this way of really *seeing* someone, never looking through or past him or her, all kinds of people were naturally drawn to Rita. She'd often start up a conversation with strangers. If we entered a store together, she'd compliment the cashier on her hair, which would lead to a discussion about the best beauty shop in the area, and before you knew it, the young woman would be telling Rita how her boyfriend doesn't really like her hairstyle, and Rita would be advising her to "Do you, and maybe get yourself a new boyfriend." Several of her friends have told me how they marvel over the way people would just tell Rita their business.

Right away, she met her grad-school bestie, Annie. They lived on the same floor in Bumstead Hall, one of the dorms at AU. Rita lived near the hall phone and would often answer it; one day she knocked on Annie's door to tell her she had a phone call, and that was that. "Rita was a talker and I talk a lot as well," explains Annie. "That's how we really connected." The friendship grew quickly. "We just really, really fell in love with each other, because I was a giver and Rita was a giver as well. We helped each other."

As the friend closest to her in proximity, Annie was a firsthand witness to the two defining aspects of Rita's life at that time. First, she learned about our family. "She *loved* her family! She would always be talking about her family," says Annie. "That's how I know your father, John T." I'm stunned when she references him by name, but Annie says Rita told her *all* about him. And she even went into detail about his funeral. "I think he had a white hearse, right?" He did. "'John T.' is a name I can never forget," says Annie. "It's almost like a brother of mine; I could never forget my brothers. And I can never forget that her dad was John T." Annie says the way Rita spoke about him, it was clear how much she loved our father. I'm touched to learn that while I was bonding with my freshman roommate, Nikki, because we'd both just lost our fathers, Rita was processing her own fresh grief by talking about Daddy with her new friend. Saying his name.

She also told Annie about me immediately, and about my being at Spelman. "She'd always say 'my sister,'" recalls Annie. "'My sister.' That's how she would say it."

Annie says she soon became aware that Rita had some health challenges. Initially, she and Rita would walk to campus together, but after a while, Rita stopped walking and drove her yellow Firebird the short distance instead. In time, Annie came to understand that

Rita got too tired from walking to campus while carrying her books, going back to the dorm, and sometimes returning to campus for later classes. "That was too much walking for her," Annie recalls. Also, Rita sometimes needed to nap between classes. Annie remembers that Rita told her she had a condition, and there was no cure. "But she was trying to figure it out," says Annie. A campus away, I was oblivious to Rita's daily struggles.

Annie also remembers being introduced to WeightWatchers by Rita, and going to classes with her in downtown Atlanta. "I said, 'Rita, why are you going to WeightWatchers? You're not big,'" says Annie. That's when Rita explained to her that she was taking medication for her condition, a steroid, and it caused people to gain weight, so she needed to watch what she was eating, and WeightWatchers helped her do that. "It seemed like that was a focus of hers," recalls Annie. As she thinks about it, Annie adds: "At Atlanta University, we were taught to wear these nice suits and dresses and taught to make sure you kept your weight down, and you looked good so you could get these corporate jobs. And Rita was going to make sure she stayed on top of that."

Annie also made note of Rita's distinct style. Sometime between college and grad school, her style evolved. She was always fashionable for sure, but Rita was developing a signature look. Where she didn't even wear lipstick in her college graduation photo, now she always wore Fashion Fair's Magenta Mist lipstick, accentuating her full lips. She wore her sandy-brown hair in a curled upsweep or the day's popular mushroom style. She often favored bold-colored tops and chic patterned sweaters paired with designer jeans that hugged her curvy behind, perfectly cuffed to accommodate her short stature; she also sent her jeans to the cleaner's, and they came back crisp, with sharp creases down the front. And, like our mother, she wore a blingy diamond ring, compliments of our mom.

And as for another key feature, Annie says: "Rita had beautiful legs, and she always wore heels. Every picture I have of her, other than one I have of her sitting at a table barefoot, Rita has heels on." Annie recalls that they were looking at a picture of themselves together one day and Rita said, "Annie, you know, your legs are just as big as mine." Annie laughs as she remembers this. "Rita was the one who got me wearing heels."

Annie introduced Rita to another friend in their class at AU, Jennifer. Because they were both from Detroit, Annie thought the two should know one another. Jennifer says as soon as she met her, Rita told her the same thing she told Annie: "My sister is at Spelman." Jennifer could hear the pride in Rita's voice. "I could tell right away," says Jennifer, "she really did love you as a sister!"

Of course, she too noted Rita's fashion sense. "She was always sharp to the teeth!" says Jennifer. "Because I knew Detroit, I knew about where she shopped—Jacobson's, the really nice Saks Fifth Avenue, and all the stores at Somerset mall. All of that." When I ask, Jennifer thinks for a moment about how best to describe Rita. "She was sophisticated, chic, sassy . . . what is the word for women who have it going on? Diva! Yes, a chic and sassy diva."

Yet Annie makes a point of saying that Rita never mentioned that she bought designer clothes. "She may have worn all these brand names, but she did not recite labels to you," says Annie. "It wasn't a part of her." In fact, she was matter-of-fact about her clothes—and generous. Annie shared two pictures with me, and in one Rita is wearing a gorgeous turquoise dress, and in the next photo, Annie is wearing it. "It was Rita's dress!" says Annie, laughing. Because they wore the same size and had a similar style, Annie tells me, "She'll have a dress on and I say, 'Oh, Rita that is beautiful'; that's all I have to say, 'That's beautiful,' and the next thing I know, she's gone and took the dress off, got something else on, and she's saying, 'Here.' And I'm like, 'You're giving me that dress?!'" Other times, Rita would send Annie one of her dresses in the mail that she thought her friend might like, and every time, "It would be perfect," says Annie.

But, Annie notes, Rita's generosity was for those she trusted. "If you crossed her, or she didn't care about you, she would not bother with you," says Annie. "She didn't pull no punches in terms of pretending that she was your friend when she was not your friend."

Memories flood over her. "She was funny, very funny," says Annie.

"And a great storyteller. That's one of the things I loved about Rita. She would just have me laughing about so many things!"

Annie's husband, Sam—another grad-school buddy, whom Rita encouraged Annie to date—tells a story about Rita's humor: "We were over at Rita's room, talking," he recalls. "It must have been late at night, and time to start getting ready for bed. Rita got up and went to the bathroom and came back and had lipstick on her lips. I'm looking at her and I say, 'Rita, you're getting ready to go to bed, right?' She said, 'Yes.' And I said, 'Why do you have lipstick on?' She said, 'Sam, you never know. If I ever wake up at nighttime and a nice man is standing over my bed, I want to look pretty. You never know.'" They fell out laughing. He says one of the guys in their friend group liked Rita and he later told him, "Okay, H, I think she put the lipstick on for you!"

Rita *was* magnetic, forever drawing men to her. During much of that first year, she dated a Nigerian classmate named George Bassey. Rita, he says, was part of a group of Black Americans who hung out with him and other Nigerians at Atlanta University. "We were like a family," he recalls. He and Rita became fast friends. "We just clicked. We could talk about our lives and our careers. And she had a wonderful personality." George and Rita soon developed what he calls a "warm" romantic relationship. "We were close, really close," he says. "There was just this love that was flowing in between us." Some of his fondest memories are of him and Rita visiting Johnnie, from the registrar's office, who'd become friends with them all. She'd prepare dinner for the two of them. "Johnnie loved Rita," George confirms, adding, "Because of that personality."

I share with George something Rita once told me: how he used to coach her in math so she could pass her statistics class. "Don't make me cry," George says. He quietly confirms, "Yes, I did help her with that." He goes on: "She would've been a wonderful wife." He slips into the present tense when he tells me, "Rita has a big heart, she's understanding. And there's something about Rita and her level of maturity."

Yet, George says that remaining in the US didn't feel like a viable option for him, with pressure from his father to return to Nigeria after grad school. "I was in such a hurry. Our generation of Nigerians who studied in America, we had to come back home and try to achieve," he explains. He remains in Nigeria to this day. But he says he has some regret, sounding wistful as he talks about Rita. "Those are real sweet memories," he says. "If I'd had more maturity, I would've thought, *Why don't we settle down and marry and make sure we live a happy life?*" He pauses. "But you know how destiny is." George says he thinks so fondly of that brief time in his life, and of his relationship with Rita, that he named his daughter Georgia. "After me," he admits. "But also, after the American state where Atlanta is."

Rita enjoyed having male buddies as well, those she could truly call a friend. Robert was one such friend. They'd been at Fisk together, and now both found themselves at AU. "I just remember if I had a bad day I could always go and talk to her, and get good counsel, and vice versa," recalls Robert. "She was a thoughtful and caring person—and so optimistic."

Meanwhile, Rita and I did pretty well throughout that first year together in Atlanta. I helped her write a couple essays, and she helped me study for my econ class. By my second semester of freshman year, when I'd moved off campus with my roommate Nikki to a new apart-ment complex near the airport called Bordeaux South, Rita visited me there—a quick interstate drive away from the Atlanta University Center. I was proud that we were back on track to keeping our vow made in that hotel room in New York. Our family was apparently grateful too. Anthony wrote me that spring. In his letter, he made a point of saying, "I'm glad to hear that you and Rita are getting along much better." And a few weeks after I got Anthony's letter, just days after Rita's twenty-third birthday, our mother wrote to me with grat-itude: "I sure am glad you bought Rita the dress. I didn't get a chance to even send a card . . . I have been down a little with my legs. I've been on them too much."

~

By the end of her first year at AU, Rita had launched into a new, in-tense relationship with a young man whom I'll call Zachary. Having met and become good friends in Nashville, they reconnected in Detroit right before Rita left for grad school, and when it became apparent to Zachary that Rita had feelings for him, that allowed him to acknowledge his feelings for her. Although he lived in another state, they saw each other whenever possible, with Zachary visiting her in Atlanta a couple times—unbeknownst to me.

On one spring visit, Zachary says that they stayed in our cousin Elaine's apartment while she was away, and he and Rita couldn't get enough of each other. They did do a few touristy things, which included going to the Sun Dial Restaurant at the top of Peachtree Plaza; he still remembers being awed by the glass-enclosed elevator that took them over seven hundred feet up, where they enjoyed a 360-degree view of the city. Zachary chuckles as he recalls that they didn't stay long despite the spectacular views. Their desire for each other was so strong that they soon rushed out of there and made their way to Rita's dorm room, because it was closer than Elaine's place. The mesmerizing hit "I Want Your Love" by the rock-disco group Chic played on the radio nonstop throughout his visit, and Zachary says the hypnotic lyrics perfectly captured their passion: "Do you feel like you ever want to try my love and see how well it fits? Baby . . . I want your love. I need your love."

"What was it about Rita?" I ask him.

His response comes quickly. "She was intellectually stimulating, sexy, a sister, from the Motor City, and so sweet," he tells me. "She was the whole package! And that laugh? And that smile? Don't get me talking." Zachary explains the real magic of their relationship this way: "She was my friend first. And everything else came with it. We would laugh and debate and argue *and* we had that intimacy." Here, he takes a moment. "When you are intimate with somebody, that's a deep experience. You become one. It's a deep thing."

Rita was feisty too. "Oh, she had some fire in her, done cussed me out and everything, man!" he admits. "She wasn't gonna let you just say anything to her. She would tell me, 'Who do you think you are?' And she'd put me in my place. Which was good."

17

That first summer we were both home from school, Rita spent much of her time helping Mama with the numbers business. She was a Jane-of-all-trades when it came to running numbers, much like our mother; she not only took people's bets over the phone, but also knew how to calculate customers' end-of-the-week tallies on the adding machine. Driving her yellow Firebird, she sometimes went to customers' homes to collect money owed, or to pay off winnings. Her friend Jill would sometimes join her, as she often did when they were still in high school. And that summer, Rita was tight as ever with our mother. Meanwhile, she and I fell back into our old pattern, often bickering over nothing. After all, our sisters-as-friends experiment was new, not yet a familiar path with a worn groove.

Annie came to visit Rita during that summer; for some reason I wasn't around and didn't get to meet her. Photos that Jennifer recently shared with me reveal that she and Annie and Rita all hung out together during Annie's visit; there's a picture of the three of them at the top of Detroit's Renaissance Center. Jennifer recalls coming by the house and meeting our siblings, and our mother. She also recalls that our mother talked to her about Rita's condition, explaining to her what lupus was, and what would happen to Rita during her flare-ups. This underscores for me that even at that early stage, our mother was worried about Rita. How did she know enough about lupus to be so concerned? Had she spoken in depth with Rita's rheumatologist? Had she read up on the disease? Had she seen into the future? To me, lupus was like arthritis, and no one treated arthritis as life-threatening. Three years into her lupus journey, from my naïve point of view, Rita seemed to have relatively mild and manageable symptoms.

Besides, Rita was ever her dynamic self. That was also the summer she took belly dancing classes. She figured it would be fun, and as was the case with Rita, when she was into something, she was *really* into it; and as usual, her excitement was contagious. One day, dressed in the full regalia of a belly dancer—a shimmery silver bra and matching thong panties beneath a sheer floor-length skirt accentuating her voluptuous curves, finger cymbals clicking—she performed for all of us in the family's living room. She was a pretty good belly dancer! It also was a great form of exercise for her, as someone who could not participate in the '80s aerobics craze. That type of exercise would've been too much for her. Yet, being Rita, she found a fun work-around to that limitation. Annie recalls how impressed she was to learn about Rita's belly dancing. "At first, I said, 'Whoa, Rita!'" But then, says Annie, she seriously considered it herself. "She actually got me to step out of my comfort zone, out of my little cocoon, and introduced me to new things," admits Annie. "Because I trusted her so much." Another fond memory Annie has of that summer visit is going on a shopping spree with Rita. "She said, 'Mama, Annie and I are about to go shopping.' Girl, your mother laid one hundred dollars on each of us, I said, 'Oh my!' and we went on out that door!"

Over Labor Day weekend of '79, as I began my second year of college and Rita was about to begin her second year of grad school, our mother sent me a letter with money inside (as she was forever doing). She wrote:

Bridgett,
Hope this will help and hold you until I can send you some more, which will probably be next week.
    I really planned on giving you a little more than this, but the hits kept coming . . .

Love,
Mama

And then she wrote:

P.S. You don't have to mention the amount to Rita. I probably won't have this much Tuesday when she leaves. I will try and send the two of you some each week until you all get caught up. Fifteen or twenty dollars a week will help a lot, when your main source comes once a month.

The main source Mama referred to was social security survivor benefit checks Rita and I received as our father's college-age children. Our mother always supplemented those checks with extra money. And more than once, Mama told me not to tell Rita how much money she was sending me, or the fact that she'd bought me new clothes, to hold that little secret between us. Mama seemed ever aware of and sensitive to Rita's feelings. She knew that Rita didn't resent my receiving gifts from our mother; she just wanted to get the same amount, in like kind, always. I also knew this, and I definitely honored Mama's wishes, and never told my sister how much I got in those letters laden with cash. Now I wonder: Was our mother asking Rita not to tell me about the money she sent her?

Three weeks later, our mother sent me more money, this time $300 (the equivalent of $1,200 in 2024 dollars). She wrote:

I know it will help some, at least until around the first, until I can send some more. Drop a note and let me know you got it.

And then she added:

I sure hope Rita feels better. I do worry about her. I can't help it. I wish she'd get back on her teas.

Love,
Mama

P.S. I found this driving license of Rita's. Give it to her.

I do worry about her. I can't help it. How did I react when I read those words? I knew Rita got bad headaches sometimes, felt tired easily, couldn't be out in the sun for too long. But I assumed Rita was basically okay because she seemed to be; the times I saw her, she didn't *look* sick. "One of the hardest things about being ill with a poorly understood disease is that most people find what you're going through incomprehensible—if they even believe you are going through it," writes Meghan O'Rourke in *The Invisible Kingdom*, a vivid account of her own chronic illness. "In your loneliness, your preoccupation with an enduring new reality, you want to be understood in a way that you can't be."

But our mother, herself a sufferer of a chronic illness—deep vein thrombosis is itself likely caused by an autoimmune disease—*did* understand. And she was trying to make sure I understood too.

I wish she'd get back on her teas. I was by then a vegetarian, and really "into" health foods; but this lifestyle choice was never put to the test, remained hypothetical, because I had no medical issues; I lived in the land of the healthy. I don't remember what type of teas Rita had tried out to manage her lupus. Perhaps kombucha? I do remember having purchased some Celestial Seasonings teas for Rita that I learned about in one of my natural healing books, but I also remember that those teas sat in a box on the floor of my college apartment's bedroom; did I ever give her those teas?

In an attempt to learn how I might help Rita, I did read Louise Hay's *Heal Your Body*; the book listed specific health challenges and the so-called mental causes for each; Hay provided affirmations to create new "thought patterns" about one's illness. For lupus, she ascribed the probable mental cause as "a giving up. Better to die than to stand up for one's self [*sic*]. Anger and Punishment." This didn't describe Rita's mindset *at all*. She was not a quitter, nor was she an angry person, so I didn't even mention the book. Thank goodness I never tried to tell her to just "love and approve of" herself. The *positive thinking* approach to illness can quickly slide into a blame-the-sufferer mentality. O'Rourke describes her own effort to use positive thinking to lift her out of her "morass" of sickness. "I found that the burden of positivity weighed on me after just a few days," she writes in her memoir. "What was I supposed to do with my fears, my darker thoughts? Tamp them down? Pretend I couldn't taste the metallic tang of terror?"

Of course, in her letter our mother was trying to tell me to check up on Rita, look out for my sister. Did I? Rita was not a complainer; besides, pride would've stopped her from calling me up to say she didn't feel well. She would've wanted *me* to call her. In my fantasy, that's what I did. In my fantasy, I'm with Rita in her dorm room and we're hanging out, having Sunday dinners together at a nearby restaurant, and I'm helping her with tasks that make her life a bit easier. In my fantasy, I understand how stressful graduate school can be, how stress triggers flare-ups, and so I'm there for her, making sure her emotional needs are being met.

But in reality, after an entire summer of falling back into our old ways, Rita and I weren't spending a lot of time together that second year. Clearly, what she and I originally had in common—being in Atlanta—soon wore off in the face of what we didn't: Grad school and sophomore year of college are vastly different experiences. We were building our own community of friends on our individual campuses. Our paths didn't naturally cross.

I do remember Rita visiting me a few times at my new apartment, in a high-rise on Peachtree Street. On one visit she brought Annie with her. "Rita came to my room, and she said, 'I'm going to be running out to Bridgett's apartment and I want you to ride with me,'" Annie recalls. "I said, 'Okay, okay!' I was anxious to meet her sister, yes, I was." Annie says she'd heard about me for an entire year, and that Rita had graduated from referring to "my sister" to saying my name, which she'd never heard pronounced the way Rita pronounced it, as Brih-jet. "I really liked the way she said it," recalls Annie. "Some people say 'Bridget,' but she always said 'Brih-jet.'"

Annie says Rita had told her, "Bridgett wanted to live off campus, and my mother got an apartment for her." Annie laughs as she remembers that Rita then told her, "She said she wanted a waterbed, and my mother bought it. It's beautiful, and I want you to see it." In her mind, Annie thought, *Oh, Rita thinks that the mother is treating Bridgett better than her.* "I didn't say nothing because I know sibling rivalry," recalls Annie. "I'm the youngest of five." But she also noticed that Rita was actually excited about my waterbed. "It was all smiles on her face. 'Oh, you got to see Bridgett's waterbed!'" No attitude.

"We parked and came up to your apartment," recalls Annie. "You all talked, and everything was very cordial. You were nice and kind and you had everything in its place. I saw the waterbed. We probably stayed no longer than an hour."

Soon after that, Rita told Annie, "They're going to be putting carpet in my room tomorrow." Sure enough, Rita had plush orangish-yellow carpet installed in her dorm room. "It's so her!" Annie says as she breaks into laughter. "I said, 'Rita, you're the only one in this dorm that has carpet on the floor. Good for you. You're living the life, lady!" Annie loved it because they could all go to Rita's room and actually sit on the floor. "It was like stepping into a little palace," adds Jennifer. "She definitely had it going on!"

Rita explained to Annie, "I can't do a whole lot of work, sweeping and mopping these floors, I can't do all that stuff. So, my mother told me I could have carpet."

Annie was likely right that the carpet was a direct response to my waterbed. Yet that anecdote beautifully illustrates the nature of Rita's so-called jealousy toward me. Rita wasn't envious; she was just a great scorekeeper, and no one understood that better about her than our mother. Annie confirms this. "I can't remember a derogatory statement or situation that she told me about you," says Annie. "I cannot remember that at all." Besides, Rita's getting carpet in her dorm room was likely what we'd now call a form of accommodation for a student with a disability. But no one spoke about it that way back then.

~

I'm sure Mama's letter I received that fall day—*I hope she feels better*—jolted me, but what did I do in response? Anything? Nothing? You can really love someone and fail to show up fully for them. To be fair to my teenage self, it had only been eighteen months since our father died. Long enough to accept that he was gone, but *not* in any way long enough to be "over" it. I kept that fact of not being over Daddy's death hidden, even from myself, even as I suspect Rita did too. I would've felt silly for still struggling with my grief, as though something was wrong with me. And yet, I think of someone like Anderson Cooper, who in his podcast, *All There Is*, interrogates his own pileup of loss as he cleans out the apartment of his late mother, Gloria Vanderbilt. His father died when he was ten, and Cooper admits that forty-five years later, he's still grappling with that loss in a visceral way. Thinking of his father still makes him cry. I have never heard a Black person say, "It's been forty-five years and still I ache and mourn and grieve." Yes, I've heard a Black person say, "I still miss him" or "I still miss her." I've said that myself. But to embrace fresh grief after so long is an indulgence in Black life that, in my experience, we don't feel privy to. Given all we're up against in this world, we feel we simply can't *afford* to grieve but for so long. In their book *African American Grief,* authors Paul C. Rosenblatt and Beverly R. Wallace put it this way: "In a racist environment that keeps many families on the edge of coping, those families cannot afford to lose a grieving person's functioning."

Rita was the first in our family to graduate college, and I was trying to be the second. I needed to function. Anderson Cooper could afford to keep his grief fresh and alive because he didn't have to get on with life in quite the same way. He didn't have to continuously brace himself for the next racial injustice, which usurps the one before. (I keep in mind that Rita and I lived in Atlanta at a time when we were warned to avoid Stone Mountain, once a stronghold of the KKK.) If I'd said out loud, "I'm still depressed over losing Daddy," Black folks in my life, my own loved ones, would've told me to *carry him in your heart, baby, but you got to move on.* They would've told me to accept that he'd passed and look forward, focus on my studies. Essentially, get over it. Still, knowing loss so intimately, I think it further pushed me to unconsciously deny Rita's condition. Just as I couldn't accept that her legs were aching "like Mama's" that day in New York, I couldn't accept that I had a sick sister whose illness was serious, that I could possibly lose her. No way. Denial was my safety valve.

Also, it's odd having a sibling with a chronic condition that appears suddenly. One minute, Rita was fine, and the next minute she wasn't. Our relationship was already in place and hadn't been formed around the dynamic of a sick sibling who'd been that way since we were children. Her new reality was jolting, and I did not make the adjustment quickly. Nor did Rita want to be seen as someone who needed help. She was hell-bent on moving forward and doing everything she wanted to do, and could do, no limitations. "I'm gonna *live* my life," she often said. Today, we'd likely be advised to go into family therapy after Rita's diagnosis, to see it as something that affected each of us, but no one knew to do that back then. Rita didn't even have a therapist herself, not for many, many years.

Mama wrote me another, a two-page letter that fall, sharing some news from home and sending more cash. "You don't have to mention to Rita about this little money," she advised, once again. "Because I haven't been able to send her any money but once since she has been there. I feel bad about it but I didn't have it." My mother also somehow knew I was struggling to fit in—did I share my laments with her, or did she just know?—because she said to me in that letter, "I know things are hard with you right now but believe me they will get better . . ."

Things did get a little better. Soon enough, I got a college boyfriend. That helped. We met in a physical science class and Byron was perfect for me—easygoing and kind and funny and loving, and really into me. Rita liked him. I gained an adopted group of friends through Byron, but in my heart, I knew they still weren't *my* tribe. I decided to go out for the Alpha Kappa Alpha sorority. I thought, *What better way to find a sense of belonging than to join a sorority?* Yet it was an odd choice for me because I was in many ways the opposite of a joiner, had never been someone with a group of girlfriends, and knew almost nothing about sororities, to be honest. I was no legacy. But searching for belonging can do that, have you chasing after something, the right something to fill a void. And there is this: my decision to pursue sorority life originated with Rita—something I admitted in my journal:

> What does being an AKA really mean to me? In the privacy of these pages, I can be totally truthful. I first got the idea from Rita, who let me know that I was the "AKA" type. In her own way, she was insulting me because she wanted to pledge Delta. I then took on the role that she assumed I had. But was her assumption valid? Afterall [*sic*], didn't she say she always thought I'd go to Michigan State or somewhere of that nature? She took me at face value and now I'm beginning to wonder if I'm not doing the same?

I was slightly hurt that my sister felt she belonged in one sorority, and that I belonged in another. Back then, I saw it as a way of her saying, *I admire this sorority, but I think you'd fit well in the one I don't admire.* Now I think she might've just as easily been thinking, *I admire that sorority, but I don't think I'd fit in there the way you would.* Either way, I actually did pursue the sorority she thought was right for me. That was the level of Rita's unspoken influence over me. After all, despite her surprise that I chose to attend a Black college, Rita had been the one who put the idea of Spelman into my head in the first place.

That spring, our sister Dianne wrote to me. Before she closed the letter, she asked: "How are you and Rita doing?" Yet again this reminds me that it really was a *thing*, a family affair, the fact that Rita and I hadn't gotten along before, but now that we were in the same city, Dianne signaled to me that she too wanted us to figure it out, whatever "it" was between us.

Bored during class one day, I made a list:

Ten Reasons Why I Should Be Happy:

1. The sun is shining
2. My mother loves me
3. I can see, feel, hear, touch & smell
4. Spring comes every year
5. I am 2 decades old
6. I eat every day
7. School will soon be over
8. I woke up this morning
9. My health is sound
10. I have a future

Looking back, number nine feels like my reaction to Rita's reality—knowing I "should" feel grateful that I wasn't the one with lupus, that that wasn't my fate. Because it certainly could've been.

18

With Rita's time in graduate school winding down, Mama wrote to me again, and this time her words were bruising:

4–25–80

Hi Bridgett,
Here is your mail, money, and Master Charge. I hope you remember to get oil in your car.

Bridgett, I hate to bring this up, because I promised myself not to try and force a relationship with you and Rita that is just not there. I am just praying that God will direct the two of you. But Rita was very sick over the weekend. Please check on her for me. I do feel really bad, when Johnnie have [*sic*] to call me and tell me how sick she was and you don't even know.

You be sweet and remember, I am not trying to give you a hard time. I love you very much. I just make the mistake thinking you are so much more mature than Rita. I admit it is a mistake because you are so much younger than her.

Love,
"Mama"

I'm still awed by our mother's tenderness and care, her yearning for me and Rita to bond. She *really* wanted me to understand how important it was to be there for my sister, even as she wanted me to feel no guilt. I'm moved by the tightrope our mother was walking. That letter flooded me with mixed emotions. I wondered why no one had called to tell me Rita had been sick, and I was hurt by that exclusion. And I also felt guilty because I felt I should've known. *Please check on her for me.* I did.

My college scrapbook shows that five days before Mama wrote that bruising letter, I was involved in an "Epitome of Unity" fashion show and banquet that my classmates and I organized at the downtown Holiday Inn. According to the program, I'm listed as the commentator. Being reminded of that makes me judge myself for frivolous pursuits while my sister was struggling with her health. But I still did not fully appreciate or even understand Rita's flare-ups. When our mother wrote to say Rita had been "very sick" that weekend, it could be that she had bodily flu-like achiness, a migraine headache, severe fatigue, joint pain, or all of those symptoms at once. This could've happened after she'd gone through a period of feeling really good, which is what makes lupus so unpredictable. What I simply didn't know or understand back then is that Rita was likely always in the throes of chronic mild-to-severe pain—experiencing it, getting over it, or about to experience it.

I do have one vivid memory of us from that spring, one that I hang on to greedily: My boyfriend Byron and I are in an auditorium on Atlanta University's campus to watch Rita practice for an upcoming presentation, and my pride swells as I stand in the back, seeing how good my sister looks onstage, in a pin-striped skirt and jacket and pumps, the "power suit" of the 1980s. I love seeing how well she performs her presentation with professionalism. I know that I'm seeing her anew.

In another memory, one that Byron has helped me conjure, he and I cut through Atlanta University's campus to get to our class at Morris Brown College (part of the Atlanta University Center consortium), and we pass by Rita working in the registrar's office, where we stop and chat. I love being reminded that there were times I'd just run into her on AUC's campus.

Shortly before my sophomore year ended, when she was already back in Detroit, Rita wrote letter number four, to ask a favor:

May 14, 1980

Hey Bridgett,
Just a short little note to say hello. What's been happening with you besides getting ready for your trip to Europe?

I talked to TR (helped give C.'s bridal shower with me). She said C.'s marriage is on the rocks. She also said C. admitted that she really didn't want to get married, but her mother was the main one pushing her to the altar.

I was wondering if I could stay in your apartment while you were in Europe.

Love,
Rita

I'd decided to work that summer as a cocktail waitress at a top-floor bar in an Atlanta hotel, then use the money I'd earned to take a whirlwind two-week trip to Europe, powering through England, the Netherlands, Belgium, France, Switzerland, and Italy as part of a summer travel program with the American Institute for Foreign Study. It would be my first trip outside the US, my first need for a passport. (Mama told me that however much money I saved as a waitress, she'd match that amount. And she did.) Meanwhile Rita was in the throes of her long-distance relationship with Zachary. Even though she didn't make it explicit in the letter, she was asking if they could both stay in my place during his next visit to Atlanta. Of course, I said yes. I could see that Rita was *really* into Zachary. Rita was *not* one of those young women hell-bent on getting married just to say she was married (hence her comments in the letter about her friend C.); she wanted to marry a man she could feel genuine excitement over. She was certainly excited over Zachary. Not only had they started out as friends, but they were also both graduates of HBCUs, so they shared that common experience too. Rita felt he had all the potential to be "the one," and because I'd never heard her speak about a man quite that way, and because I wanted her to find true love, I also wanted him to be the one—even though I still hadn't met him yet.

Annie knew about Zachary, but never did meet him. "She would go visit him, that I do know," confirms Annie. "I remember her talking about him quite a lot," echoes Jennifer, who also hadn't met him. And yet, Zachary and Rita were in love.

"Oh, I'd met your mom by then and everything," Zachary tells me. "And I remember your mom sitting there with me, eating breakfast, and she told me, 'A man doesn't decide about marriage, it's the woman who decides whether or not to get married.' And I remember how that scared me, you know, what with my being young and all." Plus, his parents hadn't had a good marriage, and that made him wary. Still, things seemed to be progressing toward the altar, as Rita traveled to his hometown. "She met my daddy, my aunt, my people," he says. "This was my girlfriend."

Remembering her trip to meet his family, Zachary says: "That girl had a style, man." He recalls, "When I brought her to my town and took her around, she'd be the best-dressed woman. No doubt about it. Stepping in high style. You knew Rita was a city lady. The women would say, 'Who is that?'" Zachary recalls in particular a pair of rhinestone-encrusted high-heeled pumps that Rita wore, accentuating her big, pretty legs. "One of my friends saw them and said, 'Damn, look at those shoes!'" Zachary laughs. "She was very opulent. When I hear that word, I think of her. Of any woman I've ever been with, she's the most opulent."

Rita's opulence was as much a characteristic of who she was as anything; over the years, everyone has commented on her style. Looking back, I do think Rita's indulgence toward beautiful clothes and jewelry and shoes tied in some way to her having lupus. From the time she was a young adult—just as she was diagnosed—she had a carpe diem attitude, and her flashy style was part of that. I've since learned this is not unusual for sufferers of chronic illness. O'Rourke explains in *The Invisible Kingdom* her obsession with spending hours in bed, window-shopping for clothes online. "I was trying to manifest the person I wanted to be," she writes. "A person who could enjoy her life . . . a person who wasn't about to die or disappear . . . The worse I felt, the less I could do what I wanted . . . the more I searched for beauty and pleasure."

Zachary didn't even know at that point that Rita had lupus. It never came up, and he says he saw no telltale signs of it. But as he thinks more about it, he says: "I did notice she'd sometimes fall asleep on you. Maybe that was the medicine she was taking or something?"

The "or something" was likely the lupus itself causing exhaustion. I understand why Rita hid her condition from Zachary. She didn't want pity, didn't want him to see her as "less than," to use her term. And she could pretty much hide it from him because she fluctuated from feeling well to not feeling well, back and forth. If he caught her between flare-ups, she could appear healthy and normal, because she was.

~

At Rita's graduation from Atlanta University, I was joined by our cousin Elaine, her boyfriend, and her mom, Emily. The ceremony where we *could've* all been in attendance was held at the Martin Luther King Jr. Memorial Chapel on Morehouse College's campus, and it included well-known Black faces lining the dais. James Baldwin was awarded an honorary doctor of literature degree, and St. Lucian economist Sir William Arthur Lewis, who'd won a Nobel Prize the year before, was awarded an honorary doctor of laws degree. Trailblazing TV news anchor Max Robinson was the commencement speaker. Robinson was the first African American man to coanchor a nightly network newscast, ABC's *World News Tonight*. He won three Emmys, and founded the National Association of Black Journalists, an organization that became important to me just a few years later, when I began my own career in journalism. Thanks to an *Atlanta Daily World* article covering the speech, I've learned that he told the overflowing audience, "The news media only provide a superficial cloak over our existence," and that was one reason, he said, why Black institutions must flourish. "And we must not define or limit them," he added. "They will house Black history." He was right, of course. The day of Atlanta University's 1980 commencement was itself an important one in Black history, honoring men who faced their own immense weathering as "firsts" and who wouldn't live long: James Baldwin died seven years later from stomach cancer at age sixty-three. Max Robinson died eight years later from AIDS at age forty-nine.

But that's not the ceremony we all attended. Both Rita and her classmate Jennifer acquired their degrees a semester later than the rest of their class, due to a missed assignment for one and a grade changed too late for the other. And so they waited a full year to walk; the ceremony we all attended was in May 1981. Afterward, I snapped a picture of Rita, which became another of my favorites: she stands in a side profile in her black cap and gown, arm at her waist as she holds her ribbon-bound diploma; she smiles proudly. Throughout my twenties, I kept that picture of her in a 3x5 gold-plated frame on the mantel, or altar, or nightstand in whatever space I was staying in whichever city I happened to be living. In my thirties, other photos took center stage. Months after my fortieth birthday, I again placed that picture on display, and have kept it that way ever since. It now sits on the mantel in my home office. Why have I clung to that particular image of Rita in her graduate-school cap and gown? Maybe because she looks so happy, her life in front of her; maybe it's because she's in love and I can see that in her eyes, can see the hope in her posture. Maybe it's because lupus hasn't won. Maybe I've clung to that image across the decades because it marks the end of an era for us as sisters, living in the same city as young adults: the end of our Atlanta years.

19

Rita was in a good place, or as she loved to say, "Girl, I'm feeling jazzy!" At twenty-four, soon to be armed with a new MBA, she was flying to different cities to interview for finance jobs at major companies like Ford and Eli Lilly and IBM. She was also still in the throes of her romance with Zachary. "It was pretty intense by then," he admits. "We were going strong."

When I turned twenty, Rita was in Minneapolis, on a job interview. She sent me a birthday card along with a note—letter number five—written on the Marquette Hotel's stationery:

> Hi Bridgett,
> Hope this birthday card arrived on time. Your gift will be
> late this year because Hudson's Department Store here in
> Minneapolis would not let me use my Detroit charge.
> *"Rita"*

I doubt it would've helped even if Rita's gift and card had arrived by my twentieth birthday, which I spent alone, in my Peachtree Street high-rise apartment. It still stands out for me, decades later, how inexplicably sad I was on that day. The following day I wrote in my journal:

> Birthday was so lonely. Another realization moment: "Bridgett,
> you are a loner." All alone on my birthday. Twenty years old
> & I thought no one cared. Rain didn't help either. Utterly
> depressing—until nearly 10 o'clock, THEN it got better. Heard
> from home and that made it all better. Kinda . . .

Our mother was the one who called me that night. When I lamented that I hadn't heard from her earlier, she said, "I figured you'd be out with friends, celebrating." I shared a bit of my sorrow with her, saying that I was really sad about no longer being a teenager, and Mama said to me: "I'd love to be twenty *anything*. Your whole life is in front of you." Wistfully, she added: "I remember when you were a little girl and I used to sing to you at bedtime." Then, giving me the best medicine for melancholy, she began singing to me through the phone, her voice both sweet and beautifully off-key: "Bridgett will eat her carrots and peas, carrots and peas, carrots and peas, Bridgett will eat her carrots and peas, so she can grow up to be prettyyyyyy."

I look back and think about the difference between Rita's turning twenty and discovering her body's immune system will betray her over time as it attacks itself, and my turning twenty in a healthy body. Could that be why I was so sad for no good reason? Did I feel survivor's guilt? Was I already mourning a future loss I couldn't name?

Meanwhile, I packed up my Peachtree Street apartment before leaving for Europe that summer, as I'd already arranged to move into an old, quirky apartment in northeast Atlanta, the opposite of a high-rise. But Rita didn't want to stay with her boyfriend in a place that looked un-lived-in. "I took all your pictures out of their wrappings and hung them back on the wall," Rita later told me. "Same with a lot of your dishes. And then, before I left, I packed everything back up." This I found both touching and funny. She wanted the place to look homey and lived-in for Zachary's visit, but she also made no attempt to get me to change my plans and postpone packing up. That was Rita. She didn't believe in asking big favors of others, but she did believe in work-arounds to get what she wanted.

Zachary drove to Atlanta in his Cadillac, along with a friend; they were to meet up with his cousin, who flew in from California, so they could all attend the 1980 Atlanta Jazz Festival. Vibraphonist Lionel Hampton, among other luminaries, was performing.

His cousin arrived first, and Rita was the one who picked him up from the airport; since he hadn't yet met Rita, Zachary told his cousin: "You'll know her. Just check out her backside." Just as he loved so much about her, Zachary loved Rita's ass. "It was big and beautiful," he says.

They had another great visit, not only attending the festival, but also hanging out at local hotspot discos like Cisco's and Mr. V's. This time the song that provided the soundtrack to their romance was Tom Browne's "Funkin' for Jamaica": "I feel it inside my soul, let it get into you . . . this feeling's funk, that's what it is." Feelings still rise up in Zachary when he hears that song, filling him with memories of desire. "That was really our heyday," he says.

Rita wrote me letter number six during that time; it was a perfunctory note: "I'm sending you 25 dollars . . . and I'm still investigating your albums." (A couple of my LPs had gone missing after she'd stayed in my place with Zachary and his cousin.) She signed the letter in her signature way: "Love, Rita."

Later that summer, Zachary went to Detroit to see Rita. I was still in Atlanta. On that visit, she got him a coveted, pricey ticket to attend boxer Thomas "Hit Man" Hearns's big fight against Mexican reigning champion Pipino Cuevas. Our mother dropped him off at the Joe Louis Arena, and Zachary took his seat in the third row. "Ali was there!" he says. "Everybody was there." From his choice spot he watched as Hearns, a hometown hero, viciously knocked out Cuevas in the second round, capturing his first world title as welterweight champ. "He hit that dude, man, and he spun around like a top!" recalls Zachary. That same summer another hometown hero, Diana Ross, was enjoying a comeback hit with "Upside Down." Zachary says that dizzying song became yet another anthem to his dizzying passion for Rita: "I said, 'Upside down, you're turning me,' you're giving love instinctively . . ."

"She made me a little crazy," he confesses.

Other memorable experiences during his visits to Detroit included going to Belle Isle (an island park in the Detroit River) and the popular nightclub Trapper's Alley. One day, spur-of-the-moment, Rita suggested they take the four-hour train ride to Toronto; once there, they stayed at the famous Harbour Castle Hotel, with its gorgeous waterfront views of Lake Ontario. Zachary had never been to Canada. "I'll tell you what, one thing about your sister," he says to me: "She's the one person that you have absolute fun with when you're going out. It's the most fun. I don't think I've ever had such a good time . . . just hanging out. You know what I mean?"

~

I moved into my new apartment—my third since starting college—just before the start of my junior year. It was in a postwar building of about twenty units on Barnett Street in the up-and-coming Virginia Highland area—more coming than up. I felt that, yes, the place needed some work—it was unrenovated—but it had lots of character, what Realtors now call "old-world charm"; my second-floor apartment had a lovely sunroom with French doors and windows on three sides, looking out onto the building's courtyard. The bathroom featured a claw-foot tub, and there were hardwood floors throughout. But Rita came to see the place, and she did *not* like it. She liked modern apartments with carpeted floors and fresh appliances and renovated bathrooms. To her the place looked run-down, and she wasn't so sure about the neighborhood. She'd glimpsed some questionable characters. Also, lower-class whites lived across the street, and they didn't look too friendly. I shot back that she just couldn't appreciate "classic" style and bohemian vibes.

"Well, I'm telling Mama," Rita announced, with finality. It reminded me of our growing-up days, when she'd say just that, "I'm telling Mama," about something going on, a tattletale, the big sister whose allegiance was to our mother, a mini-mom. And that's what she did this time too: she told Mama. If I see it through Rita's eyes, I can imagine that the Barnett Building, as it was called, frightened her a bit, to imagine her twenty-year-old sister living there on her own. After all, Rita was the same sister who wrote me from college telling me to "write me back and let me know who you're walking to school with." And to be fair, the building *did* attract quirky tenants from what we used to call *all walks of life*—including my next-door neighbor who used to loudly scream fake orgasms most nights while having sex with the landlord, which I heard as though I were in the room with them, thanks to the thin walls.

I got busy transforming the apartment and spent a couple weeks scrubbing and cleaning and painting, then decorating in my eclectic style. On a late July day, a stream of visitors dropped by my newly transformed place; Rita was the first to come and was pleasantly

surprised. "Okay," she admitted. "You really did pull this place together; I'll give you that." I felt as though I'd taught her something
that day about me, about who I was beyond her baby sister. Yet, soon
enough, our mother wrote me:

> Hi, Bridgett,
> Well, I hope you are sitting down because I am about to give you
> a shock. Burt and I are coming to Atlanta. I just want to see for
> myself how you are living. It is about to drive me crazy. When
> I get through figuring it all out, you may have to move back on
> campus . . . Please do not write or call asking me not to come.
> I will be there . . . I am looking forward to sleeping on your
> waterbed.
>
> Love,
> *Mama*

She brought with her heavy-duty bug spray to help me deal with the
Georgia roaches, which Rita had reported back to her she'd seen, and
which my mother found totally unacceptable. But for the most part,
Mama approved of my apartment. She made a point of saying that the
place reminded her fondly of an early home she lived in as a young wife
and mother in Nashville—a well-kept housing project called Napier
Courts—and that made me feel connected to her in a way that distinguished what *we* shared from what she and Rita shared. During her visit,
our mother bought me a lovely mahogany desk at an antique furniture
store, which I placed my electric typewriter atop, then hung a calendar
and bulletin board above—to create my very first writing space.

~

At the start of the new semester, I threw a party in my new apartment, launching me into my junior year on a high note. Rita was back
at home, still interviewing for jobs that matched her MBA, with its
concentration in finance and marketing. During that time, our mother

sent me two letters in one envelope. In the first letter, she shares with me her concerns about money. She also criticizes Rita—a rarity:

9/6/80

Dear Bridgett,

I am sorry to inform you that your Social Security check did not come. I called them and they said it would be mailed out this month. I hope you can stand it. I am sending your rent. I wish I had more to send.

My phone is off in the back room, all because of Rita. I have talked until I am blue in the face about these phones. Burt's phone is also messed up. Dianne's is too. She just sat on her behind in Atlanta and charged her calls to my phones. I am really sick about it. I just don't have money I used to have.

Love,
"Mama"

PS: Please send Rita's phone book. Please send it off as soon as possible, she keeps telling me to tell you to send it.

Here is another twenty. I know it will help some.

This is Sunday morning and I talked with you last night. I am thinking of going to church.

Rita is up now and trying to read this letter backwards while I am writing, so I will close.

Her middle name should have been nosey.

Mama wrote the second letter the next day, as a follow-up:

9/7/80

Hi Bridgett,

I hope you are fine but I am a little sad to-day. My friend Minnie died to-day. They called me, and I went over to the hospital and she was still in the room. She really did look peaceful.

Your check came to-day, as you can see. It was here when I got back to the house from the hospital. I did not open it. You know who. She got one too only hers was $379.00.

I am glad yours came for this amount. Please put some in the bank, so you will have some cash on hand at all times. The other letter was the first one I wrote so I am sending it anyway. It was the hardest thing for me to mail it. I kept trying to wait on your Social Security check. Well it came and it was for much more than I had anticipated.

My phone is still off in the back. I guess I will try and get it on in another day or two.

Rita is in the kitchen talking about buying some Sassoon panties.

Love,
Mama

PS: Please put some of your money up. Don't worry about me. I will make it. I was just disgusted the other night when I was crying on your shoulder.

I bought you a cute table for your apartment. I got it at a yard sale on Fairway Drive. Rita did not like the table. I told her it is not for you anyway.

Don't ever mention about the opening of the check. I told her it was wrong.

Our mother captured in these two letters several of Rita's signature characteristics. First, Rita's love of talking on the phone was well-known. She'd been enjoying this pastime since she was a child, chatting on the phone with her grade-school friend Linda. In later years it was her main form of visiting with people. But long-distance calls were *so* expensive back then. They were based on the day and time you called, as well as where you were calling from and to. And there was no way around the expense. Bell Telephone System (later, AT&T) had a monopoly. As an example, that year Bell charged $2.17 on weekdays for a five-minute call from NY to LA. That's nearly $8 in today's money. Calling from Atlanta to Detroit was similarly expensive. And yes, you could call from one phone number and charge it to a different number. Michigan Bell turned off phones when those bills went unpaid, with barely any grace periods. We had three separate phone lines; what's worth noting is that Rita didn't dare charge calls to the business line, the one our mother used to run her numbers. The telephone was literally a number runner's lifeline. Turns out, Mama's letter was foreshadowing, as long-distance calls would come back to really complicate Rita's life.

Also, Rita was known for buying beautiful things, often made by popular designers, hence our mother's noting the temerity of Rita buying "some Sassoon panties" while her phone (whose bill Rita ran up) was still off for lack of payment. This extravagant spending was something our mother talked to her about a lot. As an example, Mama used to say, "Why do you need to wear a new pair of pantyhose every time? You can learn to wash the same pair and wear them again." But Rita would say, "It's worth it to me. I like for my pantyhose to be fresh."

And yes, Rita was also known for wanting to know everything that was going on, or as Mama aptly wrote, "Her middle name should've been nosey." The fact that she was trying to see what our mother was writing to me didn't surprise me. She probably sensed that our mother was explaining to me who exactly opened my social security check to see how much it was for—apparently a lot more than hers. I suspect Rita felt a little guilty about it. And our mother clearly didn't approve of her doing that. Yet she also didn't want me confronting Rita about it. "Don't ever mention about the opening of the check. I told her it was wrong." Our mother was forever navigating our fragile relationship as sisters, trying to mediate between us even as she tried not to take sides.

20

That September, Rita was hired as a purchasing agent for the Tennessee Valley Authority, which meant she'd be moving to Chattanooga. Formed as part of President Franklin D. Roosevelt's New Deal programs, TVA quickly became the nation's largest electricity supplier, building nuclear plants and other infrastructure projects and in the process displacing tens of thousands of Tennessee Valley residents, largely in Black communities, through eminent domain.

Her classmate Annie says when Rita interviewed at TVA, the two talked about the pros and cons. "Because it's in the South, the attitude of the people of TVA, older people, their ideology was different," says Annie. And it wasn't Rita's first choice. She'd interviewed with many companies, including one in Texas, but that state's oppressive heat caused her to have a flare-up. "She immediately said, 'I'm not going to be able to take any offer in Texas because of my sickness,'" Annie recalls. "She said, 'I got to go to a place that has distinct seasons.'" Rita's first choice for employment had been Bank of Pittsburgh; I remember she even joked that she was going to become a Steeler fan, but the offer didn't come. And so, knowing that she had relatives close by in Nashville, Rita accepted the position in Chattanooga.

This was a big deal for our family. An announcement ran in the *Michigan Chronicle*, Detroit's Black newspaper, featuring that great photo of Rita taken in Vegas; the caption beneath it read: "EARNS MASTERS DEGREE—Rita Renee Davis recently earned her Masters of Business administration degree from Atlanta university, specializing in finance. After several lucrative job offers, Ms. Davis has decided to accept a position as a purchasing agent with Tennessee Valley Authority in Chattanooga . . . The 23-year-old is a 1976 graduate of Fisk University, and daughter of Mr. and Mrs. Burton [*sic*] Robinson and the late John T. Davis."

Rita's job as a purchasing agent was to work in TVA's Raw Materials Building Supplies section, which meant, according to her résumé, that her responsibilities included "procuring building materials for nuclear plants from U.S. and foreign bidders for contracts in amounts up to $500,000. This includes evaluating the low responsive bidder as well as working under the auspices of design engineers." I was impressed by her duties then, as I am now.

From the start Rita found Chattanooga a striking contrast to other places she'd lived. By 1980, Blacks made up 15 percent of Chattanooga's population, compared to whites' 80 percent. This was a new experience for Rita. She'd grown up in Detroit, a majority-Black city. She'd gone to college in Nashville at an HBCU, surrounded by Black classmates, as well as her extended Southern family. She'd attended a historically Black grad school in Atlanta, with the city's Black mayor and "new South" vibe. Still, she seemed to make the adjustment at first; she moved into a nice apartment complex close to downtown and near the banks of the Tennessee River. Given her outgoing nature, she also soon made friends; one in particular was an older woman named Miss Clee, which was characteristic of Rita. Miss Clee, I suspect, helped Rita find a church home; since her preteen days, when she wrote letters to God, Rita remained a believer, and wherever she lived, she found a Baptist church to attend. And she was already in the habit of kissing her Bible regularly, already leaving behind traces of her magenta lipstick.

Folks made their way to Chattanooga to visit Rita. Our cousin Elaine visited her often; Annie and her husband, Sam, visited her on their way to the Knoxville World's Fair one year; Annie recalls that they all went to see the soul singer Al Green preach at a local church. Her classmate Jennifer also visited Rita. So did I, joining Elaine to spend that first Thanksgiving with her. Zachary says that he also visited her there, at least once. "Some buddies of mine were going to Florida," he recalls. "And they dropped me off in Chattanooga, so I spent a week with her there."

Rita was proud of her job. In those early days, she sent our mother a letter:

Hey Mama, just me sending you a copy of my very first
requisition & invitation to bid. I've been real excited about my
first real assignment after six weeks. (smile). Love, Rita.

The job required a lot of time on the phone, on long-distance and
overseas calls, and that part likely came easy to Rita. Yet, no question, her work environment was challenging from the start. I now
ask myself why she'd had to wait six weeks to be allowed to do what
she'd been hired to do. And it turns out, her white colleagues were *not*
welcoming, to say the least. "Oh, it was very rocky," confirms Annie.
"I basically talked to her almost every night when she was there, [she
was] telling me about incidents that occurred, and some of the things
that they would say to her."

It didn't help that Rita wasn't from Chattanooga and therefore was
seen as an outsider. More fundamentally, she was an oddity: a Black
woman. In 1980, the corporate world was just beginning to hire
Blacks in any significant numbers, so Rita was one of the only ones.
Filled with negative beliefs about Blacks that the culture swam in,
and unhappy about affirmative action, her colleagues likely assumed
she was only there to fill a quota rather than because she was qualified. Ironic, given that she was more educated than her coworkers
with the same position. (This was and still is typical, as cited in a
report published a few years ago by an advocacy group showing that
young Blacks need two more levels of education to have the same
chance at landing a job as their white peers.) Some of her coworkers
were clearly resentful of her advanced degree, so she also had to con-
tend with that.

"They were jealous, absolutely," says Annie. "It was these old white
people that were so dirty to a young African American with an MBA."

The same month Rita began at TVA—October 1980—*Newsweek*
published a riveting opinion piece by Leanita McClain, a young journalist at the *Chicago Tribune*. Titled "The Middle-Class Black's Burden," the article by McClain articulated the challenge and ongoing
stress faced by Black professional women who find themselves in a
workplace that's as unprepared for them as they are for it. "I have

fulfilled the entry requirements of the American middle class, yet I am left, at times, feeling unwelcomed and stereotyped," she wrote. "I have not overcome my old nemesis, prejudice. Life is easier, being black is not." McClain goes on to note, "I am burdened daily with showing whites that blacks are people . . . Many of my coworkers see no black faces from the time the train pulls out Friday evening until they meet me at the coffee machine Monday morning. I remain a novelty."

As a fellow Black woman in her twenties, navigating a corporate environment, Rita had much the same experience as McClain. I know because she would often say to me about TVA, "These white folks are a trip."

Annie recalls, "They were treating her bad. Rita would call me and tell me about the little things they would do to her. She'd say, 'I had something on my desk. When I came back the next day, it was gone.' Sometimes, she would be crying . . . But she stood up to them, which was good." Annie says she empathized with Rita because she knew firsthand how hard it was. "We were trailblazers in terms of eradicating some of these racial things that was going on, on these jobs," says Annie. "We were on the front lines, absolutely."

Dr. Geronimus, the author of *Weathering*, refers to this phenomenon of being "a first," and what it can do to Black bodies: "Success comes at a spectacularly high health cost for those who have to fight the hardest to achieve it in the context of a society that doesn't value them," she writes. It can lead, she notes, to "accelerated biological aging . . . causing those who beat the odds through hopefulness, hard work, and perseverance to weather young, across many body systems."

～

When she came home for the holidays, only on the job for about three months, Rita told us a harrowing story of workplace trauma, so shocking I didn't want to believe it could be true. She said she was in the employee lounge with coworkers. The lounge had a large picture window that looked out onto the city below. A couple women in the lounge walked over to look out the window. "All of a sudden, those women started pointing at something below, on the street," said Rita. "And so, I went over to look out the window too." She paused for emphasis. "It was a Klan rally. They were *literally* dressed in white robes." And then, "They clapped," said Rita. "Those women I worked with started clapping for the Klan. Cheering them on. Right in front of me."

As it happened, Rita didn't say a word, and no one looked at her. She just left the room. Of course, all that performative clapping was for her, but she knew that she couldn't report the behavior to her supervisor, that no one would reprimand those coworkers, knew she'd be accused of "overreacting." But she now also understood more fully what they thought of her, and what she was up against. After that, she still had to show up every day, work beside those same white men and women. She had to accept that microaggression—or was that a macroaggression?—and just keep quiet, try to do her job. But Rita's body surely absorbed the trauma.

Annie knew about the Klan incident. "I'm really sorry that I couldn't say then, 'That's not good for your health, no matter how we want to live up to the expectations of our MBA for Atlanta University,'" says Annie. "But at that time, we're talking about how to actually deal with it because we're young." Annie adds that Rita and she both felt the pressure to be the face of Blacks in corporate America, because they were aware that their success would open the door for other Blacks. "We felt a responsibility," she says.

Rita had no idea of the racist context she'd unwittingly walked into: The year before she came to TVA, in 1979, Ku Klux Klan leader David Duke traveled to Sale Creek, Tennessee, twenty-eight miles northeast of Chattanooga, to conduct a cross burning; it attracted five hundred people. One of them, Bill Church, was so roused he decided to create his own local Klan group, the Justice Knights of the KKK, and made himself Imperial Wizard. He and his fellow Klan members would collect donations at an intersection in the city while dressed in full regalia, out in the open.

Church decided to escalate his intimidation into violence: On

April 19, 1980, he and two other Klan members, dressed in camo gear, went to the Ninth Street district, a historically Black neighborhood in Chattanooga, erected two eight-foot wooden crosses in a vacant lot, and set them on fire. The three men then drove to the intersection of East Ninth and Douglass Streets, carrying with them two shotguns, more than five dozen shells of ammo, and a letter about starting a race war. One of those men, Marshall Thrash, fired his shotgun filled with birdshot at four middle-aged Black women who were waiting for a taxi after leaving a local club. The spraying bullets hit each of them; one of the women ended up with one hundred shotgun pellets in her leg. Their names were Viola Ellison, Lela Mae Evans, Katherine Johnson, and Opal Lee Jackson. The Klansmen then traveled further down Ninth Street, and Thrash opened fire at a woman who was watering flowers in her front yard. Her first name was Fannie, like our mother's, and her last name was Crumsey. The shots missed her, but they shattered the window of her daughter's car, and she was injured by flying glass. (Her lawyer later said if she'd been standing, she would've been decapitated.) All five women survived, but newspaper photos of two of the victims sprawled out on the ground are hard to look at; I'm imagining the injuries those women sustained emotionally, let alone physically. They survived, but at what cost?

The three men were arrested shortly afterward and stood trial for attempted murder in late July. Church and the second man, Larry Payne, were acquitted by an all-white jury; Thrash, who'd actually fired the shots, turned state's evidence, confessed to the crime, and was given a $225 fine and nine months in prison (he served three, based on "good behavior"). The trauma felt by the Black community was enormous, to imagine that in 1980—not 1950—Klansmen could blatantly and openly shoot Black women in a drive-by and get away with it. Black Chattanooga reacted to the acquittals with understandable fury. Four days and nights of rioting, marching, firebombing, and confrontations ensued; a weeklong curfew was imposed. President Jimmy Carter asked Reverend Jesse Jackson to come to Chattanooga. At the same time, Klan leaders from across the country came to the city to antagonize and bomb the protesters and, as one Klansman put it, "To look out for the interest of white people and the police." That same week after the acquittal, three Klansmen were arrested with bomb ingredients one mile away from a housing project. This so terrified residents that many elderly Blacks moved out of the project to live with relatives.

Rita moved to Chattanooga less than three months after the men had been acquitted. The apartment complex where she chose to live was on Cameron Circle, barely 1.5 miles from East Ninth Street, where the women were shot—basically a seven-minute "good ol' boy" joyride away.

~

A year into the job, Rita was finding the situation at TVA more and more challenging. How do you come back from the toxicity of an environment where coworkers cheered on a Klan rally in front of you? From work one autumn day, Rita dashed off a note—her sixth letter to me—writing it on a TVA "Expediting and File Notes" form:

November 6, 1981

Hey Bridgett,
Just a few lines to say I was glad to talk with you. I have enclosed Mama's Sear's charge.
    Give me a call in a week, or before Thanksgiving.

Love,
Rita

When we talked, she vented about the stress she was under at work, and I listened, saddened to hear those things, but not surprised. This is what so many white folks don't get about life for people of color in this country, and Blacks in particular. Just dealing with assumptions about our so-called inferiority, and the daily indignities those assumptions prompt, is steadily taking its toll on us; it certainly did so on Rita. Dr. Geronimus puts it this way: "The accidents of birth that assign us to either a socially valued or a marginalized and looked down upon group can impact life expectancy, not just through the obvious economic determinants but through the slow drip of stealth ideas about race and personal responsibility." She adds: "Some of our most cherished beliefs as a culture activate or intensify these harms."

The story of those five women shot by Klansmen has a powerful coda. Having gotten no justice in the criminal court, the women, with the help of the Center for Constitutional Rights, sued their attackers in civil court. In February of 1982, the women won a judgment of $535,000 (the equivalent of $1.6 million today). The case, Crumsey v. Justice Knights of the Ku Klux Klan, was the first time the Klan had ever been successfully sued in federal civil court. That set a precedent that allowed civil rights attorneys to use the landmark case as a legal backbone for not just other anti-Klan cases, but other racially motivated crimes. Also, they won a city injunction against the Klan, prohibiting them from engaging in violence and terror in Chattanooga's Black community.

Randolph McLaughlin, who represented the women, said in an interview some twenty years later: "We broke the back of the Klan." When McLaughlin's team researched the jury pool in 1982, they conducted an opinion poll on white beliefs about the KKK. "White residents of Chattanooga thought the Klan was a good thing," he noted. "They said it was a good organization that protected white people."

Hence that Klan march and Rita's TVA coworkers' reaction in front of her. Never mind that they had to know "protecting white people" meant using terror and violence and murder against Black people. McLaughlin said that throughout the civil trial, he remembers looking at a mural on the courtroom wall depicting a white woman in a sunbonnet holding a white baby as Confederate soldiers limp home from war. In the background, Black Southerners pick cotton. There's now a very different kind of mural on display, this one near the site of the Ninth Street attack and painted by a local artist, honoring the five women. The mural was painted in 2022, forty years after the women won the case against their attackers. Just one of the women, Opal Lee Jackson, was still alive and able to see the mural unveiled.

I'm sure there was resentment among whites throughout Chattanooga toward Black folks after those women won their civil case. In that jury-selection study the lawyers conducted, the majority of white respondents said they felt Black lawyers, out-of-town lawyers, and civil rights lawyers had no business taking that kind of case in *their* city.

And I'm equally sure that some of that same resentment was directed at Rita in her workplace. It makes me think of how Chicagoans treated their Black coworkers after Harold Washington, a Black man, won the 1983 election as mayor. McClain, the young Black woman journalist, wrote an op-ed with the incendiary headline, "How Chicago Taught Me to Hate Whites," in which she noted that after Washington's win, "Even black and white secretaries in City Hall are not speaking to each other." McClain wrote that she was unprepared for the silence with which her white colleagues greeted Washington's nomination. "I've been crushed by their inability to share the excitement of one of 'us' making it into power," she wrote. McClain was deeply troubled by the city's as well as the country's racial animus, and, dealing with the controversy that ensued after her piece ran, while struggling with crippling depression, she took her own life less than a year later.

Rita didn't do anything so drastic, but she felt the stress of white resentment all around her just the same, and it took its toll.

"She did very well to go to TVA with lupus, and deal with that garbage," says Annie. "It was a lot of stress on her body, but she kept herself focused and she kept her friends close, and she got through it . . . She got through it."

One month after those five brave Black women won their civil suit, Rita sent me an ominous-sounding note:

March 23, 1982

Hey Bridgett,
Just me sending you some pictures . . . Reaganomics will not
permit me to call. They are monitoring the phones at work.

Take Care,
Love Rita

Rita, on the verge of being a teenager, stands in the walkway of our family home on Broadstreet, already demonstrating her sense of style.

Our oldest sister, Deborah Jeanne, age five, carrying the hopes and dreams that will prompt our parents to soon migrate north from Nashville, their ancestral home

Our father, John T., sitting in the living room of our family home, in one of the only remaining photos I have of him

Smokey was Dianne's teen idol, and she's beyond thrilled to take this picture with him, his arm around her, at the wedding of Warren "Pete" Moore, a member of the Miracles.

Our brother, Anthony, age twenty-three, sporting his '70s-era Afro with style

Rita, photographed at her beloved Fisk University, a teenager in college

This was Rita and my first time in New York City in 1978, we sisters traveling together just weeks after our father had died.

For a couple years, Rita took belly dancing classes, and for her performances, she made sure she had the entire belly dancer's outfit!

With our mother, Fannie, Rita and I celebrating the holidays at a family friend's home in 1979; I'm on winter break from college and Rita's on winter break from grad school. She has discovered her signature lipstick.

The first of our parents' children to complete college, Rita was also the first to get a master's degree.

Proud of her professionalism, Rita nevertheless suffered a series of micro- and macroaggressions at her job in corporate America.

Rita visited me during my study abroad; I love how she managed to coordinate with the guards' red uniforms, and I love how the wind makes her dress billow out.

This was one of Rita's favorite outfits, so striking; I can hear her now, saying, "I feel jazzy!"

I love Rita's exaggerated smile because it captures the joy and gratitude we were feeling that holiday season, so unaware that as 1986 approached we were about to have the worst year of loss imaginable.

Rita flew to New York to be at my thirtieth birthday celebration, even though our mother had been diagnosed with cancer only months before. We tried so hard to stay positive.

Rita really stepped up for our nephew Tony, especially after our mother died. Tony lived with Rita throughout his twenties and helped care for her in those later years.

We loved hanging out with our mother, and on this night especially, Rita and I were optimistic. Mama seemed to be doing so well.

I'm wearing my prom dress, which Rita convinced me to buy during our trip to New York, and which I subsequently wore over and over for years.

Over the years, Rita and I wrote many, many letters to each other from wherever we each were in the world.

Nothing meant more to me than having Rita at my wedding. She had her dress custom-made, along with a matching cane. Forever stylish. I was grateful to Tony and her dear friend Wilma for making sure Rita made it safely to New York.

THREE

~

21

In the family cosmos, one sibling's life affects and determines the trajectory of the other siblings' lives. If circumstances had turned out differently for our oldest sister, Deborah, what might have been different for the rest of us? For Rita? If I can better understand what happened to Deborah, does it help me better understand what later happened to Rita?

In late January 1982, a friend of Deborah's called our mother to tell her that Deborah wasn't doing well, and Mama went to where she was, found her lying in bed unable to move; she called an ambulance, which took Deborah to Detroit Receiving, the city's public hospital. Her blood pressure was spiking, and she stayed hospitalized for several days. Rita was living in Chattanooga, working at TVA, and I was in Atlanta, finishing my final semester at Spelman, and so our sister Dianne was the one at home, the one who visited Deborah in the hospital. One day she told Dianne, as she sat up in bed sipping orange juice from a straw, "I'm just tired."

Deborah had a lot to be tired from. By the time she lay exhausted in that hospital bed, she'd faced a series of harsh experiences across her thirty-five years—fueled by the fact of her birth in 1940s America. She was our parents' love child, born when Fannie was eighteen, John T. twenty, and they were newly married; like most firstborns, Deborah symbolized their hopes for the future. By every account, she was a high achiever from the start, both walking and talking by the time she was nine months old. Beautiful photographs exist of her, taken in a studio—not unlike those of famed photographer James Van Der Zee—that do not exist for the rest of us: Deborah, age five, holding a purse in the crook of her arm, decked out in finery, down to her lace-trimmed ankle socks; in another, five-year-old Deborah sitting at a piano, smiling for the camera. Yet, despite being one of the first grandchildren born into a close-knit Southern Black family and doted on by our grandfather, Deborah was also a quiet and shy dark-skinned child growing up in Jim Crow Nashville in the late '40s and early '50s. A second-grade teacher wrote on her report card that, "Deborah is so inattentive that she fails to progress as rapidly as she can." Her third-grade teacher was more understanding and predicted at the beginning of the school year: "I feel that she is improving. I try to keep her busy all the time. Will be among my best students." By the spring, however, the same teacher wrote, "She is a very sweet girl . . . she can learn well, but other wise [*sic*] something is wrong. Forgets where she places things, looses [*sic*] her lunch money. Leaves it on the tray at lunch time." What was wrong? Three months before, our mother had lost her baby girl minutes after she was born. Researchers have found that not only are Black mothers twice as likely to lose a baby at birth than white mothers, nearly 50 percent of Black mothers who experience an infant death suffer postpartum depression. Maybe that's some of what was wrong: maybe our mother was struggling through her grief.

Just a couple months after that familial loss, our parents migrated to Michigan, leaving six-year-old Dianne behind with our mother's sister Florence. And so, Deborah faced a completely new life up north without her little sister, who'd been her constant companion as long as she could remember. They'd been a unit in that way sisters close in age often become. Mama was soon pregnant with Rita, just as the family was plunged into poverty, facing an uncertain future in Michigan after fleeing a racist South. When Deborah was eleven, nine-year-old Dianne rejoined the family, but three years had gone by. I suspect she and Deborah never again regained their closeness. They loved each other, of course, but as sisters they didn't hang out together. Where Dianne was more social and had many friends, Deborah was more of a loner. A voracious reader, she spent hours in her room reading broadly and widely, her ever-present thick cat-eye glasses hanging down her small nose. She was an exceptional student, or as our cousin Elaine puts it, "Deborah Jeanne had straight As across the board, every time. This was in elementary, middle, *and* high school."

At Mackenzie High, Deborah did not want any attention drawn to her. But she was a tall teen and, as an anxious eater, what people called plus-size. "She was extremely shy," says Elaine, "and really conscious of her weight." At a time when no girls wore pants to school, Deborah used to demand that before her third-period class, Elaine meet her at the bottom of the stairway and walk behind her as she climbed the stairs to her next class—so no one could see under her skirt or dress. "She was very self-conscious about that," Elaine recalls. She'd do this for Deborah every day, then run to her own class so she wouldn't be late. In exchange, Deborah would let her wear one of her mohair sweaters or give her fifty cents, or best of all, do her homework for her. "She likely had social anxiety," Elaine says. "But we didn't have words like that back then." Deborah graduated as valedictorian of her class in 1964, and went on to Wayne State University, majoring in psychology and carrying that acute shyness with her. At times, she'd insist that our father drive her to the campus, because she didn't know how to drive herself, and riding the bus created more stress for her.

But then came the late '60s. In early 1968, with one semester left before graduating, Deborah dropped out of college. Our mother's incredulity quickly turned to fury, and it was palpable and constant, undergirded by a deep disappointment that only now, as a mother myself, do I fully understand. At the time, I was seven and Rita was eleven and we often heard Mama say about Deborah: "Some people have book sense but no common sense!" Who can say why Deborah didn't stay in school? I'm sure Wayne State produced its fair share of race-based challenges, with its tiny population of Black students and its casual microaggressions—like the dean who tried to keep Deborah from majoring in psychology because he told her that was a waste of time for a Negro girl. And then there was the culture surrounding her: weeks before Deborah's first college classes, the bodies of three voting-rights workers were found in Mississippi after they'd been tortured and murdered by the KKK during Freedom Summer. In the spring semester of Deborah's freshman year, she heard the city's own Malcolm X speak at Detroit's Ford Auditorium, where he delivered his "Bullet or the Ballot" speech; one week later he was assassinated. Two weeks after that, John Lewis and other peaceful protesters marching for voting rights were beaten almost to death by state troopers as they attempted to cross the Edmund Pettus Bridge in Selma. During the fall of Deborah's junior year, she heard Stokely Carmichael speak at a Detroit rally, making his famous call for Black Power, and that same month, the Black Panthers formed in Oakland, quickly starting a chapter in Detroit. In the summer leading up to Deborah's senior year, the "race riot," or rather the Great Rebellion, broke out in Detroit, still one of the largest and most fatal uprisings in US history. And in April of what would've been Deborah's final semester of college, Dr. Martin Luther King Jr. was assassinated—bringing both our parents to tears—followed within three weeks by a student protest erupting on Wayne State's campus that a battery of police violently squashed. That steady drumbeat of racial turbulence would've definitely stressed out a sensitive, highly intelligent young Black woman. Deborah, surrounded by constant reminders of clear and present danger for Black Americans, surely experienced what psychologists call "vicarious traumatization." I can understand how she might've thought, *What's the point of a college degree when The Man is so brutally relentless at keeping us down?*

I can understand too how Deborah found her way to drugs.

As 1960s drug culture abounded, with Timothy Leary pushing his consciousness-expanding use of LSD, and hippies and musicians and high-profile celebrities smoking copious amounts of weed, Deborah discovered marijuana. Our parents vehemently disapproved, given all the scare-tactic messages claiming it was addictive, even though it turns out it wasn't. I'm sure weed chilled her out, made Deborah feel better. Meanwhile, those Vietnam troops were coming back from Southeast Asia—most suffering from unnamed and untreated post-traumatic stress disorder—some bringing heroin habits with them in their own efforts to self-medicate. Thanks to that phenomenon, and dealers' quests to keep supplying the drug, heroin too was suddenly all over urban areas like Detroit. It doesn't take a conspiracy theorist to make the connection between heroin's sudden availability in Black communities right at the height of Black protest movements in the country. Deborah herself was an ally of Black activists and touted their causes. I vividly remember that she was *really* into The Last Poets, the civil-rights-era spoken-word artists. In time, Deborah started snorting this newly available drug, and I can imagine how good it made her feel.

Maia Szalavitz, a former addict who writes about drug use for the *New York Times*, has described heroin as "warm, buttery love." Szalavitz says it wasn't euphoria that kept her using it, though. "It was relief from my dread and anxiety, and a soothing sense that I was safe, nurtured, and unconditionally loved."

Deborah was likely feeling something similar. You can be loved and not feel loved. You want a reprieve from a world that doesn't accept you for who you are, that executes its everyday subtle-yet-pervasive reminders that because you are tall and dark and female and fat, you do not belong, don't fit in. You want a reprieve from a society that keeps brutalizing and killing your people for daring to seek equality. (Studies show that times of uncertainty are tied to higher levels of opioid use.) You can want a reprieve from the cumulative injustices that create in you a deep phobia of the outside world, with its potential dangers. Experts now call this reaction "a severe and chronic response to trauma." And you want relief from your crippling shyness and anxiousness, left undiagnosed and untreated. (According to a study published in the journal *Drug and Alcohol Dependence*, a whopping 93 percent of drug users report having some form of mental illness.)

Those who study these things now acknowledge what Black folks have always known: racism, a daily part of American culture, impacts our emotional and psychological well-being, and cumulative experiences of racism are traumatic. Every day that Deborah encountered the outside world back then, she surely experienced the brunt of that racism in frequent and myriad ways. How did she mentally manage the sheer volume of race-based stressors? I cannot imagine. But no one gave this kind of suffering credence back in our sister's day. Only recently, after 2020's racial reckoning, did the American Psychiatric Association issue an apology for ignoring the role of racism in mental health. "I spent a lot of years of my life working on unpacking and understanding the intersection between racism and mental health," lamented Maysa Akbar, the president of the APA, and an Afro-Latina woman who has devoted her career to proving to her colleagues that there is such a thing as racial trauma. "I truly believe psychology has a critical role to play in this entire process, [to] understand how people think, how they feel, how they act, why they do things that they do."

If we could put today's diagnoses into the 1960s landscape, I suspect Deborah would've been diagnosed with PTSD, or more accurately, acute stress disorder, because the racial stressors were ongoing and relentless, hardly "post" anything. Of course, there was zero language for such a condition back in 1968. The term "PTSD" didn't even get coined until the 1980s, and that was specifically for war vets. No one was seriously looking at the cost of racism on the lives of Black women and men. There was simply no effective treatment made available for someone suffering like my sister other than street drugs. It's barely better today. The more I think about it, the more I see that drugs are in fact an adaptive response to racism. Where else could Deborah go for relief? What else could she turn to? She couldn't talk to an affordable therapist or psychiatrist, particularly one who didn't carry his or her own inherent bias. Not only were there few self-care options, but nobody thought you even needed help for your mental struggles, even with physical violence at the hands of the state an ever-present threat. "Your ancestors dealt with much worse," was often the retort from Black people. "You're just being paranoid; get over it," was the retort from white people. No wonder so many Black folks have resorted to food for comfort, as Deborah often did. And no wonder Black folks have resorted to the same psychoactive drugs that human beings have resorted to throughout history to cope—alcohol, nicotine, cannabis, caffeine, amphetamines, LSD, and yes, opioids.

It's easy to judge from the distance of time, experience, and a cultural shift across the decades, but back then, in the '60s, who really knew how addictive heroin was? It was an unheard-of drug for most people, apart from those Vietnam vets, entertainers, and musicians. Also, contrary to popular myth, most of those who used heroin didn't become addicted. And its potential danger wasn't clear or obvious until its use became an epidemic (a similar pattern to crack in the '80s and fentanyl now). Back in 1969, based on a Gallup poll, only 4 percent of Americans said they'd ever even tried marijuana, let alone hard drugs.

Rita, watching Deborah's experience unfold from the sidelines, vowed that she'd never experiment with *any* drugs. And yet at thirteen, Rita was secretly smoking cigarettes and cursing, as a way to deal with her own anxiety. After all, she was a very young teen navigating high school, shoving desperately written letters to God into her Bible, dealing with our parents' divorce and our mother's secret remarriage, and witnessing our brother-in-law's alcoholism wreak its havoc on our sister Dianne's life. It was a lot.

22

People use drugs for a reason, and Deborah's reason was surely to self-medicate. Opioids, scientists now know, mimic the neurotransmitters in the brain that create the good feelings we get from spending time with friends and family. It feels the same—like warm, buttery love. As is the pattern with all hard drugs, I'm sure at first it was fun, exciting, soothing. There's no doubt that heroin eased Deborah's problems with acute anxiety and isolation. Heroin brought Deborah out of her room, and out of her shell. I have all but no "before" memories of her; but I have vivid memories of her after, right around the time she began using drugs. Rita and I both witnessed her loudly spewing political views of the day—much to our socially conservative parents' chagrin—and leaving the house more often, her fear of the outside world seemingly gone. She lost weight. She began a serious relationship with a young man named Jerome, and when he was briefly incarcerated, she had me take photos of her to send to him. In our living room, she lay seductively on her side, dressed in a pretty lavender negligee, while I snapped pictures with our Polaroid. I was about seven or eight, honored to be chosen for the task, and excited to see our big sister in this new and exciting way.

Inevitably, Deborah graduated to shooting up, injecting *smack*, as they called it back then, into her veins. She likely followed a predictable pattern for drug users: what began as euphoric and helpful became less effective, and she needed more just to get the desired effects; coping without it must've seemed impossible. Her cravings for heroin intensified even as it became less enjoyable, and suddenly she was addicted. And as she grappled with that addiction, she also lived with a health problem that research has also linked to racism—high blood pressure—which went unchecked and untreated.

Somewhere in late '68 or early '69, Deborah overdosed. My one vivid memory of this is seeing the emergency responders lifting her onto a stretcher and sliding that stretcher down the stairs. Rita, still a twelve-year-old, absorbed this family crisis by praying more. Seeing Deborah almost die terrified her; she also saw how upset our mother was by the ordeal, and *that* further upset Rita, ever invested in our mother's well-being. That is when Rita wrote her first letter to God, beseeching Him to help with her anxiety, to help her "stop worrying."

As is so often the case, OD'ing didn't stop Deborah from using, because the issues that had led her to drug use hadn't gone away. She was still an awkward Black girl in a world that had no place for her. And the herculean effort to overcome withdrawal symptoms wasn't something she could manage, not yet. I look back and see that Deborah was always at high risk for addiction. It wasn't just because heroin was so readily available back then throughout Black-majority cities like Detroit. Scientists have long debunked the myth that being exposed to drugs is what leads to using them. (Our sister Dianne, two years younger than Deborah, never showed any interest in drugs.) Johann Hari, the author of *Chasing the Scream*, about America's drug war, offers up a far more compassionate and radical explanation in his TED Talk: "What if addiction is not about chemical hooks, what if addiction is about your cage?" he asks. "What if addiction is an adaptation to your environment? Maybe we shouldn't even call it addiction. Maybe we should call it bonding." Hari further explains: "Human beings have a natural and innate need to bond, and when we're happy and healthy we'll bond and connect with each other. But if you can't do that, because you're traumatized or isolated or beaten down by life, you will bond with something that will give you some sense of relief . . . that might be drugs."

Hari's theory dovetails with what experts now know: the majority of people who do get hooked on drugs not only have mental disorders, but also traumatic childhoods, as the *New York Times* journalist Szalavitz has reported. And any Black girl born in 1946, uprooted to escape Jim Crow life as a child, later coming of age amidst the turbulence of the civil rights and Black Power movements and their attendant violence, has lived with a specific, racialized trauma. Especially if she is suffering from severe shyness and anxiety, mental disorders themselves likely caused by that same trauma. As our mother so aptly said more than once: every Black person in America should be in therapy at the government's expense.

Sadly, the government had quite the opposite reaction to Black folks' mental health needs—zero compassion, and derision. Deborah had the misfortune of turning to heroin for self-help at the same time that newly elected President Richard Nixon was launching his war on drugs as the "Number One Enemy," which we now know was really a ruse for his war on the people he despised. "The Nixon campaign had two enemies, the antiwar left and Black people," admitted John Ehrlichman, counsel and chief domestic advisor under Nixon, in an interview decades later. "We knew we couldn't make it illegal to be either against the war or Black but by getting the public to associate the hippies with marijuana and the blacks with heroin and then criminalizing both heavily, we could disrupt those communities. We could arrest their leaders, raid their homes, break up their meetings and vilify them night after night on the evening news. Did we know we were lying about the drugs? Of course, we did."

All drug policy, in fact, is rooted in racism. Dr. Carl Hart, a Columbia University professor and neuroscientist who has studied drug use for thirty years, confirms what Ehrlichman has said: "We can consistently and continuously wed the bad behavior of some group that we don't like to a drug. And then we can vilify that group without actually saying it. We're saying we're vilifying the drug, but, really, we're vilifying that group." The war on drugs worked beautifully in that way: the prevalent perception in most people's minds is still that drug addicts are some of the most horrible, irresponsible people in our society. These users of "bad" drugs just so happen also to be people at the margins of our society. The sympathy and compassion exerted in recent years toward majority-white drug addicts of opioids like heroin and fentanyl who are overdosing and dying in alarming numbers was unimaginable back in our sister's and brother's (and our father's) day, when we were made to believe the face of addiction was Black. No one saw it as a national crisis. The social stigma for Black drug users like Deborah was relentless, not to mention that using an illegal substance meant she was also breaking the law—itself a scary proposition, given how the criminal justice system deals with any Black person, let alone an addict.

Deborah had dreams. Often, she'd share them with me—dreams of going back to school, traveling, gifting our mother with lots of money, and always the plan to "get myself together." She was so positive. I loved listening to her promises, and I believed her every time, across all those years. Rita was a different story. She was far more practical-minded, unmoved by Deborah's promises, because Rita was grounded in our daily reality. She saw that Deborah's drug use was a source of deep stress for our mother. She remained firmly planted on Team Mama. When Rita later went to college and adamantly refused to take even one puff of a marijuana joint, it had a lot to do with what she saw our mother suffer over Deborah's and Anthony's addictions.

One of Rita's most stark responses to our siblings' drug use was to vow that she would *never* have children, because they brought too much grief to their parents. And she stayed true to her convictions. I never once heard her say that she wanted to have a child, be a mother. True, lupus makes childbirth a risky venture anyway given the demands it puts on a woman's body, but that was not her main reason for choosing to remain childless. She wanted children to be loved and protected and nurtured, and could be quite mothering, but she did not want the heartache that inevitably comes with being a parent; she'd witnessed that heartache up close and her reaction was, *No thank you.*

~

Deborah spent some time at Detroit's Herman Kiefer Hospital's Drug Abuse Clinic in the early '70s, while in her midtwenties. I've inherited a few of the books that she read from the clinic's library while she was there, reflecting her interest in Black history and culture. She read E. Franklin Frazier's *Black Bourgeoisie*, W. E. B. Du Bois's *The Souls of Black Folks*, and Dick Gregory's *From the Back of the Bus*. She also read two of Frantz Fanon's iconic books, *The Wretched of the Earth* and *Black Skin, White Masks*. I find it interesting that Fanon was a French Caribbean psychiatrist who saw back in the 1950s that racism thwarted any attempt at psychological healing in his Black patients. Deborah's interest in psychology now strikes me as her seeking a way to better understand her own racial trauma. She would've been a gifted psychiatrist.

While in rehab, Deborah wrote a poem that she sent to our mother. She noted that she'd written it "here in the clinic about two weeks ago!" My mother saved that poem for the rest of her life. Its first stanza reads:

> If I could erase the tears and
> Years from your face,
> I'd try my best somehow,
> I'd place love's crown upon
> That furrowed brow—
> And live a better life somehow.
> The hours fly into years
> And still I want to erase each tear
> That I've put there.

Rehab seems to have given our sister a brief respite—a place to rest, read, reflect, write—as well as a chance to receive medication and therapy. But rehab did not magically end her dependence on heroin. Deborah dealt with her addiction across the ensuing years, something Rita and I struggled to understand. Now, thanks to the literature, I see that Deborah's addiction was *not just* a matter of irresistible impulses or uncontrollable behavior; nor was it about being self-centered while exercising free choice. It was far more complex. "During addiction, people tend to prioritize short-term rewards over long-term gains, which means they postpone pain associated with quitting, often indefinitely," explains Szalavitz, the *NYT* writer and former addict. This makes sense for someone like Deborah, living amidst an uncertain, hostile environment with no clear career options. "When a better future seems unlikely, it's rational to get whatever joy you can in the present," notes Szalavitz.

I think about that, why our sister didn't find her way out of addiction into a passion or career that could've given her life a focus, some meaning. This makes me think of a contemporary of Deborah's: Octavia Butler. They were born just seven months apart, and while their lives were different in significant ways—one born in the South to two parents who migrated north, the other born in Pasadena and raised as an only child by a widowed mother—they were physically similar as tall, dark-skinned Black girls with some girth and kinky hair, which meant they weren't perceived as conventionally attractive. Both were painfully shy, bookworms who as socially awkward girls stayed in their bedrooms a lot. Both were gifted students, but the world didn't embrace or encourage their intellect. Where does your brilliance go when society seems to have no use for it? Butler found a channel for hers through fiction. By seventeen, she knew she wanted to be a writer, yet wrote in her journal that she thought she may never get to do that, because as her aunt told her, to protect her, "Negroes can't be writers." Yet she wrote anyway, creating science fiction that she later described as temporary escape hatches from a life of "boredom, calluses, humiliation, and not enough money. I needed my fantasies to shield me from the world."

Deborah turned to drugs to shield her from that same world. As soon as I read Toni Morrison's novel *Sula*, I recognized in her description of the title character our own sister:

> *In a way, her strangeness . . . was the consequence of an idle imagination. Had she paints, or clay, or knew the discipline of the dance, or strings, had she anything to engage her tremendous curiosity and her gift for metaphor, she might have exchanged the restlessness and preoccupation with whim for an activity that provided her with all she yearned for.*

In those years when both Butler and Deborah were in their twenties, you could argue that our sister had the fuller life, with her boyfriend Jerome, friends to smoke weed and converse with, and the easing up of her anxiety that marijuana and heroin provided. Butler spent her twenties writing science fiction constantly, but also working harsh menial jobs and feeling both lonely and isolated. She never learned to drive, and had no social life, nor intimate relationships.

Butler's daily writing habit eventually paid off. In December 1975, at twenty-eight, she sold her first book. Deborah turned twenty-nine that month, having already survived an overdose, drug rehab, and an arrest for possession of marijuana. Across those same years, Deborah channeled her brilliance into supporting *her* daily habit, itself a combination of creativity and tenacity, which is what hustling requires to succeed at it. She figured out how to beat the system in myriad ways, to support her habit without ever having to sell her body, as too many women addicts found themselves forced to do. She shoplifted, then "boosted" expensive purses, selling them to the teachers and nurses and postal workers in her orbit. She "busted scripts," which involved getting access to doctors' prescription pads and writing prescriptions for uppers like Dexedrine and downers like Valium, perfectly forging doctors' names and selling the pills one by one to friends and acquaintances. She opened department store credit cards, used them to buy gift certificates, then bought inexpensive items in the stores with those certificates, getting the remaining balance in cash. She was living off the grid, using her intelligence to sustain her hustle, sometimes more successfully than others. I remember real high points for Deborah during some of those years, which come to me in flashes: She lived at Lafayette Towers for a while, which was one of the few luxury apartment complexes in the city, located downtown. She drove a new car, a 1976 Cordoba, which she let me drive to my own Sweet Sixteen party. She once bought the entire floor display of a living room suite of furnishings, right down to the pillows and the vases.

We all benefited from her brilliance. She helped me get that driver's license in Rita's name with my picture, so I could have the ID needed to get my summer job at Red Barn; she helped Rita write research papers while she was in college; and she helped our mother write papers when she decided to take Black history classes at Detroit's Shaw College. Others paid her to tutor their children, and to write their college entrance essays. She was really good at that. In fact, along another road taken, she could've become a writer, or a motivational speaker. I have saved a prayer/affirmation she wrote for our mother to be blessed with prosperity. "Let life reveal to her the fruits of our faith, the ripe, rich succulent fruits of good fortune!" she wrote. "Let it give to her these offerings, for her to pluck to her heart's delight—to taste and savor endlessly for the rest of her days."

As years passed, Deborah moved on from heroin; to be sure, she still used substances to get "buzzed"—pills, weed, even cough syrup—but she stopped using heroin as she approached her December birthday in 1981; this is consistent with what experts tell us: according to a joint study published by the Centers for Disease Control and Prevention and the National Institute on Drug Abuse, three out of four people who experience addiction eventually recover. Deborah's outlook also improved, something Rita and I commented on. She talked more about wanting more. She had a new boyfriend, a guy named Gregory. That summer, she did two things she'd never done before: She flew on an airplane for the first time, across country to San Francisco, because she'd always wanted to see California. And she started wearing pants. Given her size, Deborah had avoided that fashion choice out of acute self-consciousness, but now she was sporting stylish slacks with new ease and confidence. On New Year's Eve, she took me to a Unity Temple service, where we wrote on scraps of paper what we wanted to discard, collectively burning them in a communal bowl on the church altar; we also wrote letters saying what we wanted to achieve in 1982, slipped them in envelopes, sealed them, and addressed them to ourselves. So when she landed in the hospital that February, I saw it as a good thing, part of a fresh start: she could rest, focus on her health issues, gear up for a new phase in life. When she told our sister Dianne, "I'm just tired," I assumed she was talking about her old life, ready to live a new one. She still had time to discover her passion, like Octavia Butler. She was only thirty-five.

But Deborah was a Black woman in the public, "poor people's" hospital, with no one steadily advocating for her. Just as with Daddy, the biggest mistake our family has made is not keeping daily vigil over a loved one in the hospital. Back in 1978, we believed that Daddy would get the treatment he needed, and now, four years later, we believed against our own lived experience the same thing about Deborah. We shouldn't have; we should've understood both the implicit and explicit bias doctors had toward her—based first on her skin color, second on the fact that she was, in their eyes, irresponsibly obese, and third based on the outward signs of her years of addiction. According to recovery experts, to this day, doctors will often treat someone who has a history of drug addiction with indifference at best, because those patients are seen as a "lost cause" and a waste of energy. "Patients dealing with drug addiction get much, much worse care," confirms Dr. Jessica Gregg, who treats addiction for a living, in an article she wrote for the Oregon Health & Science University news site. "It announces itself with, 'Well, you did this to yourself.'" Dr. Gregg notes that it's as if those who've abused drugs don't care about their health.

Did doctors and nurses see the needle tracks on her arms and hands, the missing finger lost to gangrene, her fatness and Blackness, and decide that Deborah brought her illness on herself, that she wasn't worth the effort? Was she a lost cause to them from the get-go?

23

On the twelfth day of her hospital stay, our mother got a call from a doctor on staff, to say that Deborah had "taken a turn for the worse." Mama rushed to the hospital with a family friend, Miss Bertha, and was met by a doctor who said, "I'm sorry, but your daughter didn't make it." Mama beat her fists into the doctor's chest. The doctor then explained that Deborah likely had an undetected blood clot in her leg—exacerbated from all those days of being on bed rest (which is why now patients are made to get up and walk around). He told Mama that when Deborah rose to walk, the clot likely traveled quickly through her body, blocking a blood vessel in her lungs, causing a pulmonary embolism. He then told Mama that a nurse yelled, "Code Blue!" when she discovered Deborah lying there, and that a team worked on her for forty-five minutes, trying to revive her, as if that detail would be of some comfort.

All these years, we understood that Deborah died from an embolism. Rita and I talked about it, and we both believed that the blood clot came on suddenly. "I guess there was nothing that could be done," Rita would say, sounding half-convinced. We never talked about it beyond that, but I had a nagging feeling that maybe the clot wasn't detected soon enough. Just as with our father's case of suffering a stroke while in the hospital, embolisms while in the hospital are not uncommon, and in fact, survival rates are lower if you're already hospitalized, unlike if you come in with the condition through the emergency room. Again, admitted patients get less attention than an ER patient. Learning this fact confirmed my nagging suspicions. I'd imagined a scenario in which Deborah complained about pain in her leg, and nurses and doctors dismissed her with the assumption that she just wanted "to get high" from pain medication. I imagined they were negligent in getting her family history, not bothering to make the connection to our mother's lifetime of blood clots and act accordingly (a compression stocking is a simple solution to averting them).

I imagined they let her stay on bed rest too long—more negligence. And once she fell, how long did she lie there on the floor before she was noticed? Why did the doctor feel compelled to convey that anecdote to our mother about how long they tried to save her?

Honestly, Rita and I told each other that, bottom line, Deborah entered the hospital with a "run-down" body due to her years of addiction, and so when this sudden mishap of a surprising blood clot arose, her body couldn't endure it. Somehow, this made us feel better, this narrative of inevitability we told ourselves. Really, we were blaming the drugs for her death. (Never mind that's it's due to the stigma placed on drug users that our sister avoided the hospital for as long as she did.) The alternative of what might've happened to her was somehow more painful.

I did something recently that I hadn't allowed myself to do in forty-plus years—I ordered a copy of Deborah's death certificate. What I found crushed me. She literally died from cardio-pulmonary arrest, i.e., her heart stopped beating unexpectedly. What caused her heart to stop beating was sepsis, which I know because our mother requested an autopsy, and it is the *first* cause listed. Sepsis is a severe blood infection that introduces a large number of bacteria into the bloodstream, and that leads to endocarditis, an inflammation of the heart valves; this is exactly what happened to Deborah: endocarditis is the second cause listed on her death certificate.

She died from a damaged heart, which was damaged *after* she entered the hospital, due to sepsis. Sepsis is the number one cause of death in hospitals, the biggest of many hospital-acquired infections. According to the CDC, every year 270,000 adults in the US die from it. That's more than deaths from opioid overdose, breast cancer, and prostate cancer combined. Put another way, that's the equivalent of 650 jumbo jets dropping out of the sky every year. Anyone can develop sepsis. Deborah wasn't even particularly susceptible, didn't have an underlying condition that tends to lead to sepsis. She wasn't high-risk due to being an infant or child or older adult; she didn't have diabetes or AIDs or cancer or liver disease or an autoimmune disease; she hadn't just had surgery, wasn't taking certain medications. She simply contracted sepsis in the hospital, as hundreds of thousands of people do. And it turns out, one of the conditions sepsis can trigger is a blood clot. This could explain why Deborah suffered a pulmonary embolism in the first place, with the clot then traveling through an already-damaged heart. Or there may have been no blood clot at all because the death certificate lists a *"possible* pulmonary embolus."- It's simply a medical theory, a guess. Given either scenario, the bottom line is that thanks to sepsis, Deborah went into cardiac arrest—suffered a heart attack—and there was no way she could survive that. But if she'd gotten better medical care earlier, she would've likely been released sooner, before those bacteria invaded her bloodstream.

Because I now better understand *why* her heart stopped beating, I understand why our mother ordered that autopsy. Because she knew enough to know: drugs did not kill her daughter. Our mother told people this fact whenever possible. "Deborah did not die from drugs," she'd say, repeatedly. She wanted the stigma removed, because with drugs involved, she knew folks' empathy largely vanished; she wanted people to know that her daughter did not bring her death upon herself. Looks like I needed to know that truth too, even after all these years. But knowing what really happened to Deborah makes me utterly sad. Her death was not inevitable because of her "lifestyle." Hospitalization, which was supposed to help her get better, killed our sister, as it likely did our father.

Dianne called Rita and then me, to tell us the news. Rita flew first to Atlanta to get me so we could fly together to Detroit. During those days we were back home to bury Deborah, Rita fell ill. She spiked a fever, and experienced severe achiness and deep fatigue. She told me that she couldn't really cry over Deborah, because crying brought on an excruciating migraine headache. That really broke my heart, to know that Rita's sorrow landed on an already compromised body. How *do* you grieve while battling a chronic disease? She rested a lot, trying her best to avoid a severe flare-up, because she couldn't afford to miss more time at work, already such a troubling place. Yet Rita was haunted by the fact that Deborah died alone, and in a way, she blamed her job for that. "If I hadn't been living in Chattanooga, dealing with that bullshit at work, I would've been at the hospital every day," she later said to me, more than once.

At the simple ceremony we held for Deborah, I sat next to our brother and watched helplessly as tears fell down his face. He hadn't even been free a year, had lost our father while incarcerated, and now this. It hit me that Anthony had had a relationship with Deborah, his big sister, before Rita and I were even around. My mind landed on a picture of the two of them as children in our grandparents' living room, Anthony a toddler, and Deborah a little girl of seven or so. Now our oldest sibling was gone, and Anthony, like the rest of us, had lost the chance to grow a relationship with her.

In the days and weeks that followed, we dealt with our grief differently. I stopped going to my college classes, until a beloved professor, Judy Gebre-Hiwet, sent word via a classmate for me to return. Rita worked through her grief largely by talking on the phone—to Mama, to our sister Dianne, to me, to her friends. That's how she best connected to others, and that was her form of self-care.

~

I play a "what if" game when I think about Deborah's life; I do this because what we lost in losing her is so vast and unknowable. Just as I've wondered what difference it would've made for Rita and me to have our father in our lives as young women, I wonder what our lives would've been like had Deborah lived, had we benefited from her insight and support and knowledge while still forming our adult selves. And what about Rita's health? Grieving is so stressful. There's a physiological explanation for how sick Rita became after Deborah died: Studies show that grief can have a powerful, adverse effect on the body, can really take its toll. In those who are grieving, immune cell function is reduced, and inflammatory responses are increased. And given that under stress, the body releases a ton of stress hormones, or cortisol, to cope, it's no surprise all this can lead to flare-ups for someone like Rita with a chronic condition; those flare-ups create painful symptoms that can last for many weeks. On top of that, the emotional stress of coping with the loss of a loved one *while also* dealing with these physical ailments can lead to anxiety and depression—so much wear and tear on a body whose immune system is already fighting with itself. Grief makes lupus worse.

What if Deborah hadn't been demonized for being an addict, but rather given compassion and clean needles and controlled amounts of heroin or methadone—both proven to be effective methods of treating addiction? What if, even before heroin entered her life, she'd been taught healthy ways to cope, using antianxiety medication and/or therapy? What if she'd been steered toward meaningful work by an influential mentor, perhaps a professor at Wayne State University who saw her potential? What if she'd been able to freely take gummies to ease her symptoms in an open, unstigmatized way that cannabis users can do today, with dispensaries dotting the Detroit landscape everywhere? Things might've been different. She might never have landed in that hospital.

I recently found, among Rita's possessions, a photograph of Deborah. I treat it like an extraordinary treasure because Deborah all but *never* allowed herself to be photographed. No high school graduation photos nor candid shots from her teenage or adult years. The one exception was her posing with her boyfriend Jerome for a photograph that would be added to a family album we sent to our brother, Anthony, during his incarceration—a photo that has been lost. I haven't seen an image of Deborah as an adult in over forty years. The one that remains is not a great picture, as it's way too dark, but I can just make out the outline of her body, her round Afro and owl-shaped glasses, the glare from a nearby lamp reflecting off the lenses and creating two pinpoints of light that obscure her eyes. She's wearing a blue or lavender dress, staring at the camera. In front of her, in a side profile, is her travel partner, very tall and wearing a white shirt and dark vest. On the back of the photo, written in her handwriting, is: "Gregory & Deborah / St. Francis Hotel / San Francisco, Calif. / 8–4–81." I'm awash in emotion looking at this image because it fills me with a tumble of regret for what could've been.

Octavia Butler did find some of those things in her own life that helped her cope; she found both mentors and a passion. And yet, while she got to live into her late fifties, Butler suffered a similar fate of neglect. For years, she experienced undiagnosed symptoms of fatigue, back pain, shortness of breath, hair loss; the medical advice she got was to exercise more—the equivalent of "lose some weight." Never mind that she was an active hiker. At one point, she had pneumonia that was misdiagnosed and left untreated for weeks. Days before she fell outside her home and hit her head and died, Butler had talked to her doctor about dizziness and swollen ankles and nausea. Her doctor told her it was likely the flu, and to just get some rest. Butler too was a Black woman trying to navigate a health-care system that only saw her color and gender, which meant she was largely dismissed, her pleas beside the point. There's a reverberating throughline from those Black babies delivered by white doctors being 58 percent more likely to die than those delivered by Black doctors, and the fate of a gifted, once-in-a-generation fifty-eight-year-old Black sci-fi writer. It's about not bothering to see someone's full humanity, not even if it's Octavia Butler, let alone an unknown, brilliant, thirty-five-year-old Black woman whose full potential the world will never experience.

The moment before that doctor told our mother her firstborn child had died, and right before she responded by beating her fists into his chest, our family story was not one of tragedy. Daddy's death was a loss, for sure, but he'd also been chronically ill for many years, as long as Rita and I could remember, and so losing him hurt deeply, but it wasn't completely out of the blue. We knew he was a sick man. Until then, we had vague understandings of Deborah's continuous drug use, sure, but no one really thought she was in danger of another overdose. And her hospital stay didn't seem dire or critical, but rather a precautionary measure. We were relieved that she was there, getting the treatment she needed to get better. We were doing okay. After Deborah died, ours became a family story of tragedy. Sudden death plunges you into that abyss in a way that an ill family member who's touch and go in the hospital does not. We knew Daddy's condition was serious, and so on some level, we understood what could happen. But Deborah was different. One day Rita and I were not particularly worried about her, and the next day she was gone.

24

For my final college spring break, I visited Rita in Chattanooga, Deborah's death still fresh. We spent a few days together, and on the last day, as we sat outdoors at a downtown-area park near the banks of the Tennessee River, Rita turned to me and said, "We can't fight anymore."

I nodded, understanding exactly what she meant and why. When we'd lost our father, we'd made a similar vow, but we were younger back then, and it was harder to keep that promise. Back then, I was leaving high school and entering college. Now, I was leaving college and Rita was turning twenty-six. Losing a sister is not the same as losing a father. We were one less sibling now, no longer anchored by two sisters in our lives, no longer four daughters, and Rita and I could feel the gap that loss had created in the arc of sisterly protection around us. To lose a sister is to lose a peer, to know that anything can go wrong. Parents naturally die before their children, but the world is untrustworthy when a sibling dies. We couldn't risk it.

Rita said, "We can't fight anymore," I nodded, and then she reached for my hand, I took hers in mine, and we sat there in silence.

For years we stopped bickering, didn't say a harsh word to each other, refused to take each other for granted. From that moment forward, we were in lockstep when we described our relationship. People inevitably would say, "You two don't look anything alike," and she and I both would answer the same way: "I know, but we're very close."

When Rita sent that letter in late March, writing that she was sending me some pictures, they were ones we took together while I visited her on that spring break. We appear so vulnerable in those photos, unsmiling, sad eyes looking at the camera earnestly. And when she wrote that "Reaganomics will not permit me to call," she was referring to the overall austerity that had landed on the country due to President Reagan's "trickle-down economics"; as an aside, Reagan had gotten fired from his job as host of a TV series in the early

1960s after criticizing TVA as an example of "big government." I suspect TVA was wary of the funds Reagan might cut from its budget. Anyway, when Rita wrote, "They are monitoring the phones at work," it was an omen. Soon enough, TVA investigated her for making personal long-distance calls on the company's phone. They had the phone records, showing she was calling cities like Nashville and Detroit and Atlanta, places where they didn't do business with contractors. Places where her loved ones lived. Rita was using the phone as she'd always done, as a form of connection and comfort. She was especially in need of this ritual because she was trying to process the loss of our sister just weeks before. Her boss couldn't have cared less. That June, TVA fired Rita.

She asked me not to tell Mama, and in a testament to our renewed bond as sisters, I kept my promise to her, and kept mum. Rita flew home, telling our mother she was taking an approved leave of absence. Meanwhile, a longtime friend of mine, Elliott, told us about a Detroit production of Ossie Davis's play *Purlie*, all set to go, but in need of investors. *Purlie* is an exuberant musical about a Jim Crow–era Black minister who wants to open an abandoned church and lead his people to freedom. In a move that surprised us all, our mother decided to become the sole investor in the production. Turns out, she'd taken out a life insurance policy on Deborah for several thousand dollars, and after paying for the burial, she wanted to do something meaningful with the remaining payout. Rita and I became the musical's official producers. The program read: "Rita and Bridgett Davis are sisters who recently teamed together to form Davis & Davis Productions. . . . Combining Bridgett's artistic interests with her sister's business expertise, *Purlie* is the first theatrical endeavor they have undertaken." We divvied up responsibilities; I handled the writing-related tasks like creating the press release, while she handled the business-related ones like attracting ads for the program, and together we mounted the production. *Purlie*, which starred Ruben Santiago-Hudson, premiered on July 22 that summer. The musical had a limited run of eight performances. Rita and I were at every performance; while I found it hard to see the same show over and over, it never got old for Rita, who'd already discovered her deep love of musicals when we saw *The Wiz* in New York. We lost Mama's investment despite our best efforts. Our inexperience, coupled with the massive union fees paid to Detroit's Music Hall and all the free tickets we gave away, proved to be our downfall. But what *was* a success was how Rita and I worked together, how it gave her a distraction from the humiliation of having been let go from her job, and how we as a family came together that summer to celebrate something uplifting and joyful—art!—as a way to assuage our sadness.

The musical production behind us, Rita finally confessed the truth to our mother. Mama was upset. "If I'd known about your job, I *never* would've spent money on that damn musical," she told Rita. "I would've used that money to help you." I was secretly glad she hadn't known, because the musical had felt like the best therapy. Doing the hardest thing, telling our mother, gave Rita the courage to fight back. Just as our father had fought General Motors two decades before in his workmen's comp case, she launched a racial discrimination case against her former employer with the Equal Employment Opportunity Commission (EEOC). With the help of EEOC, Rita made the claim that TVA had unfairly and harshly penalized her with termination for making personal long-distance calls; her hope was that the case would be resolved quickly. Turns out, Reagan had just appointed a new, young director of EEOC, Clarence Thomas.

Meanwhile, I returned to Atlanta to be with my new fiancé, whom I'll call J. Ours was a whirlwind romance—we didn't have our first real date until May, were engaged in June—which I later understood to be its own form of grieving over Deborah. I wanted to give our mother something to be happy about, and I thought a wedding would be that thing, but at the time I told myself I was in love, and so I chose to spend a few weeks with him before heading abroad for a yearlong travel fellowship I'd been awarded. I would travel to London, Paris, Lagos, and Nairobi before returning home to marry J. Rita was the only person in my life who asked me if I was *really* into him. "What do you like about J. that makes you want to spend your life with him?" she asked me. I couldn't answer her. "Think about it," she said to me. "Marriage is serious."

When I asked her about her own love life, and her relationship with Zachary, whom I still hadn't met, she told me, "He only visits me when it's convenient for him, when it fits into his schedule, and I don't have time for that. I broke up with him." Zachary confirms this.

"Oh, she broke up with me about five or six times!" he recalls. "She wanted to get married, and now that I'm more mature, I don't blame her, a young woman." Zachary says Rita told him, "Hey, man, look, my last name needs to get changed." He laughs. "You know how she is," he says, speaking of her in the present.

And did he ever get close to buying her an engagement ring?

"I would say no. I was too apprehensive," he admits. Having come from a broken home, he says at that point the idea of marriage still frightened him. And Rita frightened him a bit too.

"Rita would tell you how she felt," he says. "She was like, 'You are going to accept me for *me*,' instead of being coy and laying back and only thinking these things like other women do. No, she was going to say it! Some of that scared me. I could handle that now, but back then I couldn't." He pauses. "I just couldn't do it."

~

After losing her job, Rita tried to regroup. She moved to Atlanta in an effort to get her life back on track and start over in a city that wasn't Detroit. But no question, that was a dark time for Rita. The fact that her struggles coincided with my leaving the country for a year is something that, looking back, saddens me. We had just found our way to a genuine closeness as sisters, and then I left. Just as she was entering one of the toughest years of her young-adult life, I wasn't there to support her through it. That year was the longest we'd ever gone without seeing one another. Letters between us became our connective thread. I hungered for her letters, waited for their arrival, because they helped fill the gap of my own loneliness; it was hard to be so far away from everyone. I especially missed Rita. We talked about her coming to visit me in London, to keep me company for the holidays. But things simply were not going well:

November 15, 1982

Hey Bridgett,

Just me dropping you a card and note. Well it was real nice
talking with you last Sunday. However, I checked on the prices
to London and at this present time, I'm unable to afford the trip.

   Today, or should I say yesterday November 14, 1982 has
been a very bad day for me in terms of everything going wrong.
Therefore I'm going to close this letter because I'm in a very bad
mood and a little depressed. You're too far away from home to be
subjected to my depression.

   I will write again in a few days. Say a prayer for me.

Love,
Rita

I'll never know what happened to her on that particular day in
November. I do know that she'd been let go of her job on trumped-up
claims of a "telephone violation," after experiencing on-the-job microaggressions that included being forced to watch colleagues cheer at a
Klan rally, and now she was out of work, struggling financially and
dealing with the loss of so much promise after the highlight of obtaining her MBA. And I had no doubt in my mind she was still grieving
the loss of our sister Deborah.

   It chills me to think about how low Rita must have gotten, how
much she was struggling emotionally. In recent years, a study conducted by the National Institutes of Health has shown that African
Americans who reported higher levels of education also reported
higher levels of racial discrimination, and that data point links to
higher incidences of depression. Of course one would follow the other.
No surprise that Rita fell into her own depression.

   By the time she wrote me letter number ten a few months later,
I was in Nigeria, and she was home, briefly, to help out while our
mother was once again in the hospital. Rita was back on the job market, and somewhat encouraged:

February 11, 1983

Surprise!!!

Well Ms. International, how is life in the Mother Country, Africa? I am sorry I don't know how to say hello in Swahili (smile).

If you're wondering whether I went to New York for my job interview with IBM the answer is yes. As of to date, I have not heard from the company. The interview itself went pretty well. The only negative thing about the interview was if given the job I would live in an all-white city again. During my interview day with IBM, I only saw three Blacks. Two were secretaries and the other one was a janitor.

Would you believe that while in New York scared Rita took a bus to Manhattan and stayed over one night to see the play "Dreamgirls"? I had a $50 seat and believe me the play was worth one hundred dollars a seat. It's almost impossible to describe the play . . .

I almost forgot; J. sent Mama the sharpest flowers I have ever seen. The arrangement was the "Bird of Paradise" with a small Teddy Bear inside, and the card was signed, "From Bridgett and J." (Freaky.)

Well, let me bring you up to date on Rita:

Presently, I'm still unemployed and enjoying the good life.

I have an interview scheduled with Ford Motors Purchasing. I would love to stay in this area. Say a little prayer for me. I am assured that God will bless me with something enjoyable and nice.

I have also applied to Vanderbilt's PhD Program and the University of Pittsburgh. I am trying to have other alternatives if I don't decide to accept full employment. Being off work has really let me realize that working a 9-to-5 job confines you. Also, if I get a PhD in business, I could always teach on a college level and have a more flexible schedule. In addition to having a job which is conducive to my health. Wish me luck.

Since I have been back in Detroit I have dated a policeman, and D. has taken me out. Life is for living.

Well, Bridgett, I'm going to close. I have truly missed you not being at home or being able to contact you by telephone.

I love you & miss you.

Love your Sister,
Rita

P.S. I will write again in a few days. Don't laugh at the amount of money.

Clearly, Rita was trying to figure out what was next, at a crossroads between chasing another corporate job in an "all-white" environment and moving toward a career that would be less taxing on her, physically and mentally. And in a gentle push, she let me know that my fiancé, by sending our mother flowers and signing my name alongside his, was revealing himself to be presumptive, if not possessive—i.e., "freaky." After I received that letter from Rita, I got up the courage to send J. a Dear John letter, breaking off our engagement. Our mother later wrote to say that "Rita tried to tell me that you didn't really love J. I refused to listen. I guess I was looking forward to a wedding."

As for Rita's love life, she'd tried again with Zachary, but he wasn't committing to her, and wasn't making enough of an effort to be with her. Despite really loving him, Rita decided she had to move on. "I can't wait around anymore while he tries to figure it out," she told me. "I don't have that kind of time."

Recently, I just came out and asked Zachary: "What was *really* going on? Did you love her?"

He's quiet for a moment. "I would say yes," he tells me. "I would say yes. I really loved her. But I was young and scared." Rita made it clear how she felt about his reluctance. She told him, "You're gonna miss me one day." "She used to say that to me all the time," admits Zachary. *You're gonna miss me one day.* "And she was right." He sighs. "She was right."

25

One month later, just shy of her twenty-seventh birthday, Rita wrote me again with an update:

March 11, 1983

Hello Bridgett,
Just me dropping a few lines and to say I'm very sorry for taking so long to write again.

So far, I am still unemployed and didn't get the job offer with IBM. However, this job situation has not totally gotten me down since there are so many people out of work in Detroit . . . Tentatively, I have decided to relocate back to Detroit and seek employment. My decision is not yet final. I have given this a serious thought. My living situation in Atlanta is far below my standards and everyone should have a cut-off point in terms of how far they will fall. My living conditions in Atlanta is no exaggeration.

Before I forget to tell you: My complaint with TVA has turned into my favor. I truly hope I win the case because losing my job has really fucked things up for me. Say a prayer that everything will work out for me.

Well, Bridgett, I am going to close for now. Please excuse any grammatical errors. I am writing this letter at 4:00 am.

Take Care

Love you & Miss You
Your sister Rita

Rita likely couldn't find work because she had an albatross around her neck; as long as the TVA case hadn't yet been decided, she couldn't count on good references from her last place of employment. Nor could she list the work she was really doing (working for our mom's numbers business) on her résumé. In the next letter she sent to me, in Kenya, she expressed her frustration over her living and work situation. She also made it clear that, given how much TVA's unjust firing had "fucked things up" for her, she was continuing to fight back.

May 18, 1983

Hey Bridgett,
Well, by the time you receive this letter, you would have celebrated your 23rd birthday. I hope your day was a happy one.
      Sorry I took so long to write and thanks for the birthday card. I've been back in Detroit for exactly 5 weeks, and I am trying my best to adjust to living at home again. There's nothing like living alone. However, my being home is a lot of help to Mama but I continue to express to everyone that I do not plan to make Detroit my home. I am only in Detroit because of my employment and financial situation.

And then Rita laid out the details of her case:

Concerning my EEO complaint: The situation with TVA is 50–50, which means I have as good a chance to win as lose. Since I left TVA there have been 2 white women in my same department who have been charged with telephone violation. Neither one has been suspended or terminated. I wrote a letter to my chief of complaint processing about the telephone violations of the two white women. He's going to decide if the situation should be investigated since no decision has been rendered in my case. TVA has spent about $30,000 to $40,000 on my case. I have decided if I don't win my case administratively, I will go to court. My situation at TVA shows how racist the system is. For example, Harold Washington the new mayor in Chicago is receiving no cooperation from common council. Every day the news shows how disorderly the meetings are and that the common council refused to work with Washington because he's Black. Have you experienced any racism in Kenya?

Well, enough on these white folks.

Juliette's mother came over Mother's Day and the pictures show that Africa has truly agreed with you and that you are still dressing nice (smile).

I am planning to come to London in August. The travel agencies have good prices to London during the summer months.

Also, Mama sent you a package with a skirt and top and a pair of pants. Please send your clothes size because I get tired of having to judge whether you would like something, or whether something will fit Ms. Bridgett (smile).

Well Bridgett it's 5:00 a.m. I am going to close for now. I will write in about one week.

Love,
Rita

Rita visited me in London that August as promised, the one time she and I were together outside of the country, just the two of us. We did all the touristy things, which included attending Notting Hill Carnival, an annual Caribbean celebration. And I snapped an iconic photo of Rita standing in front of the changing of the guards at Buckingham Palace, her red Indian cotton dress billowing in the wind, matching both the guard's uniform and her lipstick as she smiled her perfect smile. A couple months later, my year abroad ended, and I returned to Detroit for several months before moving back to Georgia to do an internship at a small newspaper in Gainesville, and later getting hired at the *Atlanta Journal-Constitution*. I was launching my career while Rita's was still stalled. She was the most educated of our mother's children, yet she was doing the thing our mother had worked so hard to ensure none of us would have to do—helping her run numbers. Rita had to feel on some level that she was out in the wilderness professionally. Meanwhile, her case against TVA dragged on, and during that time she tweaked her résumé, making her new objective a job in marketing, "preferably in the area of sales with the express purpose of obtaining qualifying experience for upper-level management."

Back then, yuppies—young urban professional Baby Boomers—were part of the cultural zeitgeist. I wrote a trend story for the *Atlanta Journal-Constitution* showing that buppies—Black urban professionals—were also a trend. "The financial savvy attained by a small, select group of college-educated blacks has propelled them into upper middle-class 'American dream' lifestyles that their parents and grandparents never attained," I wrote. "And now they talk of climbing the corporate ladder the way their ancestors sang of climbing Jacob's." When I wrote that story, I distinctly remember thinking that Rita should've been someone I interviewed, as she fit the profile as a Black, twentysomething woman with an advanced degree. But I couldn't include my own sister in that story, because her career trajectory had been thwarted. I felt for her, for what could've been, for what she'd earned and deserved. There was no corporate ladder for Rita to climb.

As her EEOC case moved into its second year, Rita kept her hopes up that it would resolve soon. That fall, *The Cosby Show* premiered, and suddenly the country was thrust into the awareness that some Blacks lived upscale and upwardly mobile lives. Rita wasn't a big fan of the show, and I wonder now if that showcase of Black bourgeois life bothered Rita, herself in professional limbo. Around that time, she read Louise Hay's new book, *You Can Heal Your Life,* in which the author further honed her concept that our emotional problems and physical maladies can be improved by changing our thinking. Rita, continuing to suffer from flare-ups, took away the message that worry was not good for her health, and vowed that she was going to stop obsessing over her case, figure out some way to move on with her life. And so, she made a big decision: she began teaching economics as a substitute high school teacher. "I *never* thought I'd teach," she said. "But it actually makes sense for me."

It did make sense: shorter workdays, summers free, classroom autonomy. She got a regular "building sub" position at Redford High School and soon enough, with that income, coupled with what she made working for our mother, she moved her life forward another step: she got her own apartment at Northgate Apartments complex in Oak Park, three miles from our home, confident that with her two jobs she could pay the pricey $355-per-month rent (the equivalent of over $1,000 in 2024).

This was when she met another dear friend, Wilma, who taught business classes at Redford. They saw each other in the hallways, crossed paths a few times, and actually first chatted while in the school office. Wilma says that with her outgoing personality, it was easy to be friendly with Rita. "She'd say, 'Oh, girl, I like what you have on,'" Wilma recalls. Wilma would compliment her on something she was wearing—both of them fashion mavens—and before long, they became good friends. "We would talk and whatnot, and just became close that way," says Wilma.

Here is that moment in her personal narrative that we who love Rita always cast as proof of her incredible will for living, and her strength in the face of a chronic illness. She understood that lupus required a job more conducive to her health, and so she pivoted, figuring out how to create a new life for herself. This is true. But what is also true is that her career change was necessitated by a punitive act on her employer's part, fueled by bias, which is straight-up racism. She may have still ultimately switched to a job better suited for her, but she was *forced* to do so—and at what cost to the very health she was now attempting to protect by switching professions? What did her being accused of misconduct and then fired so abruptly rob her of? How much did the yearslong case she forged against TVA cost her? How much did that ongoing psychological stress take its toll on her? How much did her already immune-compromised body begin an accelerated deterioration, so early in her adulthood, as a result? As that 2019 report found, racial discrimination contributes to racial disparities in SLE outcomes.

A year after TVA's treatment of Rita had forced her to change her life's work, Dr. Geronimus, then a young researcher at the University of Michigan School of Public Health, noted in a published report that Black women in their midtwenties had higher rates of infant death than teenage girls did—a shocking finding that went against the prevailing ideas. Why was this so? She discovered that because these women were older, stress had more time to affect their bodies. For white mothers, the opposite proved true—the older they were, the better their birthing outcome. Dr. Geronimus's research showed that the longer a Black woman lives, the more interaction with racism she experiences, and as a result, the more her body wears down, leading to health complications. That's when Dr. Geronimus coined the term "weathering" to explain this phenomenon. She showed what actually happens to the bodies of Black women who deal with "long-term cascades of stress hormones," as she puts it. "This toxic stress triggers the premature deterioration of the bodies of African American women as a consequence of repeated exposure to a climate of discrimination and insults."

Dr. Geronimus has said she coined the term "weathering"—forty years ago—as a metaphor, "To suggest that what I was seeing was both weathering as in the idea of bodies being eroded by their environments; but also, it means people being able to withstand that or survive it." It's such a perfect term, because it connotes real wear and tear—both from erosion and effort—which is exactly what the cardiovascular, metabolic, and immune systems suffer as a result of all those accumulated stress hormones. It makes me think of those cars that Rita used to drive through the corrosion booth at her proving ground job, to see how much accelerated abuse they could take. And that description certainly describes Rita's experience being mistreated by and fighting against her former employer; it was a highly traumatizing experience that dragged on, chronically stressful for her. Now that I have the language for it, I'm certain that long-drawn-out ordeal weathered Rita's body, even as she weathered the ordeal.

~

The summer of 1985, Zachary got married. Rita told me in a matter-of-fact way, and when I asked how she felt, she just shrugged and said, "Men are like buses; if you miss one, another one is coming soon."

She'd definitely been dating other men in recent years, including Elijah, whom she'd dated off and on since college, and so yes, she could seemingly move on. But *I* felt gut-punched when she told me this, and *so* disappointed in him. I'd been hoping that they'd make it as a couple, even though I dared not express this to Rita in the moment, not wanting to upset her. I do remember wondering if my sister's chance to have a life partner who really *got* her, someone who would protect and defend her, care for her, love her unconditionally—had all that just slipped out of her grasp? Now that I know about the intensity of their connection, I'm certain that Zachary marrying another woman deeply hurt Rita. She had to ask herself, *Why not me?* I decided to ask Zachary that very question:

"Why not Rita?"

He sounds slightly pained and wistful when he answers me. "I think about it . . . how she could've been my wife, how she would've really inspired me," he admits. "And your mother, Fannie! She could've been my mother-in-law and I could've learned so much from her about hustling to really make it in this world . . . I do think about all that, and I do wonder, did I make a mistake?"

Zachary is still married to the same woman, which is why he asked me not to use his real name. "Oh man, what Rita and I had was a *deep* deal," he says. "I only had that once in my life with a woman. Only once."

In some good news that same summer, the investigation of Rita's case ended, and EEOC rendered a decision: Based on the evidence, she was discriminated against when TVA terminated her in 1982. Rita won!

Her case was strengthened by the fact that the two white women employees who'd done the same thing—used work phones to make personal long-distance calls—had not been penalized, let alone fired. As remedy, TVA agreed to one year of back pay. Rita received a check for $22,942 gross, and $15,596 net. In 2024 dollars, that's the equivalent of $44,000 in take-home pay.

Three years after being let go, Rita's fighting back paid off, and she was vindicated. Said differently, she suffered through three years of being unable to get a job in her field commensurate with her education because of a wrongful termination; when she finally received justice, she couldn't get back those years, nor the career she'd been forced to abandon. Fortunately, finally winning not only gave Rita the resources to support herself as she transitioned into a new career in secondary education; it gave her back her confidence. She could exhale, reclaim the psychic space that her case against TVA had taken up, no longer live in limbo. What she'd been saying to everyone—that she'd been unfairly fired from her job—had now been proven true by a federal judge, dropping the stigma that loomed over her, and leaving her with a five-inch-thick EEOC complaint file as proof. She could finally move on. Rita was twenty-nine.

That fall, while I was living in New York, pursuing a graduate degree in journalism, I let myself get conned. While walking along Broadway near Columbia University one day, I was approached by a woman who asked for help. She was African, she had a package of money with nowhere to keep it safe, and the man who'd abused her was trying to take it from her; could I hold it for her until she could get it wired out of the country? I foolishly agreed to let her keep it in my dorm room; once we were in my room (yes, I let this stranger into my room), and she was leaving the bundle of cash with me, she said she needed some collateral to make sure I wouldn't steal her money. I took my diamond ring off my finger and gave it to her. That ring had been given to me when I was ten by our mother. She gave one to Rita at the same time, saying to us both, "Now you never have to get excited about a man giving you a diamond ring. You can get excited about how he treats you." The woman left, saying she'd be right back. Of course, I never saw her again, and of course the "money" was nothing more than wrapped newspaper. I was so ashamed of my gullibility, but confessed to only one person, to Rita, what happened. "I was really trying to help her," I said, crying. "I had no intention of taking her money!"

"I know you're not like that," said Rita. "She took advantage of your kindness, so don't feel bad."

Having her confirm my good intentions, and not shame me for being stupid, meant everything to me. And then, days later, a special delivery arrived in the mail. Rita had sent me *her* diamond ring.

Later that fall, Rita wrote again, to let me know that Mama, who was again in the hospital, would be there for another week or so, but she was "doing very well, asking for her pretty gowns, blush, lipsticks, etc. Just like she's at home (smile)." And Rita wished me luck with my studies, sharing a quote that she attributed to the popular televangelist Reverend Robert Schuller: "Tough semesters never last, but tough students do."

Neither of us knew at the time just how tough I'd have to be to make it through my final semester.

~

Christmas 1985 is utterly joyful. I'm halfway through grad school, Rita is teaching high school, our futures bright. In a photo of us taken over the holiday, Rita wears a brilliant hot pink wool coat and a smile bigger than I've ever seen, an exaggerated smile to match our exaggerated happiness. We stand in the living room of her modern apartment, its cream-colored custom drapes shimmering behind us as luxurious backdrop. We're twenty-five and twenty-nine, the only time we'll both be in our mid- to late twenties, a perfect age for sisters who are closer than ever. We're giddy with anticipation, drunk on expectation. Rita's lupus is in remission, and she looks great. "Don't let me lose twenty pounds," she says. "Because then I'll *really* be jazzy!" We have survived losing our father and our big sister. Our brother and remaining sister and mother are all okay. We have an adorable toddler nephew—our sister Dianne's miracle baby. Nothing could go terribly wrong because we've already suffered our fair and unfair share of tragedy. This is our season of "blue nights," as Joan Didion coined them, a beautiful yet brief sweet spot in our lives. Rita and I have the arrogant optimism of youth, believing this magical time will go on and on. We don't understand yet that "blue nights are the opposite of the dying of the brightness, but they are also its warning."

26

Once again, in the family cosmos, one sibling's life affects and determines the trajectory of the other siblings' lives. If circumstances had turned out differently for our family in 1986, if what happened to our remaining siblings had not happened, what might have been different for us? For Rita?

While I was home from school on winter break, Anthony came by to visit us all. He and I chatted about a popular cologne he wanted to try but couldn't find in Detroit; he wrote down the name, Rothschild, and I promised him that as soon as I got back to New York, I'd find the cologne and send a bottle to him. Later that day, I was hanging out in the den when suddenly I jumped up with a start and asked our mother: "Where's Anthony?" She said, "He just left." I raced to the side door and rushed outside, managing to catch him just as he was getting into his car. "Hey!" I called out to him. "I just wanted to say bye." He smiled at me. "Goodbye, little sister," he said, then entered his car, pulled out of the driveway, and disappeared.

Days later, once I was back in New York at grad school, Anthony's girlfriend at the time called our mother in the predawn, saying that she'd just discovered Anthony on the front porch of their place; he was unconscious. "And I don't know where my car is!" she kept saying. "I don't know where my car is!" Our mother instructed her to call for an ambulance. Then she asked Rita to drive over to their place. Rita, alone, sped through the streets and got there just as the ambulance arrived; she trailed behind the emergency vehicle, its flashing lights and siren blaring as they rushed our brother to Mount Carmel Hospital. She was terrified, not knowing if they'd get him there in time, not knowing how bad his condition was, or what had actually happened to him. Was it a seizure? Was he just drunk, passed out? Worse? The not knowing was unbearable. "You have no idea what that drive was like," she told me later. "I prayed the whole way."

By the time he lay in the back of that ambulance, our brother had been out of prison for five years, after serving five years. While incarcerated he'd received his GED and taken college classes. Now thirty-three, he'd created a new life for himself: no longer with his wife, Renita, but still married to her, he'd found a job that he could manage to get as a man with "a record," working as a custodian at local high schools; he was living with a new woman, establishing a relationship with his son, Tony, and spending some nights hanging out at a neighborhood bar, the Blue Room. He liked to go there to shoot pool. Located on Wyoming, it was close to where he lived on Washburn. Every time I see an old episode of *Cheers*, I conjure up Anthony and that local bar where everyone knew his name. He'd been in the Blue Room that very night he ended up unconscious on the porch of his home.

I think about all the events in Anthony's life that led to that night. Our mother pinpointed the moment when she believed things went awry as when she took him out of Catholic school. Until junior high, she would tell us, he was a good student, and a polite boy. But then he entered high school and started "getting into trouble," as she put it. In those years of Anthony's youth, a lot happened. He was a fifteen-year-old when Detroit's "riot" broke out in the summer of 1967. Dozens of teenage boys like him were arrested or shot at during the Great Rebellion. Many were killed, including three teens shot by police at the Algiers Motel, and the last recorded fatality from the uprising was a nineteen-year-old killed by a paratrooper. Anthony was sixteen when our parents divorced, and our father moved out of the family home on Broadstreet. When one year later, our mother remarried and we moved away, our father moved back into the house on Broadstreet, and Anthony chose to stay with him. We never really talked about these seismic changes among ourselves as siblings, but our father once revealed to me that he believed the divorce and our mother's remarriage had been hardest on Anthony. Who knows? I do know that just as I understand why our sister Deborah sought relief through drugs, I understand why our brother wanted to escape the pressures both inside and outside our front door. Somewhere around that time, in the late '60s, according to Anthony's wife, Renita, our brother-in-law, George, gave Anthony heroin to snort for the first time.

Meanwhile, throughout his late teens, Anthony was like so many young Black men before and after: repeatedly stopped by police while driving, or walking, constantly harassed. And in 1970, just as Rita was making her way through high school and Anthony became old enough to vote, Detroit's police formed an "elite" undercover operation called STRESS, which stood for Stop the Robberies, Enjoy Safe Streets; it was really an excuse for the predominantly white police force to target Black neighborhoods. They used such regular, deadly force against Black men that Detroit's police department led the nation in "civilian killings." Anthony was stopped by STRESS police several times. Usually, it was for driving our mother's nice car. (Many years later, his own son would have the same experience in Atlanta, stopped often by Georgia State Patrol for driving a late-model white Camaro that his grandmother had bought for him.) Anthony was sometimes stopped because he "met the description" of a suspect, i.e., he was a young Black man. I was with him once when this happened. We were on a Michigan highway, and Anthony was stopped for speeding; whether he was or not, I can't say. I do know a state trooper approached our car, and the way he ordered Anthony to spread his legs, get patted down, then "come with me" to his patrol car made me worried about what might happen next. Anthony complied wordlessly, but I instinctively moved toward my brother. "Stay back!" the officer barked at me. "Stay back or else!" So much terror shot through my own body in that moment, an overwhelming feeling I'll never forget, that I can only imagine what was going on for Anthony. We are so used to these encounters with police that if they don't end tragically, we dismiss them as a routine part of life. In fact, thanks to Dr. Geronimus's research, we don't have to imagine what my brother suffered in that moment. She has delineated for us what likely went through Anthony's body during that and each of his so-called random encounters with police officers. During a talk with journalist Linda Villarosa, Dr. Geronimus described what happens inside the body of a young Black man who's stopped by the police:

He becomes very vigilant and very concerned about his behavior.
Meanwhile he knows that the reason he's doing that is that there's

some chance this is going to end up being a fatal confrontation for him. He's actually in . . . what many people think of as a fight or flight mode even though he's trying to stay calm and polite despite the fact that through his body there are now stress hormones raging, that in turn elevate blood pressure, elevate heart rate, catapult oxygenated blood towards his heart and other large muscles (as you would if you needed to fight or flee). Meanwhile they're mobilizing glucose triggers and fats into his bloodstream for energy.

Dr. Geronimus goes on to explain the ongoing effects on a Black man's body like Anthony's, beyond a singular encounter:

And when this is happening chronically from every fist in your face— whether it's fears of the police or actual interactions with the police or just anticipating them, and then also ruminating about them after- wards, all these things . . . leads your body to be in this chronic state of stress arousal . . .

My compassion swells as I imagine Anthony seeking relief from that chronic state of stress by using heroin. While we know that to- day one in five Americans is taking medication to treat their mental health, what I find telling is that in 2023, four million Americans admitted to specifically taking prescription opioids for "nonmedical" use; 10 percent of them went on to use heroin. But in the 1960s and 1970s, a time when we didn't have cell phones to document Black men and women's fatal and near-fatal encounters with the law, many people believed there had to be a good reason why police behaved as they did toward African Americans. Why would any young Black man have *any* reason to seek relief from the racial stressors in his life via drugs? Now we know why. By the time he was in his late teens, Anthony was using heroin regularly.

Back then I was still a child, but Rita was already in her teens, and far more aware of the dangers that faced our brother out in the world. She carried that anxiety with her every time he left the house. And Rita had to feel relief every time Anthony walked through our front door, safely back at home. No question she was also absorbing our mother's anxiety then relief, anxiety then relief. Again, that was the nature of their bond, and of Rita's vociferous protectiveness toward our mother.

Anthony was eighteen when his then-girlfriend, Renita, became pregnant. "What do you plan to do?" Mama asked him. "Are you gonna do right by her?" Anthony said yes, he wanted to do the honorable thing. He loved her. Even though he was still a teenager, battling a growing addiction, he presented Renita with an engagement ring on Christmas Day. They married, and just as he turned nineteen, he became a father to Anthony Ray Davis II, whom we called Tony. Anthony now had an incentive to conquer his addiction, and I remember at least one drug rehab program he entered. Yet he battled his addiction for several more years. What was there in the culture to support him? Black drug addicts were demonized. During that time of his young marriage, he told Renita that no matter what, she should never try heroin. "The one thing he told me when he got into the drug situation, and I asked him what he was doing, he said, 'Don't you ever let me catch you doing this here,'" recalls Renita. "For him to not want me to experience what he was going through was enough to let me know that he loved me. That's how I knew." She pauses. "We loved each other."

Sadly, drug use too easily reduces a person to what drugs cause them to do, rather than who they are. And Renita, as the mother of his only son, wants it known that Anthony was much more than a man who once battled an addiction. "I cannot even say how good a person he was," she insists. "As much as he had, he shared it all. His was a giving heart, like his mother. He was always looking out for the underdog, taking up for other people. And he looked out for everybody . . ."

Renita pauses. "He wasn't a bad guy at all," she says. "He just got a raw deal."

27

I'll never know exactly what prompted Anthony to hold up a party store (as Detroiters call convenience stores) back in 1975.

"That was not even his style," Renita says to me many years later as we talk about what happened. "He didn't have it to do. He was doing it because he was with them that were doing it," is how she puts it. "He became more of a pawn, because of those drugs. Drugs got him going out there doing things he'd never done before."

When our mother later said there was no reason in hell that Anthony had to rob anybody, because he knew he could come to her for whatever money he needed, she didn't consider Anthony's shame; he knew how she felt about his addiction, and he knew how she felt about giving him money. Sometimes in an effort to exert tough love, she refused him that money, knowing what he was going to do with it. Yet she vacillated. Many times, she handed over that money specifically because she didn't want him out in the streets trying to get it in other ways. But Anthony's addiction was a constant, with him ever seeking money to support his habit. A vicious cycle. It's so hard to know how to help an addict help himself.

Rita and I never really discussed what Anthony had done. It was too painful, a third rail. But Renita has her theories: she tells me that the way she sees it, Anthony had guts, but he wasn't streetwise like a hardened criminal. "If you don't have that street knowledge, baby, and you try something like that?" she says. "You're lost."

Our father had his own theory. He believed that the men who planned the robbery with Anthony set him up. They knew he hadn't grown up streetwise, nor in survival mode. Daddy always believed that had the police not caught him, those other men might've killed Anthony, and taken the loot from the robbery for themselves. It's a viable theory, with a bit of proof: As Anthony ran away from the crime scene, he never ditched the gun. Police caught him with that gun, a rookie mistake for sure. Desperation causes us to do the illogical, the stupid, the unthinkable.

At Anthony's trial, our parents were naturally filled with worry. The night before, they rode to the courthouse, and sprinkled a hoodoo root around the building, in a last-ditch and totally uncharacteristic effort to affect the trial's outcome. Witnesses at the trial all had the same account: When Anthony came into the store, gun in hand, he politely announced a holdup. According to eyewitness testimony, he said to the person behind the register, "Excuse me, but could you please hand over what you have?" Those who'd been there said it was odd, almost strange, how polite he was.

"Because it was not in his character to do that at all," explains Renita.

Just as with Deborah, I wonder: What if our brother hadn't been demonized for being a heroin addict back then, but rather given compassion and clean needles and controlled amounts of heroin or methadone? What if, even before heroin entered his life, he too had been able to freely take gummies in an open, unstigmatized way that cannabis users can do today, to mitigate his angst, the stress of living life as a young Black man? Things might've been different. He might've thrived. "He was very intelligent," says Renita. "He had all the qualities anybody could ask for."

Anthony showed no real emotion when the judge handed down his sentence. "I didn't want to make it harder on Mama than it already was," he later told Rita. He went on to serve his time stoically. He never complained about being behind bars. We visited him regularly, wrote letters, sent photos; our mother kept money in his commissary account. Prison did rid him of his drug addiction and gave him a lot of time to gain perspective on his young life. Three years into his stint, when he was twenty-six, he wrote me a letter both future-focused and reflective:

April 4, 1979

Hey Bridgett,
Sitting here thinking about you. I decided to drop you a few lines.
Let me start by telling you I received your card and letter. I was

very glad to hear from you . . . Bridgett, you were looking very
nice, when you came to see me. I just can't get over how you've
grown so fast. You've changed from my little "ugly" sister, into a
very pretty woman. I'm glad to hear that you and Rita are getting
along much better. Tell me, do you have a boyfriend? If so, send
me a picture of you and him, so I can tell you what I think of him.

I'm so tired of school. I'm going to take a break for a half of
semester. I'm going to start writing more often. Even though I
don't write much, I think of you quite often. You know, I hate to
write! So if I don't write as much as I should, I'll still be looking
to receive a letter from you. Let's stay in touch (O.K.)

. . . By the way, I'm working now, if you need some money,
let me know and I'll send it to you (I'm serious). Every time you
come home, I'll be expecting to see you. I really enjoy seeing you.

Let me know what's happening with you. I want you to know
whatever you tell me, is between you and I. If you want my friend
to do a chart on you send me your birthday and the time you
were born. He did one on Rita . . . What is it to do there, when
you're not in school? How do you like Atlanta? I'm thinking
about coming there when I get out. I know I'm going somewhere!
I'm tired of being a damn fool! I feel that I'm ready to settle down
now. You know I'm getting kind of old . . .

I'm just going to try to make up all this time I've been away
from Tony up to him. I don't give a damn about anything else.

I'm going to end now. You be sweet and take care of yourself.
Write me back real soon.

Love ya,
Your favorite brother Anthony

Not only am I touched by his offers to both send me money and
be someone to confide in, I see how much he wanted me and Rita to
get along. It reminds me yet again what a family triumph it was for
us all when she and I finally did find our way to each other, to a close
relationship as sisters.

After he'd served his time and gotten out a bit early for good be-havior in 1981, Anthony never once talked to me nor to Rita about prison life, and what happened to him inside. I wanted to ask him about his experience, but I never did. Once he was back home, our mother's letters to me at college often included the phrase, "Anthony is going to mail this for me," or "Anthony's here now, waiting to take this to the post office." And when she wrote to me during my year abroad, she let me know that "Anthony came to see me almost every day while I was in the hospital."

Renita said that she and Anthony remained in each other's lives, even though they never got back together. "He never divorced me. I never divorced him," she said. Neither bothered to do so, didn't really feel the need to. "He'd still come around, come visit my daddy. He'd sit at the table with him, and they'd eat biscuits together."

She confirms what I assumed to be true: Most of all, Anthony "didn't fool with no more drugs" after prison. The addiction was gone. "He would drink a little beer, you know?" she tells me. "He'd have his Colt 45, but that was the one thing he did. That was it."

And there was their son, Tony. Renita recalls the time Anthony went up to Tony's elementary school after hearing that a teacher had hit him with a paddle. "He was really nice, he didn't make a scene, but he let that teacher know, 'You're not going to be hitting my child.'" Here, she pauses. "He loved Tony to death," she says.

Tony, himself now the father of two children, says of Anthony, "Once he got out, he had to learn how to be a father." Tony remembers in those early months after his father's release, Anthony lived with our mother and stepfather and Tony. He'd sleep on the pull-out couch in the den, "And I'd go and sleep with him sometimes," Tony recalls. "Sometimes we'd wrestle, or do whatever together. . . . He'd been away a long time, and we had to form a new relationship." During those years, Tony grew from a child to a teenager, and he says about him and his father, "We started bonding."

I have a vivid memory of Anthony at a performance of *Purlie*, in the summer of 1982, a year after his release. He sits there in his seat at Detroit's Music Hall, dressed in a sharp suit and looking dapper, handsome, his girlfriend beside him. I remember being overwhelmed with happiness in that moment, thinking, *He gets to have a whole new life now.*

If any one thing had been different, Anthony might never have even been at the Blue Room that frigid night in January.

~

Meanwhile, oblivious, I turned in my grad-school thesis, returned to my small room at International House in Harlem and collapsed on the bed feeling both exhaustion and relief. My phone rang. It was our sister Dianne. I was so happy to hear her voice, to hear from home, after accomplishing something so demanding by the deadline. My voice was more exuberant than usual. "Hey!!!" I said to her. "How's everybody?"

"This is not good news," she said back.

At the Blue Room bar, on what turned out to be the coldest night of the year, Anthony got into an argument with another man while he was shooting pool. Anthony usually carried a gun for protection, but that night he didn't have it on him. The other man did. Seeing the man's gun, Anthony ran out of the bar and attempted to run home. But the man shot our brother in the back. Anthony somehow managed to make it all the way to his place before collapsing on the front porch.

A doctor told Rita at the hospital that he was dead on arrival. Dead from that one gunshot wound to the back. She had to call home and tell our mother that her son was gone.

Renita believes that Anthony banged and banged on that door, trying to get in, but his girlfriend wouldn't open the door. "I don't know if she was upset with him or whatever, maybe they were having a difficult problem, and she didn't know the significance of what was going on . . . but she didn't open the door," said Renita, convinced of this. "How long had he been out there before he died? I felt like had that woman opened the door, called an ambulance, he might still be here."

When Dianne told me what happened, I screamed so loud that someone banged on my door. Dianne instructed me to open it, and the next thing I remember is a plethora of people surrounding me, trying to comfort me. In one of the kindest gestures ever extended toward me, my classmate Frances Dinkelspiel slipped a little pill into my hand and told me to swallow. I did.

I soon learned that our mother had instructed both Rita and Dianne to not tell me what had happened until after I'd turned in my thesis. "Bad news can wait," she told them. The whole time that I was working on my thesis as I listened to my sister Deborah's favorite songs by Donny Hathaway, my brother was already dead. Had I known the news before I turned in my thesis, I might've dropped out of grad school. Mama didn't want that. I've always held on to that incredible act on our mother's part as an acute example of her ability to think about one child's future even as another child's life has ended. I'm still awed by it.

But it's not lost on me that while I was spared, Rita was not.

Rita was not only tasked with the heart-wrenching job of seeing Anthony's body lying on the ground, then riding behind the ambulance in which Anthony's body lay, but she also had to hear, "I'm sorry, but we couldn't save him," from the attending doctor, then had to relay that God-awful news to our mother. I imagine the physiological processes that went through Rita's body throughout the entire ordeal. That type of traumatic experience, we now know, creates wild levels of stress arousal, what Dr. Geronimus has described as a state in which "You're depriving some parts of your body of nutrients and you're over activating other parts of your body." Dr. Geronimus has said, "For instance, your heart can become enlarged like any muscle that's pumped too much; the blood and sugar stays in your arteries . . . all the things we think happen from eating the wrong things . . . actually can happen and happen more often and more insidiously through these stress processes wearing away at your arteries, sending plaque throughout your body." She goes on: "You've also engaged your immune system so your white blood cells are running rampant, and so the white blood cells also can form plaque and . . . all your body organs and systems start to get worn down a little more . . ."

Rita later said to me, "Why was it me who had to be the one dealing with all that, by myself?"

I couldn't answer her. Our mother knew Rita *could* do it. So Mama asked her to. But really, Rita should not have been put through that ordeal; her body was already compromised.

How many years did that horrendous and harrowing experience rob from her life?

In the days that followed Anthony's death, I could not bear to look his girlfriend in the face; in a bizarre coincidence, her name was also Rita. It pained me to see her because I too believed, as did his son's mother, that had *that* Rita opened the door when he banged on it, Anthony would be alive. People survive gunshot wounds to the back. (An autopsy had determined that the time between when our brother was shot and his death was unknown.)

My Rita and I were bereft, acutely aware of the future we'd lost with our brother. I'd gotten to spend so little time with Anthony. As a child, yes, I remember him teasing me, and playing with my two Yorkshire terriers. And Rita, just four years younger than he, had a few more memories of hanging out with Anthony. There's that great photo of the two of them that remains as proof, taken on a Christmas morning when he's about twelve and she's eight, surrounded by opened presents. I do have a few other memories, like sneaking to sit on the basement steps, watching as he entertained friends in our basement rec room. But when Anthony was seventeen, and Rita and I moved to another house with our mother and new stepfather and he did not, it meant we didn't see him as much. During his early adulthood we both saw him so few times, as he tried to manage an addiction, young fatherhood, rehab. Then he was gone for five years. And Rita was away for much of the final five years of his life—finishing college, working in Nashville, finishing grad school in Atlanta, working in Chattanooga. And so was I—in college, traveling abroad, living in Atlanta, attending grad school in New York. And yet, Rita's college and grad-school friends say she talked about him (and her sisters and mother and father) so often, they felt they knew him. As for me, I often felt my heart quietly pounding with excitement whenever I was in Anthony's presence, a too-rare occurrence. Now, Rita and I were not going to get the chance to form our adult relationships as brother and sisters with him. It was—and remains—devastating to be robbed of that. Also, I couldn't stop thinking a small thing, that I hadn't gotten around to buying him the Rothschild cologne he'd asked me to get him; for a while, that racked me with guilt.

Dianne did her best to comfort me and Rita. "He had a happy childhood," she told us. "John T. worshipped him. Fannie would do anything for him. And he had us. Anthony knew he was loved." Dianne told us to hold on to memories of his easygoing manner, his carefree ways, his smile, his quick laugh, how everyone liked him. These truths seemed to help Rita, somewhat. She said to me, "I'm glad he had those final years of freedom. I know that the last five years of his life, he was happy. At least he had that."

"Five years is nothing!" I spat back, so angry over what his murderer had snatched away from him, from us all. I kept thinking how Anthony would never get the chance to do so many things that lay ahead in his life. "You're always going somewhere," he once said to me. It broke my heart that he'd never traveled, seen other places. Had he ever been on an airplane? (Today, it gives me some solace to know that his own son, Tony, works for Delta Air Lines and travels regularly, having been everywhere from Alaska to Thailand to Europe.) I couldn't shake that sense that he never caught a break in his short life, that too few things had gone his way. As I wrote at the time in my journal, "I just hurt for his vulnerable side, the part of him that cared, that hoped, that hurt too. There was a part of him that needed protection, and the night he needed it most, no one was there."

Both Rita and I lamented that now we wouldn't have our brother nor our father to walk us down the aisle someday at our weddings. And then, out of nowhere, I said to her: "This is just preparing us for the next tragedy." She was shocked. "Why would you say something like that?" she asked. But I inexplicably kept repeating it: "This is just preparing us for the next tragedy."

Soon enough there was a trial, and the man who shot and killed our brother got less prison time than Anthony had gotten for armed robbery, where no one had been hurt, or even touched. Black life is cheap. Rita went to the trial to support both Anthony's memory and our mother. I chose not to fly to Detroit to be there. I hated myself for not being there, and for not fighting, for not using my training as a journalist to push for true criminal justice. But I just didn't have it in me, which I'm not proud to admit. I feared the experience of attending the trial might cause me to drop out of my life, completely. We filed a wrongful death suit, but we lost. A judge decided that Anthony's life, and his earning potential as a man with "a record," didn't amount to enough to make the case that his absence cost those of us left behind and made bereft—his mother, his siblings, and most of all his son, who was only fourteen when his father was murdered—deserving of compensation. Anthony never got to work out that relationship with Tony that could've grown richer and closer over time. That loss hurt me the most, what my nephew never got to know about and understand and learn from his father.

My understanding of all he'd lost prompted me to send Tony a letter three and a half years later, on his eighteenth birthday. I wrote:

I'm very proud of you. You've grown into a fine young man.
Always believe in yourself—and the way to do that is to be proud
of who you are and who you come from. Your father and your
grandfather were both good men—men whose last name you
can be proud to have. I don't ever want you to lose sight of that.
Imperfect lives are not wasted ones. It's what's in a man's heart
that matters.

28

Three months after Anthony's death, Rita turned thirty. Unlike what I would do four years later, she didn't mark the occasion with a party. We gave her gifts, and she likely celebrated with a girl-friend, or one of the men she was dating. But I don't remember any fanfare for her milestone birthday. Who was really in a celebratory mood? Rita was now student teaching, getting the credentials needed to become a fully certified teacher. That spring, she came to my grad-school graduation in New York, along with our mother and stepfather, Burt. I wrote in my journal, "Enjoyed having the people I care about there to share it all with me . . . my few days with Rita were genu-ine—no arguments and the chance to talk about our shared feelings & intimacies together. Beautiful. We're at perfect ages for that: 26 & 30." Yet when I look back on photos from that day, I see Rita putting on a good face for the occasion, with her half-smile and canary-yellow dress. What the camera also caught that day was the grief etched across our mother's face, and I still wince at that photo. It's a wonder Rita and Mama managed to show up at all for me. None of us was okay.

Done with graduate school, I was living back in Detroit for the summer, occupying the apartment above our home on West Seven Mile Road, working at the *Wall Street Journal* as a reporting intern. Rita was living in her own apartment relatively close by, but at the house every day, still helping out Mama with the numbers business. I'd originally planned to work in the *WSJ*'s San Francisco bureau, but because of our brother's death, the internship director decided it would be better for me to work in the bureau of my hometown, close to family. I was slightly bummed over his decision because I'd really wanted to be in San Francisco; honestly, what I really wanted was to escape the family's sadness, our grief. Soon enough, I was grateful beyond measure to that man who made sure I was in Detroit that summer.

On an early August morning, our mother's best friend Lula called her. "Fannie, there's a fire at the house on Broadstreet," she said.

"How bad is it?" Mama asked.

"I don't know," said Lula. "But the fire trucks have arrived. I can hear them."

Our mother leapt out of bed and drove the three plus miles to Broadstreet Avenue, to the house she'd bought twenty-five years before—the home that had anchored our leap into the middle-class. Her mind was on making room for her daughter Dianne, son-in-law, George, and almost-two-year-old grandson, Brandon. She figured they'd have to move in with her and our stepfather, Burt, while Broadstreet—as we all called the house—got repaired from the fire damage. Broadstreet meant a lot to the family, our brother-in-law, George, included. His ego had been pumped up by living in that spacious four-bedroom Colonial where his wife had lived throughout her teens—clearly the nicest home he'd ever lived in; he liked giving friends a tour, chest out as he walked from room to room, constantly calling it "my house." In fact, Dianne had repeatedly begged our mother to sign over the deed to her and George, but Mama had resisted, telling her Broadstreet was the family home, even though the two were welcome to live in it for as long as they wanted. That his name wasn't on the deed as co-owner always bothered George, and he carried more resentment over that fact than any of us realized.

When Mama pulled up to the house that early morning, she noticed that firefighters weren't bringing anyone out. She waited and waited, and still nothing. She called Burt from a pay phone nearby, frantic, saying over and over, "But no one's coming out! No one's coming out!"

By then, Dianne and George had been living in the family home for a few years, married for seventeen years. Elaine, her best friend, remembers the night that Dianne met George, in 1968. Elaine and Dianne were hanging out together at a cabaret held at a local club. They were having a good time, eating, drinking a little, dancing. George came by the table and asked Dianne to dance, then they danced again, and then he asked for her phone number. They went out for several months before Dianne told Elaine that George wanted to get married.

Elaine recalls that everyone was initially against it. George was more than six years older than Dianne, and already had a son (George Jr.); our parents thought he had too much experience for their twenty-year-old daughter. He was her first real boyfriend. Still, Dianne said she wanted to marry him. Some of her friends were already getting married, and it being the '60s, for a young woman to marry at twenty wasn't unusual at all. Elaine recalls, "The singer Dinah Washington's son, Bobby, really, really liked Dianne. They were boyfriend and girl-friend for one whole summer. But he moved to California or some-where. After that, I think she was saying to herself about George, 'Well, this is somebody that likes me.'" Rita's interpretation of their marriage, which she shared with me later, was that this was what could happen when a woman feels pressure to marry. Rita vowed that she'd never settle just to say she was someone's wife.

What trajectory might Dianne's life have taken had she stayed in college? She and Elaine had started Macomb Community College to-gether in fall 1966. Dianne lasted only one semester. The college was located on Twelve Mile Road in Warren, Michigan, a suburb twenty miles northeast of Detroit, and as Elaine recalls: "We were the only *B-L-A-C-K* people in the classes, and we were totally ignored. The teachers wouldn't acknowledge us when we raised our hand. For us, there was no extracurriculars, no campus life . . . Dianne told me, 'I'm not coming back.' I begged her and begged her, but she didn't."

Not every Black person can deal with microaggressions; I can see why Dianne chose to leave college, but I also wonder: Did that deci-sion thwart her options, her exposure to a different future, which led indirectly to her settling for and marrying George?

~

Dianne asked Elaine to go to the courthouse with her, to be her witness.

"I didn't want to go because I kept saying, 'It's too soon, it's too soon,'" Elaine recalls. "I knew your mother and father didn't approve of him either and I told her, 'I don't want to get in trouble!'" It's true that our father did not like George at all, from the start, and he and Dianne argued over him. Our mother tolerated her daughter's boyfriend, as he was very polite in her presence, deferential even. And George was nice enough to us, Dianne's siblings.

Elaine recalls that he was very late, but George did eventually show up to the courthouse, without anyone, not even a best man. The two got married.

"That was that," says Elaine.

From the onset of their marriage, it became clear that George was a more-or-less functioning alcoholic. While Rita, only thirteen, worried so much about his behavior that she was imploring God in her letters to Him to "please let George be super safe while driving my mother's car [because] he been drinking a lot," Elaine had an even bigger worry. She saw right away that George was so jealous, he didn't want Dianne talking on the phone when he was home, and always wanted her to himself. "He knew she was younger than him, and that she was very attractive," says Elaine. Also, she noted that he always seemed to be mad about something. "His height made him feel some kind of way too," Elaine believes. "He was short, and so he'd walk like he was a bad mamma jamma," she says, totally overcompensating. Meanwhile, Elaine saw that Dianne was always making excuses for him, trying to cover up his worst tendencies, including the fact that he lied all the time.

From the start, despite his flaws, Dianne really wanted us, her family, to like George—and she wanted *him* to see that we liked him. Most of all, Dianne desperately wanted our mother to approve of George. She sought our mother's approval in all things, was the only child who never went through the least bit of teenage or young-adult rebellion, always tried to please Fannie. We thought this may have something to do with her being away from our mother for three years, from age six to nine, while our parents tried desperately to get a foothold in Detroit. Dianne always stressed that our aunt Florence treated her well, like her own daughter, and they continued to have a special bond. Yet Rita's theory was that Dianne ached for our mother during those crucial years, wondering why she was the one left behind, and when she finally rejoined the family, that ache turned into a form of worship-ping. Since our mother's opinion meant everything to Dianne, that meant she really, really wanted Fannie to like George.

George seemed to want the same. Or at least, he understood how important it was for his wife's mother to think well of him. Around her, and us, he hid his worst traits, presented himself as this good guy. In front of us, George would get down on his knees and tie Dianne's shoes. And yet, if our mother was on the phone with her, and he was cursing or yelling in the background, Dianne would often say, "I'm talking to my mother, George!" and he'd go quiet. It was the same thing if she was talking to one of us, her siblings, on the phone. She'd still say, "I'm talking to my mother!" and that would chill him out, the mention of our mother enough to rein in his behavior.

At the same time, Dianne was vociferously protective of him. She tolerated no criticism of George from me or Rita. We couldn't say anything negative about him to her, and if we tried, she worked hard to defend him. But over the years, Rita and I did discuss George with each other. I distinctly remember Rita saying, "I don't like that every-thing is about him. His injury from work. His car accident. His losing another job. His DUIs. It's always about *his* drama. When does it get to be about her?"

It's true that Dianne was the one working hard, across their many years together, to keep the relationship going. It had to be so ex-hausting to deal with George's constant fuckups, his drunkenness and blackouts, his neediness and jealousy and volatility and rage, his constant demands. Never mind the worries about money, which was always tight because George spent too much of his income on the wrong things. Our mother was often the one who picked up the slack.

Elaine has thought a lot over the years about why her best friend might've stayed so long in that unhealthy marriage. Elaine's theory is that Dianne did this because she didn't want to be alone. "I think she was always trying to cover up what he was doing in the name of love and companionship. What some people don't understand is that every woman wants companionship."

is drinking.'" We don't know what happened after she hung up the phone. Recently, Elaine said to me, with the clarity of hindsight, "I think she did love him, but I think she was afraid of him."

The more depressed Dianne was within her dysfunctional marriage, the more she self-soothed with food, and the more weight she gained. "I'm sure that situation made her eat more," says Elaine. "You got to do something to keep yourself stable." Elaine and I agree that Dianne must've felt that no other man would want her, and that must've made her feel trapped. The outside world didn't help. Fat-shaming was entrenched by the 1970s and '80s, much worse than now, when more and more Black women are taking pride in their bodies, reclaiming the word "fat" in lieu of terms like "big-boned" or even "plus-size." I can only imagine the pressure Dianne felt.

29

Throughout those years, she played a key role in the family cosmos. Not only was Dianne a big help to Fannie (as she called our mother) in running her numbers business, but she was also like a second mother to me. And long before Rita and I found our way to a closer relationship, Dianne—nearly eight years older than she—was Rita's favorite sister. She was her confidante; the one Rita could tell anything and know that her secret was safe. As for our nephew Tony, Dianne was his favorite aunt. He recalls how she'd spend a lot of time with him as a child, among other things, teaching him how to use the phone and memorize his address; as he grew into a teen, Dianne's home became a safe haven for Tony. "I spent so much time in that house," he recalls. "That was my favorite house! She never judged you, never said anything negative to you. She would really talk to you." He adds: "And she made me laugh! She could be really funny." His favorite memory is how they'd eat meals together from Taco Bell, which they both loved.

Dianne had several friends, all of whom likely thought they were her best friend, because she was both fiercely loyal and reliably dependable; each girlfriend knew they could call her at any time, about anything. She loved to talk, her wit sharp, but she was also a good listener, which made her a great sounding board. And Dianne had the biggest heart of us four sisters. She understood longing and loss so viscerally. She was the one who took time to send me a letter when my Yorkie Tiffany died during my sophomore year of college. She wanted me to know she understood my pain, and that my dog's death was a familial loss too. "I know Tiffany was like a sister or dear friend to you," she wrote. "Please try to accept this loss and thank God that you had Tiffany during the most crucial part of your life (that's growing up) . . . Take care and remember you can always talk to me about anything. I love you, ok?"

And shortly after our father died, I was visiting Dianne, and got my car stuck in the snow. Dianne put on her shortie boots, threw on her coat, grabbed a shovel, and started digging me out. When an impatient driver honked his horn and complained that I was blocking his way, she yelled, "Leave her alone! This girl just lost her father!" That always struck me, how she'd just lost her father too, but she was twenty-nine and I was seventeen, and in her nurturing way she was putting my grief first, over her own.

And I know she was grieving too in that moment. In fact, it was our father who once told Dianne that she "grieved too hard," but really, she was just more demonstrative with her grief than the rest of us. Days after Deborah's death, Dianne knelt on the side of our mother's bed and cried and cried, so severely her whole body shook. "She was my sister," she kept saying. "She was my sister, and now she's gone." Each of us, Rita and Mama and myself, held her in our silence as she wept. We understood that her loss was singular, that before there'd been the others, there'd been just the two of them, Selena Dianne and Deborah Jeanne, Fannie's two girls.

And then, in 1983, a miracle occurred: after fourteen years of marriage, Dianne got pregnant. I learned about the baby while living with her and George. I'd recently returned from my year abroad, and chose to stay with them for a few months, before figuring out what to do next with my life. Dianne later told Rita that it bothered her, the way I just assumed I had a right to live in the family home; it *was* presumptuous of me, but mostly I think she didn't want me to see the dysfunction of her marriage. I saw a lot, mostly how she couldn't trust George; I saw how she hid checkbooks in my room so he wouldn't get to them and write checks for cash they didn't have. I saw how late he stayed out at night, how often he was drunk. And I saw how he kept a shotgun in the bedroom closet where I once played as a little girl, back when that was our parents' bedroom. He liked showing it off to me; Dianne would say, "George, put it away. You know I hate guns."

I also got to spend some rare quality time with my middle sister. I gave her Toni Morrison's *Song of Solomon* and Alice Walker's *The Color Purple* to read. Dianne loved them both, and I loved sharing my love of Black women writers with her. As an added bonus, I got to see

Anthony a lot more. Nearly every day he came by Broadstreet, just to spend time with us. He had a special knock at the door, which is how we'd know it was him. Rita dropped by often too, and us four siblings got to hang out together, something so rare now that we were all adults, and more poignant now that one of us was gone.

I was asleep in my childhood bedroom when Anthony burst into the room and woke me up to tell me the good news—that Dianne was pregnant! He was so excited about the baby, and even though I was groggy, I was too. We couldn't believe it! Anthony and I gave each other high fives and laughed—a rare moment of us all having something to be joyful about.

"She always wanted a baby," says Elaine. "And she was so happy when she found out she was pregnant! She just wanted to talk all night long about what she was going to do with the baby." I'm sure Dianne hoped a child's presence would make things better.

Brandon Lamarr was born on August 31, 1984. I gave him his middle name. Dianne was thrilled, but of course, it was a big adjustment. She was thirty-five and her husband in his early forties. George, in front of us, seemed to be a doting father, but Rita didn't buy it. "He's not all into that baby," she once said to me. "A man that selfish? Believe me, he doesn't like the attention that Brandon takes away from him." But Rita was like the rest of us, so excited about the baby. She declared that unlike the mistake she'd made with our then-thirteen-year-old nephew, Tony, *this* nephew was going to call her "Auntie Rita" instead of just "Rita."

Dianne suffered from postpartum depression, something she shared a bit with Jill, Rita's good friend since high school, who'd also suffered from postpartum depression when she had both her daughters. But by the time Brandon celebrated his first birthday, Dianne seemed to be in a much better space. She'd begun to get the hang of mothering, and she liked it. In the days leading up to that happy Christmas of '85, she and Rita and I all went to see *The Color Purple*, and Dianne absolutely loved the movie as much as she'd loved the book. The end credits rolling, she turned to me, tears streaming down her face. "Celie got free," she said. "That was the best part, that Celie got to be free."

Then, barely into the new year, Anthony was murdered. Something ripped loose in Dianne. Losing him was acutely hard for her because Anthony had been her steady stream of brotherly love coming through the door daily, to spend time with her. When the space shuttle Challenger exploded on live TV two weeks after Anthony's death, she came into the room where Rita and I were sitting, knelt at the side of the bed, and just sobbed—for the crew members, and the teacher and the children who watched it happen; and for our brother. Rita and I both rubbed circles into her back as she wept.

~

I have no idea what life might've been like for Dianne had Anthony lived; I do know that for the first time in their seventeen-year marriage, Dianne began to tell us negative things about George, about his constant lying, his cruelty. "I don't give a goddamn about your fucking brother," he'd say to her as she grappled with her loss, in tears. This is when we understood the emotional abuse she'd suffered at the hands of George's constant verbal attacks. She admitted to us that she'd been miserable for a long time. But she also made us vow not to tell our mother. "Don't tell Fannie! Don't tell Fannie!" she kept saying. And so we didn't.

One day, Rita said to her, "But you always acted like everything was fine."

Her response haunted Rita, and me, for years: "And you still should've known," said Dianne. "Because I wasn't that good of an actor."

That summer, while I was staying in the apartment above our family home on West Seven Mile Road, Dianne would come upstairs with little Brandon and talk in hopeful ways I'd never heard before. Sometimes Rita would join us, and Dianne would tell us her dreams. Maybe she'd travel with the baby. She had a fear of flying, but she wouldn't mind long bus or train rides to see new places. And she spoke of her future. "I think I'd like to go back to school to become a nurse," she said, which seemed like an ideal pursuit for her.

One thing was clear. She was done with George, over him. She wanted a divorce. It's as though having Brandon's future to think about made her braver, able to think about her own. Friends, as well as Rita, tried to advise her to take it slow, not make it so apparent to George that she wanted to leave him, to be more strategic. But she had a newfound fire within her, a desire for a better life, and she couldn't bear the sight of him anymore. She didn't care whether he knew it. And George absolutely knew it.

Jill remembers that she and Rita were on a three-way phone call with Dianne during that time. "I told Rita, 'Dianne is depressed,'" Jill recalls. She thought maybe Dianne was still suffering from postpartum symptoms. And to this day, she remembers something that, as she puts it, "tingles my soul": she told Dianne, "You got to watch out."

Dianne in fact shared something with Rita one day, as they were sitting together in the front room on Seven Mile. She said George had threatened her. He told her that if he found out she was seeing another man, or if she tried to leave him, he would kill her. Rita asked her, "Well, do you believe that he would do something to you?"

"I don't know," said Dianne.

Rita told our mother what Dianne had shared with her, and I recall a discussion about having Dianne and the baby come stay with Fannie and Burt for a while. But what would that mean? Was George's vow just an idle threat? He'd never hit her, never been physically violent toward her, as far as anyone knew.

Elaine talked to Dianne shortly after that, an hours-long conversation, but she says her best friend didn't tell her that George had threatened her. Instead, she and Elaine ended up singing a song together, a favorite of Dianne's that she'd learned as a child attending Elaine's church. "It goes, 'Let not your weary heart be troubled, believe in God, believe in me,'" recalls Elaine. "'For in my Father's house are many mansions, I will prepare a place for thee. Let not your heart be troubled, let not your heart be troubled, nor let it be afraid.'" Elaine says Dianne told her, "'Let's sing it again.' And we kept singing and singing and singing it," recalls Elaine. "She loved that song."

30

On a sweltering Monday evening, August 11, fifteen-year-old Tony was a couple blocks away from Broadstreet, at his grandfather's house, where it was really hot inside. Tony was used to airconditioning, and he called Dianne and said, "I'm about to come over there." She said, "Not tonight." "You know me, I'm hardheaded and I'm coming anyway," recalls Tony. "And she repeated, 'I said, not tonight.' I'm frustrated, and normally I would've gone over and knocked on the door anyway," says Tony. "But I didn't."

Meanwhile, Rita and I were together that same evening, driving around delivering bedazzled sweatsuits she was helping a local designer sell to some of her friends. Suddenly, something came over me and I got extremely anxious, impatient. I told her, "Let's go home. I want to go home now." Rita, who'd never seen me like that, didn't even say, "Girl, why are you tripping?" That itself was odd, how she quickly honored my demand, no questions asked, as if she understood too that something was off. We'd just pulled in front of one of her friends' houses, but she didn't even go in, rather pulled away from the curb so we could head back to the house. We rode in silence.

Also, that same evening, a friend of Dianne's called her; George picked up, and she asked to speak to Dianne. He said she couldn't come to the phone. The friend could hear the baby wailing in the background. That was odd because Dianne never let the baby cry, always picked him up. "What's wrong with Brandon?" she asked. George hung up on her. What we came to learn later is that a man named Ronald, who worked with George as a building attendant at Detroit's Herman Gardens housing project, and described himself as a longtime friend, had been with George that same day at Ronald's home. George, he said, was "highly depressed" about Dianne having told him she wanted a divorce. George told him he was going to burn the house down, and Ronald said he tried "for hours" to dissuade him. George went home.

Around two a.m. the next morning, George called Ronald and asked him to meet him at Livernois and Davison to get gasoline. Ronald went there, but when he didn't find George, he drove to the house on Broadstreet, where Ronald found him holding Brandon in one arm and his shotgun in the other. A can of gasoline was nearby. Ronald said George told him that he still planned to burn the house down, saying, "If I can't have the house, there ain't nobody going to have it." George also told Ronald that he was going to harm his family. "Not the baby," Ronald said he told George. "It ain't worth it." Ronald said he talked George into handing over the shotgun, but he gave it back to him because George claimed he needed it for protection, telling Ronald that Dianne was seeing another man and he believed that man was going to attack him. Ronald said he left the house after George calmed down. He told him he'd call him the next morning, and George said, "Okay, if I ain't dead."

Police officers on a routine patrol discovered the fire at 6:40 that morning and called the fire department when they were unable to get into the burning house. Just as firefighters were extinguishing the fire, our mother's friend Lula called her. Mama arrived and stood outside the house, waiting for them to bring everyone out, but no one was coming out. That's when she called Burt, frantic. By the time we all arrived, the firefighters had managed to enter the house; we waited beside other onlookers. The fire chief came out, took Mama aside, and told her the gruesome facts: three bodies had been found in the house, each with a gunshot wound. By then, Tony had heard it on the news and rushed over from his grandfather's house. We were all still standing on the sidewalk in front of my and Rita's childhood home when their bodies were brought out on stretchers, covered by white sheets. Dianne had been found on the bed in the back bedroom—what had been Anthony's room when we were growing up—and Brandon was found in their bedroom, in his crib. George had kept his word to his friend Ronald and doused the house with gasoline, set it on fire, then shot his toddler son before shooting himself with the shotgun. Brandon, just three weeks shy of his second birthday, died from smoke inhalation before he could die from the gunshot wounds to his back and left shoulder. Dianne was likely already shot by George earlier in the evening, long before he stood outside the house brandishing his shotgun—the one he'd once gleefully showed me—holding Brandon and threatening to burn down the house. I believe this because of the feeling that came over me that Monday evening, when I insisted Rita and I go home; I believe this too because of that phone call her friend made to the house, and Brandon's screams she could hear in the background.

According to the coroner, Dianne had a "shotgun wound to left forearm-chest," which suggests that she placed her arm across her chest reflexively in the moment before he shot her. Her beloved friend since age ten, Elaine, has always believed that in that same moment, "God snatched her soul up out of that shell and took her home."

Someone whisked us to a neighbor's house, sat our mother down as we all stood nearby, stunned and speechless. Incredibly, a reporter from the *Detroit News* found his way to us. I was a reporter by then myself, and it hit me that I would've likely felt compelled to do the same thing, impinge upon a family's tragedy to get an interview. I did not want us to be the subject of the news and told the reporter that I didn't have a comment. "Everyone is shocked," I was quoted as saying. "We don't know anything."

But our mother did speak to the reporter, saying, "I just hope and pray he was completely out of his mind."

I never believed he was out of his mind. It wasn't lost on me that George had recently let the homeowner's insurance policy lapse, so that the badly burned house was uninsured. Our mother struggled financially and psychologically to repair that house before deciding to just let it go, to eventually sell it two years later; the new owner also gave up on trying to restore the house, which suffered yet another arsonist's fire, and six years after George doused it with gasoline and lit matches throughout trying to destroy our family home, the city razed 12836 Broadstreet. *If I can't have the house, then ain't nobody going to have it.*

George had hid the worst parts of himself from our mother. She must've thought, *This man I invited into my home, treated like a son, trusted*

with my daughter for all these years, how could he do that? How could he?
She needed to believe he'd lost his mind. When it was just us, the family, sitting in that stranger's living room right after it happened, Mama said quietly but in earshot, "I don't want to live through losing another child." She'd now lost four, including the baby girl. As paramedics placed our mother on a stretcher to be taken to the hospital for observation, Rita whispered to me, "Let's go"; she and I drove to the family home on Seven Mile Road, and together we gathered every prescription medication bottle, as well as the aspirin bottles from the bathroom medicine cabinets and placed them in a brown paper bag. We also gathered all the little toys and clothes of Brandon's scattered about, and put them in the bag too, discarding it all in the trash. (I did save one little T-shirt that read, I'M GRANDMA'S FAVORITE, keeping it across the decades.) Rita later said to me, "It's the oddest thing. I could never picture Brandon going to school. I could just never *see* it, you know?" I agreed that was odd. In 2024, Brandon would've turned forty.

The *Detroit News* included a map showing the exact location of our beloved Broadstreet, off Glendale near Livernois, with an arrow leading to a boxed graphic with the words "Murder, suicide, fire." The *Detroit Free Press* called our family home a "well-kept two-story west side house."

Soon enough, it dawned on us—Rita stated it out loud—that Anthony had been going over to Dianne's daily as a way of checking on her, as a way of saying to George, *I'm watching you, motherfucker.* Anthony saw and knew something. As his son, Tony, puts it: "If I had to assume, I'd say, George would probably get drunk and talk, and my father heard George say stuff like, 'Man, I'm ready to end it all,' and he'd be like, 'This nigga's crazy.' And so he decided to keep his eye on him. Especially if he was saying stuff like that more and more."

We buried Dianne and Brandon together, in the same casket. For the obituary program, we used Dianne's high school graduation photo, and for Brandon, the photo I'd taken him to sit for just weeks before. I'd dressed him in a little sailor suit, and the photographer had captured his wide-mouthed smile, with his chubby cheeks and baby teeth showing. At the time, Dianne wrote to me in New York:

Hey Bridge,

I know I'm slow, but I had to get you these pictures. I think they are beautiful. I know you're laughing because I'm the mother, but the girl at the photo place thought the suit was perfect and the pictures were beautiful. She was a mother. I can't thank you enough.

Love your sis,
Dianne

Years later, when the decision was solely ours as the remaining family members, Rita and I bought a new marker for Dianne and Brandon's grave; we put her name as *Selena Dianne Davis*, deciding to scrub her murderer's last name from her final resting place. More recently, I found George's firstborn son on Facebook. He's named after him, a junior. He is, as they say, the spitting image of his father, and it startled me to see that face after so long, and after everything. I wonder what that's like, to know that you are the namesake, the son of a man who murdered your stepmother and your toddler half brother before killing himself. How do you move forward in the world carrying the weight of that legacy, ever contained within your name and face? I have compassion for George Jr.

~

Looking back, Rita and I saw warning signs, even if we didn't realize that's what they were: Why did Dianne always announce to George that she was talking to her mother on the phone? Why did she sleep so much, a clear sign of depression and exhaustion? Why was her eating so disordered, another sign of something terribly amiss? Now we understand domestic violence can be emotional, physical, sexual, financial, as well as psychological; now I look back and see that she was using coping responses to deal with her abuse-related stress.

But why didn't she share with us sooner what she was going through? And most painful of all, why didn't we as her family members take more action after she told us he'd threatened her? We didn't understand how real the threat was. Today, we would. According to the National Coalition Against Domestic Violence (NCADV), more than half of all homicides of Black women are related to "intimate partner" violence, and 91 percent of Black women killed by men knew their killers. Back then, in 1986, domestic violence was something that we certainly heard about, but no one was talking about it out in the open. And wasn't that something that happened to other women—desperate women who were poor and without family support? Not our Dianne.

But it turns out, our Dianne was vulnerable to domestic violence for reasons that experts say fit a pattern: she was married to an alcoholic, and alcohol use is associated with violence against an intimate partner; he owned a firearm; she had recently had a baby (studies show new mothers are often victims of abuse); he was underemployed and uneducated, and filled with rage over what he didn't have, compared to others. As Feminista Jones put it in a 2014 *Time* magazine article, "In a society that measures 'manhood' primarily by one's ability to provide, being denied access to the means to provide can cause some (Black) men to seek power through dominating women. For some men, the venting of anger turns violent, and their partners suffer the greatest blows."

Dianne likely feared speaking out for reasons that are multiple, and particular to Black women: she didn't want to air her dirty laundry, nor admit to the stigma of a failed marriage in a world where so many Black women were single and aching for husbands; she didn't want to admit that her dark-skinned husband fit the stereotype that society portrayed of Black men—not even to her family. Maybe he threatened to harm Brandon, and that gave her pause; if George did become violent, she likely didn't consider calling the police on him because of all the killings of Black men by "officers of the law" in Detroit. Where could she turn? She was unable to support herself and the baby financially, so what would leaving her abuser even look like? She must have felt terribly isolated and alone. When she did finally gather the courage to speak up, when she managed to have some agency and plan to divorce George, she was at her most vulnerable and unprotected. We didn't understand that's when she needed an intervention plan to empower her to keep herself safe. Experts now tell us that women going through a divorce or separation are at elevated risk for experiencing lethal violence, particularly when the abuser is highly controlling. As a 2014 article in the journal *Violence and Victims* bluntly put it: "The process of separation has been found to be a significant factor in the killings of Black women by their intimate partners." A husband uses murder as the ultimate form of control.

Dianne's culturally specific predicament—so typical, it turns out—helps to explain why the rate of Black women being killed by a man is *three times higher* than that of white women. As the NCADV puts it: "By intentionally denying Black people access to economic opportunities . . . healthcare, education, and a sense of safety from governmental systems, *racist policies increase the prevalence of risk factors for domestic violence.*"

Being a Black woman in America put our sister at higher risk of being killed by her partner.

Rita later said to me, "I wish Dianne had lived to see the *Oprah* show. That would've been like therapy for her." I agreed. She would've loved Oprah's talk show, and she would've likely watched it daily, discussing the show with her girlfriends, finding Oprah a form of company, the way TV personalities can be. Oprah broke new ground by using television to discuss the very so-called taboo issues that Dianne was facing in her own life—from postpartum depression to emotional overeating to domestic abuse. Had she been able to watch the queen of daytime talk exploring those subjects with candor and empathy, Dianne might've felt less isolated, might've even gotten advice on how to leave her abusive marriage; she might've changed her fate. *The Oprah Winfrey Show* premiered nationally one month after Dianne died.

That's the thing about yet another sibling's struck-down life: There are so many what-ifs. And the biggest one for me is the same one I ask about our father's and Deborah's deaths: What if we'd had Anthony and Dianne in our lives for longer? Minus all that loss and grief, would Rita—with her good medical care and life filled with love and friendship and meaningful work and family—have remained in remission longer?

～

Christmas that year is utterly mournful. Rita and I spend the entire day in our mother's big bed, lying side by side, as though we're young girls again but with the covers pulled over our heads. We have lost our sister, then brother, then another sister in the span of four and a half years, two of them just seven months apart. Yet life in its cruel mundanity has forced us to go on: I've been working as a reporter in Philly, a city I decide not to like, driving every day past a cemetery to get to work and lying still every evening in the pitch-blackness of my Center City apartment, mind filled with dark thoughts. Rita has been teaching high schoolers while also taking required classes and napping every day after work, exhausted by her students and her training and her lupus, but mostly by the added weight of her sorrow.

"There is a vastness to grief that overwhelms our minuscule selves," writes musician Nick Cave. "We are tiny, trembling clusters of atoms subsumed within grief's awesome presence. It occupies the core of our being and extends through our fingers to the limits of the universe."

That's it exactly. Our grief feels limitless.

31

Two months after Dianne's and Brandon's deaths, Rita was observed as a student teacher at Finney High School. "I thoroughly enjoyed observing Rita Davis teaching Economics," the supervising teacher wrote on her evaluation. He added:

> *Rita seems to be a true professional. She is confident, comfortable, and effective as a classroom manager. She displayed an excellent command of the subject matter. She was very careful to make sure that all students understood key concepts before moving on to the next item. Rita's discussion techniques were also very good—students were actively involved throughout the class hour. Her attentive control of the class seemed very natural—there was a feeling of genuine student respect for her as a teacher.*

Two months after that, Rita received her final "term report of directed teaching" from her supervisor at Marygrove College, where she was studying to acquire her accreditation. She received an A, getting a check mark for "excellent" or "good" in every one of the twenty-five traits or skills being judged, including VOICE ("pronounces and enunciates correctly") and GROOMING ("dresses according to accepted professional standards; is neat, clean, without being 'flashy' or 'mod' in clothing or hair-do") and POSTURE ("stands and sits erect; an attractive bearing"). In his narrative, the supervisor wrote that her stay as a student teacher at Finney High "has been highly successful . . . I am confident that Rita Davis will make an excellent member of any high school's staff." He went on to describe her relationship with her students as "mostly good," noting that, "A few problems arose when students tried to test her ability to control the class. Throughout she remained firm and calm. She demanded, and received, an atmosphere conducive to learning. Students quickly learned she meant business."

He continued with, "Ms. Davis was well liked by all who came in contact with her and displays friendliness and graciousness to ALL members of the staff—administrators, other teachers, and noncertified personnel."

Rita was one of those people who naturally made friends not only with fellow teachers, but with the secretaries and the cafeteria workers and the custodians and security guards in the building. There was nothing calculated about it; it's just who she was—friendly, approachable, outgoing, and completely devoid of airs or pulling rank or acting like she was above others. She didn't think of herself as better or less than anyone else. People were people. As I write this, I can't remember a time when she was excited about meeting someone based on their status; if they were in a position to help her, cool. But being impressed by a person's title or position just because? Not her thing.

I especially find compelling what the supervisor wrote about her "excellent personality characteristics," specifically under the category of POISE:

> She meets problems and emergencies with resourcefulness; confronts new challenges with maturity; manifests a deliberate manner; [is] at ease without evidence of tension or undue anxiety; is dignified without being formal or stiff; displays self-confidence; maintains a pleasant manner.

And under ENTHUSIASM, he wrote: "She is alert, optimistic, cheerful; shows genuine interest in teaching and the pupils' activities; is animated; displays a sense of humor without being giddy."

At the end of his report, the professor added a coda:

> Ms. Davis entered this student teaching assignment with some trepidation since she had recently experienced some tragedy in her family. Despite this setback she managed to handle her student-teaching assignment with professionalism.

Despite the family tragedies, Rita had done it. She'd made the transition from corporate America to public education. She was soon hired as a new teacher in the special education department of Western International High School, in southwest Detroit's Mexicantown. In the school newspaper, featured in an article headlined "Western Adjusts to New Staff Changes," alongside seven other new teachers, Rita is described as someone who comes to teaching as a second career, after working "in industry as an economist." She's quoted as saying that as a new teacher, she wants to "make an impact on the students, to motivate them to want to learn." Rita liked that Western was a small school and "very homey-like," with students that were "extremely polite." According to the article, the moment that changed Rita's life was the day in 1984 when she walked into her first classroom as a substitute teacher and realized "how much the students needed her." The mini profile goes on to describe Rita as an avid listener of gospel music whose role model was her high school English teacher, Arnetter Higgins. "Davis is single and enjoys shopping and attending estate sales," wrote the student reporter. "When she's not working as a teacher, she works as a business consultant for minority owned businesses."

The piece ends with Rita's words of advice: "Nothing beats a failure but a try."

~

Although Rita's professional life was finally back on track, she was still grappling with her grief, as we all were. I remember her in those early weeks just getting through what had to be done, uncharacteristically saying very little, the dynamism in her personality on hold. One day, Linda, her friend from childhood, showed up at our home. They hadn't seen each other much in recent years, certainly not since Linda had returned home from law school and begun working as an attorney for city government and Rita had returned home to teach. After she heard about our latest family tragedy, Linda came over to pay her respects. Really, what she did was come over to sit in our living room in silence. I thought this was slightly odd, and so did Rita.

"I was remembering our friendship, and one Friday I just went over to the house," says Linda. "I didn't call. I just showed up. Now Miss Rita wasn't all that friendly."

Still, Linda came again. And again. And again. "Linda's coming over," Rita would say on a given day, and we'd look at each other, our minds thinking the same thing: *She's a little weird.* Then Rita would let her in, and Linda would sit, still not saying much, while Rita continued doing whatever she'd been doing. This went on for weeks.

"I would just sit up in the living room," Linda recalls. "I would come every Friday, sometimes Thursday too. She'd talk a little bit, but not much. Maybe she wasn't trusting me; we hadn't really seen each other in a long time and then I just show up out of the blue. Your mom would ask me things, but Rita would be busy doing stuff. I didn't take it as a negative. I would still just come, sit up there. I wasn't asking for information about what happened or anything like that . . . All of a sudden, we just began to talk, and she began to trust me because she saw that I kept coming."

Linda's steady, quiet visits turned out to be the balm Rita needed. Their friendship reignited and took off from there. Rita later revealed to Linda, "The fact that you would come over and sit with me, and I didn't say that much to you, but you kept coming? You don't know what that meant to me."

Linda and Rita soon forged a special bond. Both single, thirty-something professional Black women living in Detroit, they understood each other's lives. They became each other's confidante, running buddy, fellow gossiper, coconspirator, Bible study partner, therapist, relationship counselor, truth teller. They talked about their jobs, their families, their desires, their angers, and life's absurdities.

"We talked about everything. You name it," says Linda. "We could joke, we could laugh, we could talk crazy, we could talk nasty," says Linda. "We could share silly stuff, and we could debate real things. She'd say, 'Wait a minute, Linda! Nope. It's like *this.*' Rita was always up on the news too. I loved the intelligent conversation with her." Linda goes on: "To her, I could be much too serious. She was a free spirit on a lot of things."

In fact, they always compared themselves to the friends in the movie *Beaches*. Linda was Hillary, the character played by Barbara Hershey, a straitlaced lawyer with a sense of decorum and proper behavior; Rita was CC, the Bette Midler character—larger than life, entertaining, a great storyteller. And opinionated. Of course, the two characters in the film eventually butt heads. So did Linda and Rita on occasion. Linda says sometimes she felt Rita got too bossy, trying to tell her what to do. And Rita sometimes accused Linda of being "prudish," and too afraid to speak up for herself.

"But one thing about her, even if we argued or fussed or had differences, I knew she was there for me," says Linda. "If anything went down, she was on my side, ready to fight . . . She was an ally. You don't find that a lot in a friend."

Their friendship was vital too because Rita could share her struggles with lupus, knowing Linda would get it. Linda understood health challenges. She was born with neurofibromatosis, which causes tumors to grow anywhere in the body; in Linda's case, the tumors appeared on her face. "People would see these raisins in my face and ask me about them, and I'd get offended," she says. "Rita would say, 'Linda, you don't owe anyone an explanation.'" Rita would often speak with compassion to me about Linda's condition. "You have no idea what it's like to have something on your face, where you can't hide it," she'd tell me. "The way people can act, the things they say? My heart goes out to Linda."

When I share this with Linda, she says, "Rita was like that. That's what I loved about her. When she loved you or cared about you, she was protective of you."

Rita once went with Linda to see a specialist who attempted to remove some of the tumors, and that meant so much to Linda. "Rita was right there with me with that, and she understood," she says. Later, in her early forties, Linda also developed a condition that causes inflammation. "It's a chronic disease, and so is lupus," says Linda; she and Rita further bonded over their shared experience. And they spoke to each other over the phone nearly every day for the next fourteen years.

"She was home to me," says Linda. "She felt safe."

When I think of Linda and Rita, I think of a quote by Toni Morrison: "Black women have always been friends," she once said. "I mean if you didn't have each other, you had nothing."

Except that Rita and I had each other, as sisters. Our relationship was strong. We lived in different cities, but we stayed connected through the phone—although Rita was now more cautious about making too many long-distance calls; they were still so expensive that you needed a good reason to call someone in another state, so we sometimes wrote each other brief letters instead. Also, back then, we were forever loaning each other money. At the beginning of 1987, she wrote me in Philly, where I was living at the time:

Bridgett,
Happy New Year!!!
   I hope you have a happy and prosperous year ahead.
   Would you believe I just got your fifty dollars together? (Thanks again).
   Whatever you do, read People magazine with Oprah Winfrey. Call collect after you read it.

Love your Sis,
Rita

P.S. Twenty pounds from my goal and I'm taking my weave off at 150 lbs. (smile)

I did read that issue of *People*, with Oprah on the cover, its main cover line blaring: "Oprah Winfrey—The Best Talker on TV (and a Movie Star to Boot)." And I did call Rita to talk about the article. Rita loved Oprah from the start, and she was emphatic that the criticisms of her, especially the charge by some Black people that Oprah catered to her mostly white audience, were completely unfair. "She's on national TV!" Rita said. "Black folks need to understand that and stop tripping."

32

A couple months later, Rita wrote me again:

> Hey Bridgett,
> Just me sending you your money for American Express. I
> could kick myself in the ass for buying two pair of earrings for
> approximately $200.
>
> Oh well. Life Is So Short Why Not Enjoy IT?
>
> Love,
>
> your sister,
> *Rita*

For us, saying "life is short" wasn't a clichéd, pat phrase. We were each other's remaining sister—all we had left to define ourselves as siblings. We were our mother and father's only surviving children, the others (apart from the baby girl) having each died in their thirties, the decade Rita had now entered. In my mind today, that has something to do with Rita's decision to begin a secret relationship with an older man, a much older man, named Willie. Rita called him by his last name, Whitmore. In a twist of the plot, he was Renita's uncle— her father's younger brother. That meant he was our nephew Tony's granduncle. Willie was a barber by trade, and nearly forty years older than Rita.

Of course, we found out, and our mother was undone by it—he was ten years older than she was!—saying one thing she hated was to see a "nasty old man" with a young woman. She tried her best to convince Rita that she didn't have time to waste. "He's robbing you of your best years, stealing your youth," she warned. "I've seen it many times." But Rita, for once, didn't listen to our mother. She really liked being with Willie. She once half-jokingly told Linda, "I like older men because I know I can count on them having a pension and benefits."

When our mother said, "But he's not educated," Rita said, "I have enough education for the both of us." Why did she say that? Mama went off. "I paid for that damn education!" she snapped back. "And I didn't do that so you could waste it on an old-ass nigger!" She gave Rita the silent treatment for days, her feelings hurt. That was the first and only time I saw Rita and our mother "have words" or not get along. It was so bizarre to see them, two peas in a pod, not speaking; it stunned us all. I saw it as a delayed teenage rebellion, which Rita never *really* had. Our mother didn't stay angry at Rita for long; she couldn't. I was relieved when they patched things up because it returned the household to its equilibrium.

Honestly, I was disappointed in Rita for dating Whitmore. I wanted her to see that she could "do better" in a mate. For the first time in a long time, she and I bickered. Tony remembers an incident that I'd conveniently forgotten: I showed up at the front door one frigid late night without my key and rang the doorbell; everyone was asleep, and so I rang and rang, but it was so cold that when Rita finally did awaken and let me in, I was angry that it had taken her so long. We started arguing, and at some point, I yelled at her, "At least I'm not laying up with a seventy-year-old man!" I'm sure she had a retort because she always did.

That was also around the same time that Rita and I went to see *Fatal Attraction* together, and afterward, we sat right there in the theater and argued about the movie, on different sides of the debate. I thought Glenn Close's character, Alex, should've known not to expect much when she got involved with a married man, that the way to protect yourself was to not enter into a vulnerable situation in the first place. But Rita was on Alex's side. "Why should she be ignored?" Rita said. "She has feelings too!" She felt the Michael Douglas character, Dan, had a responsibility to deal with Alex and do right by her. "Hell, he was the one cheating on his wife!" Rita pointed out. "She wasn't cheating on anybody."

Rita had compassion for any woman looking for love; after all, this was also in the wake of an infamous *Newsweek* article that appeared in 1986. Based on one Harvard- and Yale-led study, the magazine claimed that white, college-educated women who remained single at thirty had only a 20 percent chance of ever marrying, and that a forty-year-old single woman was "more likely to be killed by a terrorist" than to ever marry. Offensive as it was—and so clearly a backlash to the feminist movement—that statement became entrenched in the popular imagination, prompting panic and desperation. Twenty years later, the magazine finally admitted that claim was overblown hyperbole; meanwhile, the damage to the cultural psyche had been done.

Beyond that, Rita understood that your choices in a partner come from your options, and she likely felt that for her, those options were narrowing. I didn't really feel it as acutely because I was still in my twenties; Rita was "already" in her thirties; mind you, back then we were constantly being told there were more Black men in prison than in college. Coupled with that was a *lot* of discussion in pop culture about the friction between Black men and women. In an interview with the *Los Angeles Times* that year, editor in chief of *Essence* magazine Susan Taylor said Black men and women needed to stop pointing the finger at each other in anger and frustration. She then admonished Black women for "castigating" Black men for failing to provide them with the creature comforts known to the heroines of the TV shows *Dallas* and *Dynasty*, and for their part, she said Black men "must not see black women as a threat."

As I look back, Rita was also still tender with grief, and just as her friendship with Linda had turned out to be a true balm, so too was her relationship with Willie Whitmore. I never met him, but Tony, who knew his great-uncle pretty well, said he understood why women liked him. "He was always attentive, respectful, funny. And the nicest guy in the family," says Tony. "He just had charisma." Plus, Tony adds, he had the one quality that Rita really liked in men: he was patient. Her lupus symptoms sometimes caused her to move more slowly, and she appreciated not being rushed.

There was something else too. Willie was old enough to understand what it meant to live with loss. That matters. I'd broken up with a young actor I was dating in New York because he said to me after

Anthony died, "I hope after what happened to your brother, you're not going to become all clingy now." I decided to be the opposite of clingy and cut him off.

That was such a strange time, when we were losing our loved ones at a mindless, stunning rate. After the horrendous year we'd had, within seven months from 1987 to 1988, two of our beloved aunts died—our mother's own older sisters, Alice and Big Sis. Big Sis had been my favorite aunt, everyone saying I looked and acted just like her; and Aunt Alice had mothered Rita during her entire five years of living in Nashville. Both aunts were still in their sixties when they died, having carried their own traumas. We were dizzy with death. At one of their wakes—their services collapse together in my memory, so I can't distinguish which—Rita and I were in the back of the room laughing about something, and not quietly; I distinctly remember sharing that laughter, so inappropriate that our uncle Gene admonished us with harsh words. That laughter was like a code language between us, as though Rita and I both understood the absurdity of losing so many loved ones in a span of so few years—from our beloved daddy to our beloved siblings to our beloved aunties. "The condition of Black life is one of mourning," the poet Claudia Rankine has written, in quoting a friend of hers. "Not a house in the country ain't packed to its rafters with some dead Negro's grief," says Baby Suggs in Toni Morrison's *Beloved*. This was certainly true for us, our family.

It was as though Rita and I couldn't take it anymore, as though we'd become inured from the solemnity of loss, and the only logical response to such illogical circumstances was maniacal laughter, Black humor, as it were, which Rankine calls, "the laughter of vulnerability, fear, recognition and an absurd stuckness."

Giggling at our aunt's wake makes me think of Christina Sharpe's soulful book *In the Wake*, where she notes that in Black culture, a wake is that space where we, yes, "keep watch with the dead," but a wake is also "the path behind a ship" and more specifically a slave ship; it's also an aftermath. Sharpe brilliantly connects these varying definitions to present-day Blackness, showing that Black people are swept up and animated by the afterlives of slavery, a precarity that too often leads to premature deaths, which this culture then normalizes. Racism, she writes, is the engine that drives "the American ship of state" that authorized both liberty and slavery, and thus "cuts through all of our lives and deaths . . . in the wake of its purposeful flow."

33

In late 1987, our mother had a windfall in her numbers business, which meant she went long enough not having to pay out large sums to customers who hit so that she could build up a nest egg; she decided to invest some of that money in buying a house for me and Rita. Rita would live in the house, and although both of our names would be on the deed, it would effectively be Rita's. She started looking. Rita had a clear idea of what she wanted—a place located on the city's west side, with curb appeal, and most of all with rental income. And she was clear that she wanted something affordable. "I don't want to be house poor trying to pay the mortgage on something beyond my means, just to impress people," she said. She found what she was looking for in a modest two-family house with side-by-side identical structures, each with its own address, located on Evergreen near Six Mile Road. The owner, a white man I'll call Frank Scott, told her he'd raised his children in that house many years before; he sold the house to Rita directly in a land contract for $25,000. Our mother provided the $12,500 down payment (the equivalent today of $32,000). The interest rate was 10 percent, and the monthly mortgage payment was $300; she paid by personal check to Scott, as Rita called him, who now lived an hour southeast of Detroit.

We closed in February 1988, but it took Rita a few months to move in. She began right away decorating the house—custom vertical blinds, new carpet, fresh paint—but hadn't yet spent any nights in her new home. Turns out, she was scared to stay there by herself, scared even to be in the house alone. Living in a house was, as she pointed out, not the same as living in an apartment complex. She was concerned about her safety, despite the fact that the house was located in a stable neighborhood of well-kept homes. Some of it was anxiety on her part, but some of it was an understanding that crime was real. She had decorative security bars placed on all the windows and doors—a must-have in 1980s Detroit. In time, she graduated to having someone drive with her to the house and watch her enter. Once she got a tenant on the other side, she got comfortable enough to not only stay there on her own but enter the house alone. Soon enough, she began to call Evergreen—keeping with family tradition of referring to our homes by their street names—her sanctuary. "I want my place to be peaceful," she'd say. Seven Mile, our mother's house, was not that; it wasn't chaotic or tumultuous either; it's just that when your mother is a numbers runner who works out of her home, it will almost always be busy— phones and doorbells ringing, knocks on the side door, adding machine trilling, TV blaring midday, folks dropping off, picking up. That coupled with the fact that our mother was a people magnet—friends liked to "sit up under" her, as we used to say—meant it was a busy place. It really did feel a lot like Grand Central Station, as Rita dubbed it.

In comparison, Rita's place *was* calm. Even the color scheme was peaceful—taupe and cream, with little pops of turquoise, her favorite color and, later, mine. I loved walking into her living room, with its beautiful and comfy crush velvet sectional couch, its gleaming gold metal coffee table and mirror, and its statement-size abstract art hanging on the wall. Rita had impeccable taste, and she knew how to create a stylish yet inviting living space. She also collected angels and had these bronze and gold and ceramic figurines strategically placed throughout, including over archways.

The exterior of Evergreen looked great too. Tony recalls that Rita asked him and our mom to grab small boulders whenever they were driving along a country road, and so they did; Rita placed them along the edge of the driveway, all the way up to the garage, which gave her house a distinctive look on the block. Also, with the grass always freshly cut, the house painted a vibrant white against black shutters, and colorful flowers planted out front, her place had dynamic curb appeal. And while she didn't do yard work herself, she always knew someone she could pay to do it, and other handywork for her. In general, Rita believed in paying people for tasks, to help you get the quality you wanted. To her, that was money well spent.

Speaking of which, Rita was good with money, in that she thought about her own financial security, more so than many single women back then. She'd begun an IRA at age twenty-eight, was saving money out of each paycheck, and in a practical and prescient decision prompted by her friend Linda's advice, took out a long-term care policy when she was only thirty. Now, at thirty-one, she was a proud homeowner and landlord, steadily paying down her mortgage. On the other hand, she also was free-spending when it came to shopping, and buying what she wanted, when she wanted. We all indulged her for it, loving to see Rita in her signature style, walking into rooms turning heads, standing out in her eye-catching outfits, including the perfect accessories. Our mother even enjoyed buying her clothes, as evidenced in a note she wrote to me in late '87:

Hi Bridgett,
We are ok and I hope you are too.
 I bought Rita a real cute dress. It was (knit) navy blue. She swears she loves it. It is an Anne Klein long sleeve. It is a little tight but she is losing well.
 Well I have to go and will talk to you later.

Love,
"Mama"

And in another letter around that time, our mother wrote:

Bridgett,
Rita claims she wants another pair of those shoes with the gold heel. She said she was going to ask you to pick up a pair for her in navy.
 Maybe you can get her a pair if you have time. She doesn't know about this so don't worry about it if you don't have time.

Mama

~

Rita was *not* one of those people who balanced her checkbook. She just knew to have enough money in her bank account at a given time for the expenses coming through, a system that worked for her. Until it didn't. One day in early '89, out of the blue, Scott, the seller, asked to meet her in front of Evergreen.

"Don't you balance your checkbook?" he asked her.

When Rita wanted to know what he was talking about, he announced: "I haven't been cashing your rent checks for the past nine months." He literally held up all the checks she'd made out to him and fanned them out in front of her. "You owe me $2,700!"

Rita was stunned. "Why would you do that, not cash my checks?"

He grinned. "If you don't pay up now," he said, "I can take back the house."

"I could take you to court," she said.

"Try it," he snapped back. "You have no proof that you've paid!" He waved those undeposited checks in front of her. "I'll just tell the court you've been in arrears this whole time."

That's when it dawned on Rita: "You've done this before, haven't you?"

With that nasty grin, Scott told her that, in fact, yes, he'd sold and reclaimed that same house three times over the years.

"Well, you're not getting it back this time!" she yelled, then ran into the house and slammed the door behind her. Shaken, she climbed the stairs, and just lay across the bed in shock, her head pounding with a sudden migraine. First of all, she didn't have that kind of money (the equivalent of $6,800 today). Second of all, was he bluffing? Freaked out, she called our mother and told her what had just happened, crying the whole time. Mama advised her to go back and look at the land contract, to see exactly what rights she had so they could come up with a game plan. Rita then called me, a nervous wreck as I pulled out my copy of the contract and read it out loud. Sure enough, it stated that "If the purchaser shall fail to perform this contract or any part thereof, the Seller immediately after such default shall have the right to declare the same forfeited and void, and retain whatever may have been paid hereon . . . and consider and treat the Purchaser and each and every other occupant *to remove and put out* . . ." The contract further stipulated in an acceleration clause that "If default is made by the Purchaser and such default continues for a period of 45 days or more, and the Seller desires to foreclose this contract in equity, then the Seller shall have at his option the right to declare the entire unpaid balance hereunder to be due and payable forthwith."

Because Scott had made sure more than forty-five days had gone by since Rita technically paid her mortgage, he could now demand the entire $12,500 balance owed, and without that being paid, begin proceedings to put her out of the house ASAP. We didn't have much time. Rita did a title search and discovered that just one year before Scott sold the house to us, he'd gone to court to apply for a "writ of constitution" and entered a judgment against the previous buyers. He was awarded "peaceful possession" of the house by a judge that ordered the bailiff to evict those homebuyers, a couple I'll call William Johnson and Lydia Jones Johnson. Detroit was a majority-Black city, its trendy appeal to white residents still decades in the future. The Johnsons were, to be sure, Black. The man wasn't bluffing. He had done it before.

Scott was engaging in a longtime practice of exploitation and abuse vis-à-vis "land contract" sales. First brought to national attention thanks to Ta-Nehisi Coates's 2014 *Atlantic* magazine piece "The Case for Reparations," contract selling, or "buying on contract," and its attendant exploitation and plunder proliferated throughout the country. On maps, red lines were drawn around communities where even one Black family lived and thus were deemed high-risk by the Federal Housing Authority. That meant the FHA refused to insure mortgages for those houses. And *that* gave lenders their reason for refusing loans to African Americans. Because of this millions of Blacks had to resort to buying on contract. Those contracts were shaky deals that amounted to installment plans, and as Coates put it in the *Atlantic* article, the buyer entered into an agreement that "combined all the responsibilities of homeownership with all the disadvantages of renting, while offering the benefits of neither." With contract sales, you build no equity, the seller holds the title, and he or she can quickly reclaim the house for nonpayment—often using shady tactics like Scott was doing.

I only recently learned the extent to which these contract sales were embedded in the nationwide real estate industry. For example, a startling 2019 report conducted by researchers at various universities found that African Americans in Chicago lost between $3 to $4 billion in wealth because of these predatory sales from 1950 to 1970—where houses were reclaimed by sellers, buyers' investments never returned. I think about those billions of dollars of wealth lost *in just one city*, let along other cities like Detroit; I think of the massive theft that took place against hardworking, aspiring Black homeowners and their communities, the loss of generational wealth that could have benefited their heirs—all while federal policy allowed it. And in 1989, more than twenty years after the passing of the Fair Housing Act, Rita was falling victim to the same predatory practice.

Time was of the essence if she wanted to keep her house.

~

Within a few days of Scott pulling his dirty ploy, Rita called and told him to meet her at Evergreen. When he showed up, he was grinning ear to ear, confident he had her over a barrel. But when she handed him a postal money order for those nine months' worth of mortgage payments, he was stunned. "You should've seen the shock on his damn face," Rita later reported back. He hadn't counted on this Black woman coming up with the funds, because apparently that had never been the case before with the other three Black buyers he'd apparently duped out of the house. But, of course, he didn't know who he was dealing with. Rita famously used to say, "I'd sell my body before I let a child go hungry, or I let myself suffer." Her point was that you do what you have to do to take care of yourself and your own; you tap the resources you have.

"Hold on to this and don't deposit it if you want," she said to Scott as she put the paper in his hand. "Then you can explain to the US government why you sat on a postal money order."

"Where'd you get all the money?" he asked her.

"None of your fucking business," she snapped.

Coming up with the money had been hard. She'd felt deep anxiety around the need to pull together the funds so quickly, before Scott could take her to court. I felt terrible that months into my having quit my Philly job and moving to New York, I didn't have any money to contribute. I was trying to cobble together a living from freelance writing. Our mother, whose cash flow ebbed and flowed, didn't have the entire $2,700 at precisely that moment either; Fannie was now competing with the state lottery, doing her best to ensure the "legal numbers" didn't siphon off too much of her core business; but she ultimately scraped together hundreds of dollars, and likely borrowed the rest, determined that Rita would not lose her home this way, as millions of Black men and women before her had.

"This is how they do you dirty," our mother told Rita. She'd of course bought our family home on Broadstreet through a similar land contract, unable to get a traditional mortgage thanks to racist policy and not, as most might assume, because of her unorthodox source of income. And while the seller had subjected our mother to myriad microaggressions—ripping out the doorbell chimes before delivering the house; forcing her to find a third party with a stable job to put his name on the contract, and waiting three years before putting her name on it; demanding the monthly payment in cash; deducting taxes and insurance from her payments; and charging exorbitant interest—he at least hadn't tried to reclaim the house. (Again, based on the predatory contract *she'd* signed, he could have, had our mother missed even one payment.)

From that day forward, Rita still had to deal monthly with Scott, this white man who tried to snatch back her house, and that brought with it a level of constant stress. Best believe, every one of her mortgage payments going forward was in the form of a money order or cashier's check. Rita was so excited, and relieved, when four years later, the house on Evergreen was paid for, deed in hand.

"I couldn't wait to get his racist ass out of my life," she told me.

Of course, it's this type of practice that illustrates in literal terms how discrimination in housing works, but one area of societal injustice Blacks navigate on a regular basis. It's easy to forget that individual *people* have racist feelings and behave in racist ways, which is what leads to and sustains discriminatory policies, which in turn creates systemic racism. And it's also just this type of encounter that Rita had—experiencing the terror of losing her home—that creates the fight-or-flight stance that wreaks havoc on our nervous systems. Frank Scott, with his malicious tactics, added more wear and tear to Rita's body, just as her fight against TVA had done. All this by the time she was thirty-two. There's quantifiable proof of the damage this does: Dr. Geronimus found in looking at chromosomal markers for aging that middle-aged Black women appear seven years older than their white counterparts. The obvious explanation is years of racism-induced stress, but also the body's hard work of trying to overcome it.

Racism ages you. It aged Rita.

And yet, outwardly, in her early thirties she was at the height of her powers. For one thing, Rita looked great. With that beautiful behind, those big pretty legs, and that tiny waist, she really did turn heads; and by then, she'd perfected her style, which was as dazzling as ever. Her tops and dresses and purses and shoes and earrings and nails all often had some glitter or sparkle on them—just enough to be both dramatic and tasteful—what her friend Wilma called "diva fabulous." And Rita kept her hair looking good, wearing it shoulder-length with the help of a natural-looking weave she added to her own light brown hair, styled into soft bangs to frame her face. One of my favorite outfits of hers at the time was a royal-blue-and-black-sequined dress with a Wilma Flintstone–style hem that she wore with sexy black high-heeled pumps. She accented the look with her hair swept into a side ponytail. I later found a picture of her wearing that beautiful sequined dress in a small Ziploc bag she carried in her purse, alongside other treasured photos.

~

242 ~ BRIDGETT M. DAVIS

In her work life, Rita was popular at Western International High, where her colleagues loved her, thanks to that combination of bubbly personality, kindness, and realness. In every staff ID card saved from her early years at Western, she's smiling, lips gleaming with her signature Magenta Mist lipstick, dark eyes shining; she looks happy. Rita found she really loved being a special ed teacher, and that her students really loved her. Some of them were in wheelchairs, dealing with learning disabilities, and/or impaired in other ways. One of her qualities I envied and admired was Rita's comfort level with those who had physical or mental challenges. She knew how to make people with disabilities feel comfortable around her, how to joke or be nonchalant with them, offer advice, admonish them if need be. In other words, she knew how to treat her special ed students like she'd treat any other student. Tony, our nephew, would sometimes visit her classroom, and he said he witnessed a new side of Rita when he watched her with her students. "You could tell she'd found her niche, because she loved dealing with those special-needs kids," he says. "It's like she turned into Mary Poppins. She was real gentle and kind to them." Tony, who'd borne the brunt of Rita's fussing many times, recalls jokingly, "I was like, 'Wow, who in the hell is this?'"

Rita also felt nourished by her friendships with women. "The thing with Rita is, everybody can believe that she was their best friend because Rita could make you feel like that, that she listened to you," explains Linda. "I knew that about her, that she had other close friends, but it didn't bother me because I just treasured what we had, and I felt comfortable and sincere with it."

Men continued to *really* adore Rita. "Guys were always flirting with her," Tony points out. Somewhere in there she'd quietly ended things with Willie Whitmore, the decades-older man she'd been seeing, although they remained good friends. She didn't talk to me about what happened, and, relieved it was over, I didn't ask. Rita dated a few different guys throughout her thirties, and remained friendly with most, including Elijah, the man she'd dated during her college days and beyond. He'd come and help out with things that needed fixing at Evergreen, do whatever she asked of him. "We had our little dates and stuff through the years," says Elijah. "Oh, we got to be good friends." I suspect they moved in and out of a romantic and platonic relationship. "I have some good memories, baby," Elijah tells me. "That's all I can say."

Despite the societal panic around the scarcity of available Black men, Rita remained clear that she was not going to settle, be with just *any* man. "Just to say I have a man? No thanks," she'd say. "I'd rather be alone." Since her relationship with Zachary had ended, Rita hadn't yet come across another man who possessed that combination of qualities she was looking for—mature, kind, patient, genuinely into her, and maybe a bit of a hustler (but with a steady job!). "She wasn't necessarily into the lawyers and doctors and whatnot" is how Tony puts it. "But she did want someone with drive."

Most of all, whoever he was, he had to be intelligent. "Rita's whole thing was she did not want an ignorant man around," recalls Linda. "She might not care if he didn't have no degrees, but he could *not* be ignorant." Linda laughs. "She would take note of that *right* away."

Also, Rita had learned through her own experience and what she'd witnessed with other women, including me and our sisters Dianne and Deborah, that first and foremost no man was going to mistreat her, no matter what. "I don't care if I weigh three hundred pounds, you are *not* gonna just say and do whatever you want to me," she declared. "Fuck that."

34

Seems we barely had a reprieve before more bad news came our way.

In early March 1990, I was sitting in Rita's dining room at the table when she said: "Mama has cancer." I knew our mother had a tumor, but Rita had known for weeks that it was cancerous; Mama had forbidden anyone from telling me over the phone. She made sure the only two people who knew—her husband and her daughter Rita—waited until I was back home on a visit from New York. Once again, as the baby sister, I had been spared, even briefly, while Rita had to deal with knowing, had to absorb the blow of that knowledge. Rita, it seemed, was always the one having to hear first, the one to show up to the scene of tragedy, the one handling the gory details. Now, yet again, Mama had Rita be the bearer of this news.

Nothing was more frightening than hearing that sentence: *Mama has cancer.*

Turns out, she had colon cancer. Our mother did seemingly well after the initial surgery, performed by Dr. Omar Kadro, a renowned Michigan surgeon who specializes in colorectal surgeries. He told me after stepping out of the operating room that he felt he'd "gotten all of it." We were optimistic. Mama had a close friend who'd survived colon cancer, seemingly caught early; her prognosis was good. Meanwhile, a month after her surgery, in an ominous sign, I was held up at gunpoint by a wild-eyed man as I entered a subway station for the local C train near my apartment in Fort Greene, Brooklyn. I screamed so loud that the gunman ran one way, and I ran the opposite way into the subway station, leaping down the entire flight of stairs, falling, and spraining my ankle. When I told Rita about the ordeal, she said, "Thank God you're okay! Girl, can you imagine if I had to give Mama *that* news?" Of course, the thought of delivering bad news was at top of mind for her. She'd had to be the one to do just that a few years before—tell our mother that a child of hers was dead.

That May, I threw myself a thirtieth birthday party, which took place at Greene Avenue Grill, a lovely neighborhood spot in Brooklyn. Rita flew in from Detroit. I still remember the pretty floral dress with matching jacket that she wore, how excited I was that she was there, how much my friends enjoyed talking with her; I especially recall how great it felt for us to both be alive in our thirties, and for her to be in good health. Plus, Mama was doing well. It felt as though we had a lot to celebrate. After the party, I sent her some photos. "I hope you like the pictures," I wrote. "I think you look really beautiful. Love you!" That June, Tony graduated from high school, and Mama is there in the photos, she and Rita flanking Tony in his green cap and gown. But our mother is not smiling; in fact, the camera catches a worried look on her face. By that fall, she was back in the hospital for the removal of "adhesions," or scar tissue from the original surgery. She didn't return to Dr. Kadro for that second surgery, rather opted for a different surgeon referred to her by her longtime internist, Dr. Cecilia Buot—a Filipino American general practitioner who'd inherited the practice from our Black family doctor after his death. No one used the word "recurrence," but talk began of our mother receiving "light" chemotherapy. At that point, Rita and our stepfather, Burt, were Mama's primary caregivers. Rita would often call me early mornings in New York before either of us went to work. "Hey, I'm not gonna talk long," she'd always say as soon as I answered the phone. That was my slim contribution—to be on the other end of the phone for my sister to vent, express her feelings, her frustrations, and her fears. My job was to listen. She once wrote me a follow-up letter after one of our talks, the first in nearly four years:

1–22–91

Hey Bridgett,
Surprised to get a letter from me?
    Mama is scheduled to go to the hospital this Friday. As usual, she has stated that her mind is <u>not</u> fully made up about the therapy. I have put this situation in the Lord's hands.

For the past two days I woke up with a bad headache. My nerves can't take too much more. All we can do is pray that Mama will make the right decision.

Well I'm going to close for now.

Love,
Rita

P.S. I will probably call you Sunday after church.

Our mother opted not to go to the hospital that Friday. I try to imagine why Mama didn't decide right away to begin chemotherapy. I suspect that she was thinking about quality of life rather than longevity; chemo *is* scary and in its way sickening, sometimes brutal even. I don't like to consider the other possibility—that maybe she was thinking how hard it was to live with having buried four children. She knew, too, a lot more than we did how serious lupus could be. Or let's say she was facing that truth more so than the rest of us. Whatever our mother's reason, the burden of walking that tightrope between convincing her to do the "therapy" and honoring her wishes fell on Rita, and it clearly took its toll on her. Rita leaned on her faith to help her get through it.

Mama did ultimately decide to enter Grace Hospital to begin receiving chemotherapy, nearly a year after her original diagnosis—again, not under the care of her specialist surgeon, but under the care of Dr. Buot and her recommended oncologist. In those early weeks, our mother seemed to handle the treatments well, and so we believed that the chemo was working. Rita sent me a quick, optimistic note that spring, saying, "Mama is doing great."

Across the next several months, our mother had three more hospital stays to receive chemotherapy, and another stay to receive radiation. Throughout that time, when she wasn't teaching at Western High, Rita was caring for Mama. When our mother was in the hospital, Rita was going to see her right before work, and right after. And when Mama was home, Rita was essentially living in two places—

going back and forth between Evergreen and Seven Mile. Oh yes, and she was also keeping our mother's numbers business afloat, taking customers' bets in the early mornings and in the evenings after work. Burt, our stepfather, was certainly doing his share too. But that was it: just the two of them holding it down. I was living in New York as a new professor, coming home sporadically. Tony was in college in Atlanta, unaware how sick his grandmother was (our mother's mandate). In a photo of Rita during that time, taken at work, she stands against bright red lockers in the hallway at Western, dressed uncharacteristically in all black, her smile barely there; I see exhaustion in her eyes. Yet Rita never once complained about the burden of so much falling on her shoulders. She took pride in taking excellent care of the one person who meant more to her than anyone in the world.

And as part of that care, Rita became Mama's protector. Our mother had given her an untenable directive: *Do. Not. Tell. Anyone. I. Have. Cancer.* And so folks unknowingly kept showing up, calling, asking to see or talk to Fannie, spend time around her, chitchat, turn in their numbers bets with her. Some people also wanted their usual favors from Mama, many asking to borrow money. Rita stood guard at the doorway, literally. It was hard to honor Mama's wish to keep everyone in the dark, and folks often took out their frustrations on Rita, including our own extended family members. It wasn't fair to her. How she stayed healthy enough to function during that time is beyond me. Either that was the case, or she kept her own lupus flare-ups secret. I still don't know the full extent of what Rita experienced—emotionally and physically—during the two and a half years that our mother battled cancer.

"No matter how many people have traveled ahead of us on the caregiving journey and have shared their experiences, it always feels like a pilgrim's path, lonely and strange," says Patti Davis, Ronald Reagan's daughter, who founded a support group for caregivers.

All she ever said to me about caring for Mama was that it was "a lot"; I know now it had to be so hard, as well as lonely and strange. Who *really* knew what Rita was going through?

~

In December 1991, we went to Las Vegas as a family for Christmas, a trip Mama had wanted mostly so she could be away from all the well-meaning people who would've surely come to visit her; at that point, I wanted to believe the cancer treatments were working, but when I witnessed our mother take a dose of morphine from a little vial she carried in her purse, I didn't understand fully what that meant, yet I knew it wasn't good. Turns out, Dr. Buot had given Mama the morphine, to administer herself.

Rita decided that Dr. Buot was part of the problem. She felt that our mother did herself a disservice by putting her trust in a "family practice" doctor who had not once in all the years under her care required our mother to receive a gynecological exam, nor, more importantly, a colonoscopy. True, those were not yet widely used or known procedures. It would be ten more years before Katie Couric famously had a colonoscopy on national TV to spread awareness after her husband died of colon cancer at age forty-two. Still, Rita felt that as an internist, Dr. Buot should've been practicing more preventative medicine, scheduling annual screening exams for our mother, and referring her to a gastroenterologist, given her years of suffering from constipation. "All that chatting and buddy-buddy talk is not the point," Rita lamented to me more than once. "How about you just do your damn job as a doctor?!"

When Dr. Buot would visit Mama in the hospital during her chemo treatments, she'd often spend time rearranging the myriad flowers in the room that friends had brought; she'd pull out dying ones, add more water, combine two bouquets. That drove Rita crazy. "Why isn't she conferring with the oncologist?" she wondered out loud. "Why isn't she finding out from Mama how she's handling the treatment? What the hell is she doing messing with some damn flowers?!"

Finally, one day in the hospital parking lot, things exploded between Rita and Dr. Buot, whom she accused of not doing enough for our mother. "Your mother is dying!" Dr. Buot yelled. "She's dying!"

"She won't die under your watch!" Rita shot back.

When Rita relayed this to me, we both couldn't believe Dr. Buot would say such a thing. "She's really tripping," I said. Neither of us said out loud or allowed ourselves to even think that maybe Dr. Buot knew what she was talking about, that our mother was terminal. We decided instead that Mama's longtime doctor was utterly unprofessional.

Rita was so unnerved by the encounter that she convinced Mama to finally return to the care of Dr. Kadro. Basically, she begged her, and so Mama returned to him—two years after he'd performed the initial surgery. He asked her, "Mrs. Robinson, why'd you stay away so long?" Rita, who sat beside her in the examining room, said Mama just shrugged. Dr. Kadro explained that he'd be admitting our mother to Beaumont Hospital immediately, but when Rita asked about his specific plan for more treatment, Dr. Kadro "wouldn't even look me in the eye," Rita recalled. Our mother stayed in the hospital for two weeks, but it turns out she just received palliative care; the cancer had spread. Neither chemo nor radiation had worked to halt its progression.

Some may believe that because Fannie, our mother, received quality care upon diagnosis, we can't really blame implicit bias in the unsuccessful outcome of her cancer treatment. After all, she chose not to stay with her top-notch colorectal surgeon. But the reasons for that speak to the ways in which the health-care industry has repeatedly and historically failed Black people. It's the personal memory and handed-down narratives that inform Black men and women's choices as much as the care they receive, which then often determine outcomes. Our mother had witnessed firsthand and heard countless stories of friends and acquaintances suffering excruciating final days at the hands of white doctors who withheld adequate pain medication. Of course, American history as well as the plethora of studies that prove the phenomenon bear out our mother's fears. As recently as 2016, a major study showed that among first- and second-year medical students, 40 percent believed Black people's skin was thicker than white people's, and those students who believed Black patients were less sensitive to pain were less likely to treat their pain appropriately.

Our mother had a deep-rooted fear of physical suffering. One of her sayings—long before she was sick—was that, "Money even makes dying easier." She had money in the form of good health insurance, and she was determined that a doctor she knew and trusted would manage her cancer care—a doctor who'd make sure she got the pain relief she needed. Dr. Kadro was indeed renowned, but he was also a white male doctor; she didn't know what he'd say to her requests for painkillers. Our mother had spent a *lot* of time in hospitals over the years; I can only imagine what some of her experiences had been. Fannie may have been so-called cured had she stayed with Dr. Kadro, but she also may have suffered unnecessarily through an inevitable outcome. I'm not sure Mama ever believed she'd beat cancer. She certainly didn't know many people who had. Besides, she believed that a mother's worry and sadness and grief over a child could kill her, that a mother's sorrow could stop her heart's beat. Given that belief, Mama may have felt an inevitability about her prognosis, and if she did, then there was no reason to suffer, and no reason to assume Dr. Kadro would make sure she didn't. Painful as it is, I understand her choice: Dr. Buot made sure our mother didn't suffer. In that way, she provided the best care she knew how to—by honoring Mama's wishes and making her as comfortable as possible.

Our mother's prognosis was never good.

African Americans are about 20 percent more likely to get colorectal cancer and about 40 percent more likely to die from it than most other groups, according to the American Cancer Society. As late as 2021, a major colorectal surgery practice was attributing the higher incidence of colon cancer in Blacks to the three usual blame-the-victim causes—diet (high fat), genetics, and "lifestyle," as a way to explain why Blacks are dying from the disease at such a higher rate.

Meanwhile, no one blamed diet, genetics, or lifestyle for Audrey Hepburn's death in January 1993 at age sixty-three from what was then thought to be colon cancer. Media accounts looked to her childhood of malnutrition while growing up in Holland under Nazi occupation during WWII to likely explain why the rich, famous actress died of a cancer in the digestive tract. Her son said he believed her poor health later in life was a consequence of her impoverished upbringing.

I so wish Black folks were given that kind of life-experience understanding. As Dr. Geronimus so bluntly stated in *Weathering*, back in the era when our mother was diagnosed, "Those most invested in the blame game opined that Black Americans . . . didn't make the effort to become healthy . . . in the eyes of those who took this view, it was hard to claim injustice if white Americans *earned* their health through personal restraint while Black Americans were dying from the effects of their own choices." As Mama lay in bed at the end of her life in Beaumont Hospital, even I talked about how her diet had gotten her here—"Not enough fiber," I lamented. My stepfather just glared at me.

Dr. Geronimus has busted all the self-blame myths that have kept Black folks caught up in efforts to somehow just "make better choices" to stay healthier. She has emphatically laid the blame where it belongs, on those physiological processes that weather the body, and compromise it, make it more vulnerable to disease. "Weathering is not measured in number of steps walked, cigarettes smoked, opioids used, alcohol drunk, or calories eaten," she tells us. "It's not primarily measured by your years of education, the size of your paycheck, or your bank balance. It's not essentially about your emotional despair, either," she writes.

The American Cancer Society, in the aftermath of actor Chadwick Boseman's death at the young age of forty-three, had to admit as much as it moved away from the self-blame trope; its website now states the obvious: that African Americans "often experience greater obstacles to cancer prevention, detection, treatment, and survival, including systemic racial disparities that are complex and go beyond the obvious connection to cancer." Yet Dr. Geronimus tells us it's not so complex, that in fact it's pretty straightforward how those systemic racial disparities connect to cancer: "Weathering is about hopeful, hardworking, responsible, skilled, and resilient people dying from the physical toll of constant stress on their bodies, paying with their health," she writes. "Because they live in a rigged, degrading, and exploitative system."

That certainly describes our mother's life. Born into late-1920s Nashville as the granddaughter of a slave, she grew up hearing and knowing about brutality—including lynching—all around her. Her own brother died from gun violence. Shortly after giving birth in a segregated hospital to a daughter who lived for one hour and fifteen minutes, our mother left her extended, nurturing family and community to migrate north with her husband and small children, seeking a better economic life; she felt forced to leave her youngest daughter behind because of the harsh life that was to meet them in Michigan; there, she found herself newly pregnant with Rita when she saw Emmett Till's disfigured and brutalized face in *Jet* magazine, which almost caused her to have a miscarriage. When she gave birth to Rita, the delivery was a breech one in a county hospital; both of them nearly died. By the time Rita was two, our mother launched a numbers business to thwart the poverty they'd slid into thanks to the racist treatment they faced in Detroit. This while our mother suffered throughout adulthood with blood clots caused by deep vein thrombosis. While she did ultimately thrive as a number runner, our mother faced constant stress from myriad factors in a high-stakes enterprise—near wipe-outs, the threat of arrest, possible robberies, and dealing daily with anxious men and women for whom playing the numbers was no game but rather a way to experience windfalls for their own survival. In a just world, our mother wouldn't have had to resort to an underground business for financial stability. It breaks my heart that she had to work that hard, with that much daily risk, for not *that* much. As one retired investment banker said to me, "Given her acumen, in a different era, your mother could very well have run a casino or worked as a trader on Wall Street."

And even with her successes, which enabled us to live a middle-class life, she'd suffered the loss of not one, not two, but three adult children. When our mother found herself diagnosed with diverticulitis, and soon after doctors discovered the colon cancer, she repeated to Rita what she'd said after Dianne's and her grandson Brandon's murders: "I don't want to live through losing another child."

~

Rita called me at daybreak on my thirty-second birthday to first say "Happy birthday," and then to say Mama had been rushed to the hospital with a faint heartbeat, and "she may not make it through the day." I rushed to Detroit, praying during the entire flight from New York that she wouldn't die before I arrived, that she wouldn't die on my birthday. Once at her bedside, I stayed with our mother in the hospital every day for the final week of her life. When those last moments came, Rita leaned in and kissed our mother's smooth forehead, whispered goodbye. So did I, telling Mama it was okay to go. She died squeezing my hand as she took her last breath, surrounded by Rita, Mama's baby sister Florence and her daughter Jewell, and Mama's dearest friend Lula Mae.

Later, Rita said to me: "Mama's passing was beautiful." She and I were brand-new to this way of experiencing death. We'd never before had the chance to be with a loved one when he or she transitioned. We'd never been given time to prepare for the moment; Rita and I, in our short lives, had always been forced to deal with the devastating shock of a sudden death. I agreed with her; Mama's passing was beautiful.

At our mother's funeral, hundreds were in attendance; people spoke earnestly about her impact on their lives; a friend and City Council member, the Honorable Brenda M. Scott, acknowledged everyone's acts of condolence; our cousin's wife Earline sang sweetly; and our mother and Rita's beloved pastor, Reverend Stotts, gave a heartfelt eulogy. It was a moving service. But suddenly, as the recessional began, Rita stood up, walked toward the casket, and said, "Mama, get up. Get up, Mama! Get up!"

To see my sister's anguish and desperation on display was heart-wrenching. I think of Joan Didion's quote from *The Year of Magical*

Thinking: "I know why we try to keep the dead alive: we try to keep them alive in order to keep them with us." For as long as I could remember, it had always been *Fannie and Rita, Fannie and Rita, Rita and Fannie.* They weren't just close as mother and daughter; as Tony puts it: "They were mirror images of each other."

Instinctively, I rose and moved toward Rita as she stood there, so lost, behind our mother's casket; I gently guided her back to her seat. We stood together, shoulders touching; I put my hand in hers, and as deacons rolled the casket out of the church, us following behind, I didn't let go.

35

In the weeks following our mother's death on May 29, 1992, Rita
said to me, "Mama's not really gone, just moved on." Gathering
strength from that belief, she became the fierce protector of our mother's legacy, which for Rita meant carrying out Mama's wishes. First
and foremost, she wanted to make sure our mother's grandson, our
nephew Tony, was taken care of as Grandma had taken care of him.
When he came home from college on his summer break and learned
that the man whom he called "Daddy Burt," Grandma's husband, was
already involved with another woman, he told Rita how awkward it
felt to be at the house. Rita told him, "Just come over here to stay with
me." That's what he did. "It's what Mama would want," Rita assured
Tony. She now fully embraced her role as his aunt. I've often thought
about how she stepped up in the moment, without hesitation. Rita was
on my mind as I listened recently to an episode of the podcast *The
Stoop*, devoted to the topic of Black aunties. The hosts explored how
these often-childless women tend to be true caretakers, vital to their
nieces' and nephews' lives. During the episode, the sociologist Dr. Regina Davis-Sowers shares what she sees as the unique role of aunties
in the Black community. White aunts are often gift-givers, she said,
whereas Black aunts are often sustainers. She interviewed three dozen
Black aunts and concluded that "We as aunts are the second mother,
the cheerleader, the one who stands in the gap . . . the one who loves
you, but also understands you're not perfect." That was Rita.

Meanwhile, she had taken over our mother's now-modest numbers
business. She wanted to carry on Mama's work, her world, and her
wishes. What this meant is that every morning before she headed out
to teach her students at Western, Rita took a few customers' three-
and four-digit bets on the phone. After work, in the late afternoon
she took more customers' bets, then often purchased lottery tickets
from a nearby party store to offset winners breaking her small cash
reserve. Each evening after the winning numbers were announced on

the local news, she checked the business to see if anyone had hit. Her weekends were largely spent taking more customers' bets, collecting money owed and paying out winnings, and providing customers with weekly "tapes" or tallies of their plays. She did all of this while keeping it a secret even from her closest friends. Running numbers was easier for her to do in the summer, when she wasn't teaching, but I thought it was untenable, and that fall when she was back at work full-time, I tried to convince her to give it up. I didn't mention the lupus, but that was my unspoken concern when I told her, "It's too much on you, trying to maintain your job and that damn business." But as she pointed out to me, the revenue from the numbers enabled her to continue paying for Tony's living expenses and tuition at Clark College in Atlanta. She was right, of course. I recently found a copy of a letter she wrote to the Jade East apartment complex in Atlanta, where Tony was living at the time:

> To Whom It May Concern:
> This letter is to verify that I, Rita R. Davis, will be responsible for the balance of the rent for apt. #47, leased to my son, Anthony R. Davis II. The amount is $575.
> If there are any questions, please feel free to contact me at (313) 535-3739.
>
> Sincerely,
> *Rita R. Davis*

I find it apropos that she referred to Tony as her son in that letter, which of course was meant to add veracity to her promise that she'd guarantee the rent (Tony's own mother, Renita, was alive and well), but truth be told, she did take on a kind of mothering-of-an-adult-child role—a continuation of how our mother cared for and raised Tony. Still, that didn't stop me from worrying about Rita's workload. One night I dreamed that *she* had surgery to remove a polyp. The next day, I again argued with her about giving up the numbers, but to no avail.

At the same time that she was keeping our mother's business afloat, Rita was navigating the treacherous terrain of handling Mama's estate in probate. A family member became convinced that Rita was trying to claim property that our grandfather had left his own children, and was furious with Rita. I believe the family member was really just heartbroken that Fannie had died, but Rita bore the brunt of that misplaced sorrow, a scapegoat for their grief. I tried to defend Rita, arguing with the family member, but nothing could change their mind. And it pained me to see Rita suffer those slings and arrows by a loved one at a time when she herself was so grief-laden, devastated by the loss of our mother, burdened with being misunderstood while steadfastly staying true to what she deeply believed was Mama's wishes. She was so hurt—up until then, Rita and this family member had been close. I wanted her to drop the whole thing because I could see that it was costing her, that comingling of grief and hurt. I kept telling her the stress on her body wasn't worth it. But for Rita, it was about the principle, about the desire to do what Mama would want as a way of honoring her, no matter the resistance, no matter the price. That was the extent of her love for and loyalty to our mother. I stood by her side, supporting Rita 100 percent. I knew her intentions were pure. It really is an intense, tender feeling to realize that all you have in the world of complicated family is each other, to support and protect one another.

Looking back, we were both wounded animals limping through those first few months of our grief. Especially Rita. I recently found a "driver improvement order" issued to her by the Michigan Department of State. That August, she'd been stopped by police for not signaling as she made a turn on Ferndale, and that violation meant she now had an "unsatisfactory driving record," with a total of fifteen points against her (twelve was the limit). She was facing suspension of her driver's license, but the analyst wrote:

> *Ms. Davis appeared for re-exam and disclosed a recent ticket for the record. She stated that past incidents were largely due to stress and pre-occupation with long-term illness of family member. At one time,*

Ms. Davis was not giving full attention to law and safety, but effort has been made to drive in a safe, responsible manner. She is aware of the risks associated with hazardous driving and expressed a commitment to traffic safety. Therefore, based on the discussion and survival period, a three-month restricted license is issued in lieu of suspension. Warned that subsequent incidents will result in suspension.

I always thought of Rita as a cautious driver, the one who would go out of her way to avoid left turns at one point, but this tells a slightly different story: the stress of caring for our mother, and the intense stress of dealing with her death, affected Rita so fully that it impeded her ability to drive safely.

During those days of mourning, the two of us talked on the phone constantly. Yet I avoided returning to Detroit until I absolutely had to, gathering the things in our mother's house that I wanted to keep. Everything about that home was and felt different upon my return, including our stepfather, Burt, who showed me the birthday gift he'd gotten for his new "woman friend." I had to tell him in the nicest way I could that it was too soon for all that. Rita was furious with him, feeling his betrayal in full force.

Back in New York, having faced the literal fact that our mother was gone, I fell into despair; that led to my recurring fear of dying young, as our three siblings had done. I'd not yet accomplished any of the things I'd hoped to as a writer, and that terrified me. I wrote in my journal: "I'm afraid I'll die before I vindicate everyone else's death." I desperately wanted to "make it," to become successful, because I had goals, or as I wrote, "a mission": "I'm going to retire my sister and buy her a house." What I understood was that work was becoming too much for Rita, as was the upkeep and expense of her beloved Evergreen. I knew that she was dragging herself to work each morning, and taking a nap every day after she got home; I knew she was using all her allotted sick days; I knew dealing with her tenants could be stressful. I wanted to make her life easier.

Her friend Wilma recalls a conversation she had with Rita around that time. "We were talking one day, and I asked Rita, 'When was the last time you saw Dr. Indenbaum [her rheumatologist]?'" says Wilma. "She told me, 'Girl, I haven't seen him in a while.' She said, 'I was taking care of my mother.'" Wilma says Rita confessed that she actually hadn't seen her doctor in about nine months. "Oh, I fussed at her," recalls Wilma. "I said, 'Rita, I will take you there myself.'" Rita didn't take her up on her offer, and Wilma doesn't know for sure *when* Rita finally got around to seeing Dr. Indenbaum again.

~

Keeping with the tradition we'd begun when our mother chose to spend her last Christmas away from home, in Las Vegas, Rita and Tony and I spent that first Christmas without her in Florida, at Disney World. I flew from New York, meeting them in Orlando. With no one to watch my Yorkshire terrier, Magick, I decided to bring him with me on the trip, since the Disney World hotel allowed pets. I placed him in a little red carrier that I could then slip under the seat in front of me. Having him there with my two remaining family members felt poignant for sure, yet festive. We were a unit. "This is unlike a year ago because I'm not, we're not, in denial," I wrote that morning in my journal, referring to how Rita and I had not discussed the possibility of our mother's dying. We had Christmas dinner at Epcot Center, enjoying its faux Paris.

As we were returning to our respective homes after the trip, I discovered while we were at the airport that while Delta in Detroit had allowed pets on the plane, Delta in Orlando did not. What to do? Rita and I devised a plan to hide Magick underneath her voluminous (and fashionable) gold lamé raincoat. Rita and I went to the women's restroom and placed my Yorkie against her belly, the elastic band of her leggings holding him in place. I told Magick to "be quiet, and don't move." We figured if anyone noticed the "bump" around her belly, they'd think she was pregnant. I told Rita to "act normal." And then we went through security, holding our breaths. Rita went first. She was great, chatty with the security agent, and walking as casually as she could with a little dog against her midsection. The security agent made her stop; he examined his screen, and then, after an interminable pause, he waved her through. Magick hadn't moved! Once we were all through security, we went to another women's restroom, and I slipped my dog back into his red carrier. "Girl, you have some nerve!" Rita said to me because I'd talked her into the whole thing. But, of course, so did the one who pulled it off. I loved that we were in it together, this risk-taking escapade.

I had to then sneak my dog onto the plane back to New York. I did so easily. But while we were in flight, Magick crawled out of his carrier and ran into the aisle. The flight attendant squealed, then actually picked up the dog and went to show it to the pilot before handing him back to me. In this post-9/11 world, I marvel at that now, how lax air travel was back in the day. And how much more enjoyable.

With the new year, Rita finally decided to give up the numbers, the thing I'd been pressing her to do. "Did I ever think I'd see the day?" I wrote in my journal. "It's symbolic." For the first time in our collective memories, there'd be no numbers running in our family. Rita admitted it was just too much. She finally understood that that was *not* the legacy Mama would've wanted her to carry on, not if the weight of it was dragging her down. And it was.

Without the revenue that came from the numbers, I stepped up, and together we pooled our resources to split the cost of paying for Tony's expenses in Atlanta while he completed college. Rita and I never once fought about money; we came together on that; whatever she needed, I was there to help her with, and vice versa. Yet I did write in my journal about a dispute we had that April, a few weeks before her thirty-seventh birthday. "The argument with Rita was really hard. She's going through a lot. Mourning doesn't just end. It lingers." Seeing that I wrote how *she* was going through a lot, despite the fact that we'd *both* lost our mother, reminds me of when our father died, and Rita had said to me that if she was feeling bad, she couldn't imagine how I was feeling. She knew how indescribably close I'd been to Daddy. And I knew how indescribably close she'd been to Mama. My loss of our mother was very hard, but for Rita it was all but unfathomable. "Really, truth be told, how great is life?" I wrote in my journal. "A banquet of sadness, tragedies waiting to feast on our hearts."

Rita came to visit me in New York that May, and after she left, I missed her so much I fell into a slight depression. She wrote me a brief, upbeat letter afterward, even mentioning my Yorkie, Magick:

5/12/93

Hey Bridgett,
Just me sending $200 towards Tony's rent. I had a great time in New York last weekend.
    Well cheer up! Tell your little one (smile) hello.

Love,

Your Big Sis,
Rita

~

On the one-year anniversary of our mother's death, I wrote: "Everything's changing. Has changed. In one year, it's all different. Without her. The house is on the market. Burt is remarrying. Tony is our responsibility. I have no plans to return to Detroit." And, inexplicably to me now, I wrote: "It's as though she died so Rita and I could live."

Detroit was home, but it was also the geographical and emotional site of so much pain and sorrow that I just wanted to stay away from the place. Rita liked New York, and so it felt like I could keep my stance of avoiding Detroit, and simply host her on her visits to my new home. But I was struggling with my life in Manhattan, having abruptly left my Fort Greene, Brooklyn, community behind in a rash decision to "start over." I was lonely and floundering, and Rita was a bit worried about me. I'd also had a recent breakup, and as I lamented my broken heart, I'll never forget what she said to me: "Someone better is out there for you." She was right.

When she wrote to me next, beyond the financial details regarding our nephew, Rita encouraged me to have a fling with a guy I'll call K:

June 18, 1993

Hey Bridgett,
Just me sending the money for American Express and $150 towards the $200 you gave Tony. I still owe you $50—will send on June 30th.

   By the way, I am writing a check for Tony's rent which I will give him this weekend. The same with his spending money.

   Please cheer up. I am here for you at any time.

Love Your Bis Sis,
Rita

Enjoy K! Everything in this world is supposed to be used not misused. Life is too short to be unhappy for one minute. We have been through too much.

I love you!

Come fall of that year, despite my reluctance, I could no longer avoid returning home; a lot was going on there: Our nearly seventy-six-year-old stepfather, Burt, was preparing to remarry (seventeen months after Mama's death), and he was holding an estate sale at our family's Seven Mile home. Rita, ever the protector, was far more engaged with the process than I. Basically, I got to check out because she was on top of it. Every few days, as the estate sale loomed, she asked Burt if she could have a treasured piece of our mother's furniture: Could she have the French Provincial sofa in the basement that Bridgett loved from our childhood days? He said yes, and she placed it into storage for me. Could she have the hand-painted glass-cased secretary? He said yes. Could she have the black hand-painted Chinese mini cabinet? Yes. The two Louis XV–style chairs? Okay. When she asked for the pale blue Tiffany-style floor lamp, he told her: "Let this be the last thing you ask for." (Each of those treasured pieces is now in my home.) Rita wanted us, Fannie's daughters, to inherit our mother's treasures, for sure. But she also was deeply offended by the idea that this new woman in our stepfather's life would get to claim any of our mother's beautiful possessions, while benefiting from the sale of other items and furnishings our mother had worked so hard for. It *was* infuriating.

A couple weeks before Burt's wedding, the estate sale pending, I did finally fly to Detroit—returning for the last time to the house that had been my home since I was nine years old, the place where Rita and I had shared a bedroom with twin beds, the place where she'd once chased me through the entire house after I "accidentally" hit her in the face with a flying brush, the place where I'd watched her twirl through the living room, dancing with a broom to the funky tune "Clean Up Woman."

One day, after Rita left for work, our stepfather and I talked, and he revealed that the doctor had told *him* that our mother was going to die. He'd known her prognosis for some time. Whether the doctor actually told Mama, I have no idea. "Why didn't you tell me and Rita?" I asked him. "I didn't think that was my place to tell you, Chicken," was his response. He then said he hoped I would accept his soon-to-be new wife. I suddenly burst into tears. Later, without telling Rita, I called his fiancée and "made nice"; I was, as I wrote in my journal later, "striving for peace, for resolution and closure." But I knew I was betraying Rita, who staunchly believed there was no reason to engage with that woman. "Don't forget, he was dealing with her before Mama passed!" she reminded me. When our stepfather gingerly asked, I did tell Burt that no, I would not be attending his wedding. On the morning I was returning to New York, Rita went into a tirade, her anger over everything, the injustice of it all, spewing out. I'd never seen her that enraged before, and it scared me. Of course, she was utterly depressed because our mother was dead. Meanwhile, I could not wait to get back to New York, despite the fact that my life there was a mess— still recovering from a breakup and still terrified of running out of time. One night, I dreamed about my own corpse.

But as the weeks wore on, and we spoke to each other almost daily, Rita and I used each other to feel better. We talked often about how Mama would want us to go on with our lives, try to be happy. And Rita had a triumph to celebrate: after all her student teaching, temporary classroom placements, and subbing; after receiving a contingent contract and an impermanent high school placement; and after endless courses with tests and papers to write, she finally completed her certification. That semester, she took her last class, on learning disabilities, at Madonna University; she scored a ninety-six on the final. Nine years after walking into her first classroom, Rita was fully endorsed as a special ed teacher by the Detroit Board of Education. "Thank God," she said to me. "I was so damn tired of taking classes."

I remember that for the holiday season, Rita had two dates to formal affairs with two different guys, and we talked about how she planned to wear her dazzling blue-and-black sequined dress with matching sequined pumps for both dates. As she pointed out, she was certain those two guys' worlds didn't collide, so no one would be the wiser. We laughed about that. For Christmas that year, we kept up our tradition of traveling, and joined my friend Jane and her ninety-three-year-old mother in Merida, Mexico, located along the Yucatan. It was a wonderful week of witnessing another culture celebrating the Christmas holiday. We stayed in an old, beautiful hotel in the center of town, and walked around absorbing the colors and language and Mayan rituals. Some Mexican guys who called our nephew "brother" took Tony out for a night of party-hopping and drinking. And in the open market, I bought Mayan pottery while Rita bought beautiful little-girl outfits for two of the Black dolls she collected. Rita's dolls were exquisite, lifelike creations. One, with her long sandy hair and pecan-colored skin, resembled Rita. For her, she bought a soft pink eyelet two-piece outfit. And the other, with her flowing black hair and rich brown skin, resembled our mother. For her, Rita bought a white eyelet two-piece. Our mother loved white eyelet.

During that trip, my friend Jane asked me whether I knew that Rita was jealous of me. The question took me aback. She never shared what made her say such a thing, and I never asked. I already knew:

Jane saw two sisters who were very different in style and appearance and personality, and she assumed that Rita envied me, but she was wrong. I remained clear that Rita admired me and had no desire to be like me. She really liked who *she* was. I answered Jane simply: "That's not something I even think about, because I know she loves me."

In between sightseeing and meals and shopping, Rita spent a lot of time in our hotel room devouring the novel she'd brought with her—Tina McElroy Ansa's *Ugly Ways*. All week, Rita wore her long ponytail under a brightly colored sequined baseball cap. When I look at photos from that trip, she looks good, healthy. But weeks after the trip, she said to me, "I knew I wasn't feeling that great, when I was on a vacation, and I didn't even bother to do my hair."

FOUR

~

36

I can pinpoint exactly when Rita's disease began to shift in its severity: May 1994. That's when she entered the hospital for treatment because, as she said to me, "The lupus has gone wacky." This was the first time she was hospitalized for her condition. And this was also the first time I'd ever spoken directly to Dr. Indenbaum, her rheumatologist. He told me they were treating her appropriately, carefully increasing her prednisone, using the steroid to calm down inflammation. What he didn't tell me was that the lupus was behaving more aggressively in the ways it was causing her immune system to attack itself. At this point, she'd been living with and largely managing lupus for eighteen years.

What changed? Was it as her dear friend Wilma believed? That Rita had neglected her health while caring for our mother, and took too long to see her doctor even after our mother's death, and this was the upshot—the lupus "going wacky"? We'll never know for sure, but what I do know is that an autoimmune disease can be progressive, and manifests differently in each person. I also know that mother loss is one of the most traumatic experiences in our lives, and it's as much a physical experience as an emotional one. Once again, grief landed hard on Rita's body, and her compromised body suffered its wrath harshly—doctor's care or no. Force of will kept Rita going for two full years after she lost the most important person in her world— honoring Mama's wishes, doing right by her—but inevitably all that effort exhausted her, took its toll.

I, the healthy one, was at a critical juncture in my own life. I'd wanted, since I could remember, to be a writer, not only a journalist chronicling others' lives, but also using words to create new worlds. But I'd spent my young adulthood unable to write creatively with any consistency; each time a loved one died I'd find myself pushing "the work" aside as I tried to restore my soul. Yet, ironically, with each subsequent loss, the urge to use my writing to immortalize their lives intensified, even as the grief got in the way of the writing. In the few years since our sister Dianne's death, I'd managed to gain some rhythm in my writing life; I even made a bold decision: in the early months of 1992, I told my mother I planned to make a film based on a script I'd written. She was so weak, yet she encouraged me. I desperately wanted to make her proud. After her passing that May, I wanted to make Rita proud. Honestly, I was also bursting with the need to create *something* that mattered. I'd lived in New York for five years at that point and had produced next to nothing. Finally, at age thirty-four, I had a screenplay in hand, with the massive goal of turning it into a feature film. I had a plan: to spend the entire summer off from teaching to prep for the shoot, while continuing to learn every single thing I could about the world of filmmaking.

That research included a trip to France, to volunteer at the Independent Feature Film Market, where American films were shown to distributors during the Cannes Film Festival. My goal for this trip was twofold: I'd pitched and been assigned to write an expansive article about Blacks in Cannes for the tenth anniversary issue of *Black Film Review.* I desperately needed the opportunity because I was up for tenure at my college, and both my department chair and my mentor felt my package of journalism was "weak"; I'd been following my eclectic interests since being hired as a journalism professor— contributing fiction to an anthology, writing alt-jazz artists' liner notes, and doing short newspaper profiles of fascinating women like Suzan-Lori Parks, Diana Ross's daughter the singer Rhonda Ross, Queen Latifah, and talk-show host Ricki Lake. But I was told none of that work was "substantial." I needed to do this meaty, 2,500-word, deeply reported magazine piece.

I asked Rita's rheumatologist whether he felt I should still go to France. Dr. Indenbaum told me there was no need to cancel the trip, that she'd be fine after a few days' treatment. He reminded me that Rita always restabilized after a flare-up. My older friend Jane, a mentor, said to me, "Go. She's under the doctor's care, and there's really nothing you can do. Just go." Tony was home from school for the summer, staying with Rita, which meant she wasn't alone. And so I flew to Detroit, spent some time with Rita at the hospital, found her engaged in her own treatment, and also animated and talkative, and with some slight guilt, I went to France for ten days.

When I returned at the end of the month, Rita was indeed stabilized, and I was relieved. But after a couple of nights of fitful dreams and missing our mother terribly, I called Rita, already in a bad mood; so was she, complaining about Tony not cleaning up after himself, not being more considerate overall. I told her she was being unfair to him. That upset her, my not taking her side. This dynamic between us had begun when Tony was born. Our mother always felt Rita was jealous of the attention Tony got. Rita felt our nephew was too spoiled and indulged, not made to be more responsible. Both were right. But we were in a new moment in all our lives, and I should *not* have fallen back on my old pattern of thinking. I should've put myself in Rita's shoes. I had no idea what it was like to be a thirty-eight-year-old young woman dealing with health challenges while living with a twenty-three-year-old nephew who'd been spoiled by his grandmother. "Of course, I feel guilty, like I should just humor her because she's not well," I wrote in my journal.

> But like Aunt Katherine said, she's bossy. Such a huge ego. Her whole point-of-view in life (probably her first memory) is that another person came along and took her place and that she refuses to never again not be the center of attention. Anyway, if I do go back into therapy, it'll be to better understand my relationship with my sister. . . .

Now I see that it wasn't attention Rita was after, it was empathy. She simply needed to vent, be heard, have her feelings validated. But I was honestly terrified of taking her side, because that meant I had to accept a larger reality: if she and Tony couldn't get along, I'd have to move back to Detroit. I already understood that living alone was not the ideal situation for her. I needed her to put up with him as best she could. I needed the two of them to get along. But Rita needed to feel just the opposite, that she wasn't willing to put up with his immature behavior *just* because she wasn't fully well.

It was a mess, and we were a mess.

During our argument, I blurted out my fear: "If you can't get along with Tony, then I have to give up my life in New York and move back home," I said. She was quiet. I immediately regretted saying that to her. But nothing terrified me more at that point than moving back to Detroit. It remained the site of so much pain, and so much loss. Besides, in the wake of our mother's death, I'd spent the past two years in bouts of depression, castigating myself for my inability to honor our dead family members through my writing—and more than ever I could hear a ticking clock. Seeing myself lying in a casket was now a recurring dream. At this point, in 1994, I'd finally broken through: I'd not only begun my first healthy relationship in a long time, I'd also finally written a story I was passionate about, that I believed could translate to the big screen. Here was my leap into the creative life I deeply desired. I was moving forward at last, in the city I loved—and in the process making my life matter while I still had time, outrunning death.

I *needed* Rita to bounce back with proper treatment, as she'd always done before. I needed her to be okay. And yet, in my heart I knew something was different this time, with this latest flare-up. In my journal, days after our argument, I dared to write, "Loving my life, wishing Rita was 100 percent."

And then, when I saw her that summer, Rita *was* herself again; heavier than before due to the higher doses of prednisone causing weight gain and swelling, but good. She'd gotten a local designer to make fashionable, African-print dresses for her, and she was wearing a long-haired wig beneath her signature colorful sequined baseball caps; that was also the summer Rita wore a fabulous pair of platform sandals with circular cut-outs in the heels; she was still fly! We had a good time together. We ate meals at La Shish, her favorite Middle Eastern restaurant in Dearborn, with its delicious chicken shawarma, seasoned with yummy garlic sauce. And she helped me raise seed money for this film I wanted to make, managing to get eighteen different people in her network to invest, including her former boyfriend Cordell (years before he did what he did); Elijah; the funeral home director E. H. Chenault, who'd handled nearly all our loved ones' services; and women who'd played numbers with my mother.

With her support, I became engrossed in shooting my film that fall—an all-consuming, ultra-low-budget, guerrilla-style production. Once that train left the station, I was responsible for more than twenty crew members and nearly two dozen actors, as well as a host of investors big and small who were relying on me to keep this train moving forward. And I was still raising money throughout the shoot. I didn't see Rita for a few months, but we talked on the phone regularly. "You talk about ten thousand dollars like it's ten dollars," Rita once said to me about money I needed for the production. "You remind me of Mama." That made me smile, realizing I too was gambling big-time with a dream, much like our mother had with her numbers business.

~

One day, Rita told me that she was having trouble with her vision, bad enough that she realized she could no longer drive; in fact, she recounted for me the harrowing experience of driving that last time and praying all the way home from work because she couldn't really see the road or signs or streetlights; everything was fuzzy. Turns out, the lupus was causing inflammation of her blood vessels, a condition known as vasculitis, which can affect a person's organs. In Rita's case, this caused constricted blood flow to her retinas, which then became swollen, and led to vision loss. Dr. Indenbaum began a round of treatment that included higher infusions of prednisone combined with the chemotherapy drug Cytoxan—often used for lupus patients—in hopes of reducing the inflammation so that her vision would return enough for her to function. I remember feeling slightly alarmed that she was being treated with a cancer drug.

Although she didn't complain about suddenly being visually impaired, I knew that was a real heartbreak for her, because Rita had always been able to literally see what others couldn't. Unlike me, she'd never had to wear glasses. "Rita prided herself on her vision," confirms her friend Linda. "She'd say, 'Girl, you didn't see that? I got twenty-twenty vision. I don't miss nothing.' She could go into a room, and she'd case it and when she came out, she could tell you everything that was in it, down to the smallest details. She was very sharp in her ways of observation." Linda sighs. "That's why it really hurt me so bad when she started to get sick and lose that ability. I was saying, 'Oh God, please don't let that go.'"

Given this new health challenge, Rita decided that despite how much she loved special-ed teaching, she had to officially go on disability— one year after she'd finally completed her courses for full accreditation. Thankfully, the long-term disability insurance Linda had encouraged her to purchase sustained her financially, as did her rental income from the other side of Evergreen. Within a few months she also began receiving disability benefits from social security. Meanwhile, I had the wild notion that if I could *just* finish shooting my film, complete its postproduction, premiere it at the Sundance Film Festival, then sell it for a lot of money, I'd have the resources to first pay back all my investors, then help Rita financially. "Rita needs to know she's not alone," I wrote. "I have to show her she's not."

Around that time, Rita shared something she claimed to have heard through the grapevine: Someone who remained nameless had told her that a family friend, C., had told *them* she couldn't believe I wasn't moving back home to help Rita while she was struggling with her health; after all, she'd helped *me* raise money for my film. I went crazy, directing all my anger at C., saying, "How dare she?! She doesn't know my life! What's she trying to imply?!" I was so hurt by the implication that I didn't love my sister enough to drop my life and move back home to care for her. Everything I was grappling with, including my own underlying guilt, came to the fore. I'm not a yeller, and I started yelling. Rita was stunned by my response, especially when I threatened to confront C. about her accusation.

"Please don't say anything to her," Rita begged. "Just let it go, Bridgett. Just let it go."

I now know that Rita was, in her way, floating the idea out there, essentially saying, *Maybe you can come back to Detroit to be with me for a while?* She must've been so scared, dealing with the loss of her sight.

I wish I'd had the wherewithal to read between those obvious lines, but my fear came out as fury, and I couldn't allow myself to see it. I knew what people were thinking: *After all the family members they've lost, why isn't Bridgett moving back home to care for Rita? They're all each other has* ... And I was certain that Rita's closest friends were judging me for not doing just that. But—and it took many years of therapy for me to acknowledge this and give myself some grace—Rita never *did* ask me to come home. And I don't know what I might've done had she been more direct with me, had she in fact asked. I know it would've been one of the hardest decisions of my life, but because she never asked me to make it, I know now that that was a huge act of sacrificial love. Because she did need me.

Meanwhile, I was relying on a form of coping I'd developed in the wake of so much loss: Because of the successive tragedies in our lives, I'd found myself more than once having to change plans once faced with a new reality. Years before, when I'd canceled plans to spend a summer in San Francisco working for the *Wall Street Journal* as an intern because of Anthony's murder, and come home to Detroit instead, more tragedy struck. In my traumatized mind, I linked changing plans and returning home with bad luck, with death. I told myself that as long as I didn't *have* to change any plans and rush back home, things weren't too bad and there'd be no more tragic outcomes. That was the game I played with myself in order to function, to not be crippled by the fear that something terrible could happen to Rita, my last remaining sibling. My mind went into self-protective mode, and I decided she *had* to get better, and I told God as much, my prayers more demanding affirmations than pleas. I told myself this was positive thinking, and trust in God's ability to heal; I can see now that it was as much magical thinking as anything.

~

That Thanksgiving, my new boyfriend Rob and I first went to Cleveland so I could meet his parents, and then we visited Rita so he could meet her. She liked him instantly, and I was happy about that. But that's when I saw firsthand how her eyesight had gotten worse. She was so positive about it, insisting that she could see well enough, but when I saw a legal document that she'd just signed, the deteriorated condition of her handwriting shocked me; whereas her usual exuberant signature included loops around the *R* and the *D*, now it was more severe, as though a different person had signed her name.

I'll never forget coming into Rita's room to say goodbye after that November visit and waking her as she lay asleep in her bed, in the dark. I kissed her, told her I loved her, Rob kissed her too, and then he and I headed to the airport. That was the first time I felt genuinely worried about leaving her there alone. Tony was still living in Atlanta. But I had a job and a relationship and a film in production back in New York. My life was there. I told myself our stepfather, Burt, was nearby and our uncle John not far away if Rita needed family help. Plus, Rita had several cherished friends around her. But I felt like shit for leaving, and angry that all our other siblings and our parents had been snatched away, that there simply weren't enough of us anymore, and I felt ill-equipped to singularly fill the void. On that ride back to the airport, as I sat next to Rob, I did seriously consider giving up my New York life and moving back to Detroit. But I felt bereft, heartbroken by the thought.

By the time the plane landed in New York, I had renewed determination, and a new game plan: I really needed my film, *Naked Acts*, to become a financial success. That way, if Rita wanted, I could set her up in New York, where we could be together. While teaching full-time, and awaiting the tenure committee's decision, I threw myself into our final days on the set, wrapping up production in early December. With Rita's health shakier than ever, my goal was to sacrifice whatever I had to, and work harder, in order to help her in the best way I knew how. Ironically, all that work—especially the film's demands—kept me away from her even more.

Meanwhile, a week after I finished production on the film, Rita was readmitted to the hospital, for more Cytoxan and steroid treatment. During her stay, some of her students wrote to her, not yet aware that she wouldn't be returning to her classroom, or to teaching. She saved those letters, each written in block print on three-ring lined paper. One, written in pencil, read:

December 13, 1994

Dear Miss Davis,
I miss you. I got the Moby Dick book out of the library and it had many hard words . . . I will read the Moby Dick book next time, when you get out of the hospital. I would like to take our class next year to. I am still reading my reading book. I am writeing to let you know I care about you. I hope you get well soon. I miss you Miss Davis. I know you are my favorite teacher. I like you. You are nice to me Miss Davis. I will write again to you Miss Davis.
Colleen

Another student wrote hers in ink pen, on the same day:

Dear Miss Davies,
What's up. Not much here. The reason why I'll write you is because I miss you. While I hope you are doing fine. Because I'm doing very good. I hope you get out very soon. Now I have a new class for 5th hour. We all had to split up into different class. Now I got writing for 5th hour. While Miss Davies I will come and see you whenever I can. That's probley be December the 29 or 30, so don't forget. Oh yea, I have bought you something for X-mas. You see it on Dec. 29 or 30. Oh, Miss Davies, my birthday have past, it was Dec. 7, 1994. Miss Davies can you give me your address so I can come and see you. While it's time for me to go; see yea, peace Miss Davies.
P.S. Don't forget to write me back. Oh yea see you later.

By Naomi Fletcher

That holiday season, our cousin Buddy was getting married, the ceremony taking place on December 26 in Nassau, Bahamas. Rita and I had been excited to keep up our tradition of traveling together for the holidays, and we'd made our reservations. But now that the date had arrived, Rita knew her shaky health wouldn't allow her to travel that far. And so Rob went to Cleveland to be with his family for a couple days, and then I went to Detroit to spend Christmas with Rita. As the new year unfolded, I vowed to deepen my spiritual practice, largely based on a metaphysical Christianity I'd learned from Unity Temple and its longtime leader, Eric Butterworth. "I have to strengthen my faith," I wrote in my journal. "And this time I'm going to give myself a focus: Healing Rita." My plan was to throw every "woo-woo" thing I knew at my faith practice, and I made a list of what I planned to use, including an altar for conjuring good; meditation and prayer; and calling on the ancestors. "Directed energy towards the healing forces that are to return her vision," I wrote. And then I added a desire to learn herbology and homeopathy. "Educating myself so I can better help her."

In the ensuing months, I instead became consumed again by the film and its ever-growing needs, coupled with the demands of its new executive producer, now financing most of the film's postproduction costs. When I look back, I remember worrying constantly—about the film, money, and most of all Rita. "Think about Rita a lot," I wrote at one point in spring of '95.

> Think about how this is my chance to go home, put her on a holistic ritual, heal her . . . It's a redemptive fantasy. More for me to try to rectify my inability to save Mama, and Daddy—and even the others. Yet, I know I won't leave my life here for even the whole summer unless I have to. I know I'll fly home for a couple weeks at a time this summer and try to make up for lost time. Of course, I can't do that . . .

I did fly back and forth, guilt my constant companion on the plane even as the film—my lifeblood, in so many ways—continued to take me away from her; in May that year, I was back in Cannes, France, for the second year in a row, this time showing *Naked Acts* in the famous festival's adjacent film market. The day after my thirty-fifth birthday, while still in the South of France, I wrote, "I'm a bit guilt filled. Because Rita's at home, struggling with her health. Alone. And there's little that can be done that hasn't been. Still, I do feel some guilt. I am the child of advantage, and there's not any particular reason why. None."

A couple weeks later, I wrote in my journal a commitment to visit Rita "two or three times this summer." And then I wrote, "Of course, that's another story, another issue I need to deal with, but what do you know? Time for me to put down my pen . . ."

I was overwhelmed by the reality facing me. *What to do, what to do, what to do?* I didn't know what to do. I just knew that life had dealt us a cruel blow—down from each of us growing up with two parents and four siblings to just she and I. And I felt ill-equipped to be what Rita, and everyone else in my life, needed. I constantly felt torn, and in terror of failing everyone.

37

Luckily, that summer Tony decided Atlanta wasn't working for him, and he moved back to Detroit to live with Rita. Knowing he was there with her made me feel a *lot* better. In a sense, Rita was continuing the role that she'd played in Tony's life since our mother had died. He'd lived with her during his college summers since he was twenty-one, and now he was living with her full-time. He'd do so for the next five years. Essentially, Tony spent the decade of his twenties living with his aunt Rita. The woman who said she never wanted children ended up caring for a young-adult one. It was a responsibility she hadn't asked for, and also one she didn't shirk from. But just as importantly, that's when Tony also began to care for her, and he didn't shirk from his role either.

To be sure, their living arrangement wasn't without its drama. It was jarring for Rita to be thrust into a full-time auntie role. And Tony, who'd lived on his own as a college student for several years, was a twenty-four-year-old young man unused to responsibility for anyone but himself; it was a major adjustment for him too. She fussed. He resisted. She complained to me. "He doesn't listen to me. He's not cleaning up after himself. He's trying to be an 'entrepreneur' when his ass needs to get a damn job." I felt stuck in the middle. On the one hand, I wanted to support her. But when I spoke with Tony, I wanted to acknowledge what he was doing—being there when I couldn't be— even as I tried to encourage him to do more. I wasn't very effective. Now that I'm the parent of a young man in his midtwenties, I understand so much more, and when I look back, I wish I had taken Rita's side more, and also *really* insisted Tony do more.

Rita used to share her frustration over Tony with her friends, including her bestie from grad school, Annie. "She'd tell me about how her nephew wasn't doing what he was supposed to do, that he didn't want to work," recalls Annie. "I'd say, 'Well, Rita, he's young,' and she said, 'Well, yes, and I'm going to have to put him out!'"

But, of course, she didn't, and she wouldn't. She just needed to vent, and for someone to listen.

Tony says when Rita fussed at him, he never really took it to heart. He could see the big adjustment she'd had to make due to the lupus; suddenly Rita, who used to jump in her car and go wherever she wanted to go, now had to wait for him or someone else to give her a ride. He saw how hard that was for her—going from a self-sufficient woman to one who had to depend on others. "In hindsight, when you look at it from her perspective, she was like, 'I'm still a person,'" says Tony. "'I still got desires to do what I want to do.' Losing your independence is crazy, literally."

I ask him if he ever felt burdened by Rita taking out her frustrations on him.

"I've always had some type of filter where I know *why* you're doing it, so I never took stuff personal," says Tony. "It's like a kind of empathy, I guess. I'm not easily offended. It's like, I know, okay, you'll get over it."

She always did.

"She'd be back doing for me in a heartbeat," he said. "She was always saying, 'Do you have any pocket money? You need anything?' Then she'd hand me some cash. She was just kindhearted like that."

In July of '95, Elijah, still a good friend, drove Rita to Chicago to see the debut festival screening of *Naked Acts*. I got to thank Rita from the stage, as the one who'd raised seed money for me to get this little movie made. "I'm particularly pleased too that my number one associate producer and my biggest supporter is here from Detroit," I said to a full house. "That's my sister, Rita Davis." People clapped; it felt good.

I remember later watching from behind as she walked, holding on to Elijah's arm, to her hotel room, wearing heels that she was clearly struggling to walk in. We got to her room; she kicked off those beige-colored pumps with relief. And that was the last time that Rita, known for an array of dazzling shoes showing off her shapely legs, ever wore high heels. She simply couldn't anymore, thanks to the steroids. Prednisone is a miracle drug and a demon drug. As a corticosteroid, it effectively reduces inflammation, but the key is to find the balance between using prednisone at the right dose for as long as needed—to "put out the fire," as one doctor described it—before weaning off of it as soon as possible. Sadly, long-term use and high doses can cause a litany of side effects, some of which carry serious health risks. The Mayo Clinic lists twenty different potential side effects of this potent drug, including: swollen legs, high blood pressure, mood swings, delirium, upset stomach, increased risk of infection, high blood sugar, osteoporosis, fatigue, loss of appetite, nausea, thin skin that easily bruises, and wounds that slowly heal. Prednisone also famously causes people to have round or "moon" faces. Most visibly, the steroid causes significant weight gain. In Rita's case, it eventually made her obese; as someone who'd always watched her weight, dieting over the years with the goal of losing at most twenty pounds or so—even introducing Annie to WeightWatchers—she was moving in a body she didn't recognize, and that made her mobility even more challenging. Worst of all, few people understood that the steroids caused the weight gain; people judged her; sadly, that included those in the medical profession. When she was at her sickest, hospitalized and on lifesaving high doses of prednisone, a white male doctor told me with a straight face that she needed to "get her lupus under control, and also lose weight."

Later that year, Rita had another setback: she suddenly couldn't walk. As Dr. Indenbaum explained it to me, she was suffering from yet another lupus-related condition called ataxia, which affects the central nervous system, specifically the cerebellar and spinal cord. Given that it caused a form of partial paralysis, Rita entered a rehab facility, Heartland in West Bloomfield, for aggressive physical therapy. She did well across a few weeks, and when she came out, her mobility had vastly improved. But her doctor had to write a letter to Blue Cross Blue Shield, imploring the insurance company to fully cover the cost of her time in rehab:

To Whom It May Concern:
Ms. Davis has been under my care for systemic lupus erythematosus. Over the years, she has had multiple complications of this condition, treated on each occasion.

At present time she has two major disabling problems—one is visual impairment . . . and the second is walking impairment . . .

The patient was on treatment with Cytoxan and steroids, which have brought her a long way, and she is seeing a little bit at this time. Her ambulation is gradually improving but required a prolonged period of rehabilitation with physical therapy, to gain enough ability to ambulate again . . . At this time, she shows the fruit of this treatment, with marked improvement in her ambulation ability . . .

It would be my opinion that without this rehabilitation program and its prolongation because of the requirement of trying to get her walking again, she would never have been able to walk again. I believe that her treatments should be covered in full.

Sincerely,
Samuel D. Indenbaum, M.D.

~

Rita came with Tony to visit me in New York for Thanksgiving that year, and what I remember most is a lot of laughter. She used a cane to help with her walking, but it looked like a fashion accessory more than anything; she'd found a local designer to make it, and it was wrapped in a beautiful and colorful fabric that invited compliments wherever we went. I felt such relief that she'd rallied, that she was doing well. The next day, I left for Brazil to attend my first international film festival, where I'd been invited to screen *Naked Acts*. I traveled on that trip with Michelle Materre, a film programmer and Black indie-film champion. She was just a couple years older than Rita, and Michelle reminded me of her the entire trip. She, like Rita, was a Taurus, and she had the same joie de vivre and grounded sultriness that Rita possessed. Even her style of fashionable dresses in bold colors brought Rita to mind. I couldn't stop wishing I were on that Brazilian trip with my sister, wishing she were healthy enough to join me.

Our small family spent that Christmas together in Detroit, guests of Rita's friend Wilma for Christmas dinner. Rita's vision was so poor, she couldn't really see what was on her plate, and I gently guided her hand, holding the fork toward the food in front of her; none of us said a word about it, although it filled me with worry. On New Year's 1996, I wrote, "1995 was Rita's sickest time—beyond the initial shock of the lupus attack and into the long tough road towards recovery." I told myself the worst was behind her, and that's what I believed. Rita, ever the optimist, believed it too. By now, she'd adjusted relatively well to her disabilities. Her ophthalmologist had prescribed a few visual aids to help with her vision. One was a mini magnifying glass that she kept in her purse; another was a binocular-style aid that she hung around her neck, each allowing her to see things a bit better. At home, she also had a small machine with a built-in magnifier, so that she could put papers or books beneath it and read the enlarged print. She'd begun listening to books on tape in lieu of reading, and to get around, she used the city's paratransit van for the disabled, where she got to know and become friendly with the driver and her fellow passengers. Also, she still had style: turns out, her designer friend had made an array of walking canes for her, so that she had one to match each outfit; with her long, straight-haired black wig and with the prednisone causing her skin to be as smooth and round as a baby's, she looked cherubic and beautiful. She was managing, choosing to see the bright side. Even as I couldn't really know how hard it was for her to lose so much freedom so young, I also was awed by her positivity. Rita remained deeply steeped in her faith, and that helped her trust in God's love as well as His healing power. "Her relationship with God was very important to her," says Linda. "We studied the word of God together."

She also had a community of support; there was Tony, of course, but also our stepfather, Burt, and our uncle John, and her close friends and ex-boyfriends. Each helped her in different ways big and small— grocery shopping, running errands, doctors' appointments, trips to the bank. She was always effusive in saying "thank you" for whatever anyone did for her. If someone gave her a ride, she would offer that person too much gas money. She never wanted anyone to think she was a burden, nor that she was taking advantage of them. "That's why I overpay people," she used to say. "So, when I call them, they're more likely to come." Meanwhile, she continued her treatment of Cytoxan and the steroids.

Everyone I've spoken to about Rita says the same thing: she never complained about her situation, or her condition. I can vouch for that: Rita never lamented to me about her health struggles or her compromised lifestyle. Of course, it would've been understandable if she had, and who knows how she was feeling inside? But Rita never said, *Why me?* Not once.

38

On April 29, 1996, Rita turned forty. I sent her a bouquet of flowers, and a card I'd found from the Mahogany division of Hallmark that featured two brown-skinned women's legs, each wearing dynamic high-heeled shoes, one leopard-print, the other purple, with the words "For A Sister Whose Style Wows Me!" Inside, the card read: "You have a way of making life more special with your own unique style and the thoughtful touches you put into everything . . . that's why I love having you as my sister! Celebrate your day, Birthday Girl!" I signed it, "Love, your sister, Bridgett." She indeed celebrated, with a few friends. Because none of our siblings had made it to their fortieth birthday, hitting that milestone was *extremely* important to Rita. She wanted our mother to have a child who lived to age forty. That's how we talked about it, that it was a triumph for Mama's legacy. It never occurred to me that Rita actually worried about making it to forty. One of my big regrets is that I didn't fly in to be with her on her milestone birthday.

In keeping with the power of her personal number, Rita experienced four seismic events after turning forty. The first was that because of the chemotherapy treatments, she entered early menopause. When she tried to talk to me about how that felt, her sadness, I rushed to tell her how liberating it was, since she didn't want to have children anyway. I told her no more menstrual cycles with painful periods was a bonus, that if I were her, I'd be relieved. I didn't want her to feel bad, even as I secretly felt guilt for still having the childbearing option in my own life. But of course, it wasn't about me, it was about her; and for Rita it was both a symbolic and literal winding down, robbed of another vital part of her life as a young woman.

The second big event for Rita was that she officially retired on June 1 of that year. Again, to be so young and facing early retirement—not unlike our father, who faced disability at age thirty-seven—had to be hard on her. One of the things Dr. Indenbaum had told her over the years was that so many of his patients didn't *want* to work, and he'd marveled at how she'd been the opposite, always determined to keep working throughout the two decades since her lupus diagnosis. But now she just couldn't do it anymore. The way we talked about it was as a positive, a relief. She no longer had to struggle to keep a job alongside dealing with a precarious and unpredictable chronic illness. And luckily, Rita just barely managed to get in ten years of steady employment with the Detroit Board of Education to be eligible for retirement. It was, ultimately, a life-sustaining step.

Meanwhile, I geared up for a summer visit. I hadn't been home since Christmas. "Thinking about going to Detroit and being there with Rita and having to acknowledge that reality of her condition," I wrote in my journal. "Trying to be ready. Know that it's been too long since I've seen her and there's no good reason for that . . ." I knew that being home forced me to face a fuller reality than the one I lived in New York, and I dreaded it, even as I constantly missed and worried about Rita. Both were true.

The third big event that took place happened while I was visiting Rita that August. I was lying in her bed one morning, as she sat in a nearby chair. I remember exactly what I was feeling in the moments leading up to what happened: sorry for myself. I hated that I felt so alone and inadequate when it came to doing right by Rita. I hated that my whole adulthood had been shaped by family crisis and loss, and now, at age thirty-six, I had this gigantic new responsibility. I resented anew all the deaths. We should be a big family going through this with Rita, not just me and Tony. Having just turned twenty-five, he opened up to me on that visit how hard it was sometimes to live with an unwell person; he said he was going to do all he could for her, but he also wished he had someone to just "blow off steam" to about it all; I assured him he could talk to me. But it was all *so* unfair, and I was literally wallowing in self-pity when I heard Rita struggling to breathe. I looked over and saw her eyes roll back in her head; then she suddenly lost consciousness. I screamed, jumped out of bed, and slapped her face, yelling, "Rita! Rita! Rita!" over and over as a full minute or two passed—an eternity—before she regained consciousness. I called 911; only after she'd been admitted to the hospital did we learn she'd developed a blood clot that had traveled to her lung—i.e., a pulmonary embolism. Even though our mother had suffered many blood clots, they'd never traveled through her body, had always been caught and dissolved while still in her legs. Deborah likely suffered a blood clot while in the hospital, which did travel, fatally, through her heart. Now it was Rita. It wasn't lost on me that my being home might've helped save her life. "I can't afford to stay away that long again," I wrote anxiously in my journal afterward. "Certainly not while she's still struggling with her health." And then I added: "For myself too, I need to come home more; I face my grief here in a real way. I need that."

After experiencing that episode with Rita, in writing about it, I referred to her condition as "delicate," convincing myself that "good doctors are VITAL" but not in any way considering her long-term prognosis. Also, I noted anew my own good fortune, of being the healthy one. And then this odd thing happened: I remember standing at the foot of the staircase of Rita's home—she was still hospitalized—and as I was about to climb, an excruciatingly sharp pain hit my abdomen. I doubled over, gripping the handrail and gritting my teeth, as I waited for the pain to subside. And when it finally lessened, I slowly ascended the staircase, reality hitting me hard: The stress was getting to me. I could also develop a serious illness; I could die before *my* fortieth birthday.

I spent nine days in Detroit on that visit, and even though Rita was hospitalized for some of those days, I noted in my journal how good it felt to spend quality time with her. "We got to talk, to share, to affirm our love for each other," I wrote. "Home sweet home."

~

I remained rattled by Rita's experiencing a blood clot right before my eyes, but I tried to convince myself she was okay. Our mother had survived all her blood clots, after all. To deal with my anxiety, I threw myself into an overly busy life in New York. It was an easy thing to do. I found a list I kept around that time that included working on *Naked Acts*'s promotional needs (still hopeful the film could break out and save Rita financially), working on deepening my relationship with my boyfriend, Rob, writing both a novel and a new screenplay, doing the work to get promoted on my job, leading a writers' workshop in my home, and getting in "more visits to Rita." This I vowed to do while teaching three to four classes a semester as a newly tenured English and journalism professor. "I must keep my energy up so I can <u>endure</u>," I wrote at the bottom of that list. In all caps I wrote, "VITAMINS!!"

But despite my every effort to keep busy and not think about the hard stuff, a nightmare penetrated my subconscious; I saw this as both a wake-up call and proof that my faith in God needed an infusion. I wrote:

> Spirit really wants me to get this. Gave it to me in the form of a horribly frustrating dream. Deborah was lying in my childhood bed, suffering from an illness that involved massive bleeding and it was so bad that the ambulance wouldn't come; they told Rita to just prepare for her death. And Rita did; she was the calm one. She talked soothingly to her, telling her she'd be fine. And the point came when Deborah actually said, "Yeah, I do feel better." And then she died.
>
> It was scary.
>
> I don't know all that symbolizes. I know I fret over Rita in ways that aren't productive. I know that dream is about fear and helplessness. My own. And I know that without a spiritual base from which to deal with her and her illness, I'm at a loss. I can't deal.
>
> So here I am—given such clear markers over the past few days that even I with my blind eye to it all cannot ignore it anymore.
>
> I have to get back on path. Not so I can deal with Rita; and not so I can make myself successful—my two towering obsessions—I have to get into the flow of consciousness so I can live with myself.

~

The fourth big event that took place that year came when Rita moved from her three-bedroom house on Detroit's northwest side to a two-bedroom high-rise apartment downtown. In consultation with Dr. Indenbaum, Rita decided she could no longer handle the stairs in her Evergreen home, both in terms of doing laundry in the basement and climbing upstairs to her bedroom and bathroom. The struggle to walk was likely due in some part to the lingering effects of the ataxia combined with the side effects of the prednisone. (Research shows that women suffer more adverse effects from prednisone; I am convinced that means Black women do so at an even higher rate.) "It just wasn't conducive to what she was going through," says Tony, who had a front-row seat to her struggles.

Having elevators and everything on one floor just made sense, and Rita's first choice for a new place to live was Riverfront Towers. A luxury complex of three high-rise skyscrapers situated along the Detroit River, Riverfront is a special place in Detroit lore. Its most famous resident, Rosa Parks, lived there for eleven years until her death. Former Detroit mayor Coleman Young once lived there; and Aretha Franklin later lived there in the final weeks of her life. The apartments each have spectacular views of the river, the cityscape, and Canada's skyline. Rita was excited about the change. "I remember, she kept saying to me, 'I'm going to move to where I can have a view of downtown, and the water,'" recalls her grad-school friend Jennifer.

An apartment in Riverfront's newest tower suddenly became available that fall, so Rita and Tony had to move quickly. I flew home, grateful to have something concrete to do for her. She was so happy that I'd come. "I can't believe you got here so fast to help me!" she said more than once. She also bragged to her friends about how I'd dropped everything to be there to help her move. Her immense gratitude made me understand for the first time that our roles had shifted; I was now in many ways the big sister, not her. It frustrates me still, across the distance of time, that something so obvious took me so long to understand. I guess it's hard to think of yourself as anything but the role you were designated at birth. I was "the baby" for so long, I got stuck in that image of myself far longer than I should have.

The Riverfront turned out to be perfect for Rita. Its luxury design—walk-in closets, stacked washer/dryer unit, en suite bathroom off the master, and those stunning, expansive views from both the living room and bedrooms—made it feel like a genuine step up in life for her, rather than a downsizing. Rita called it her place of peace. This way, she didn't have to move as a forty-year-old single woman into an assisted living facility, which would've been such a blow, and yet, Riverfront had key in-house amenities, so that in many ways it functioned as a high-end version of one. There was a small grocery store on site, and the man who worked there would make special deliveries to Rita's apartment; there was also a hair salon, and a video store. Best of all, Riverfront had a bar and grill, and on the nights that Tony worked, Rita got many of her dinners there, delivered to her door. "She would do it all the time," Tony recalls. "They had some great meals too. They had a chicken salad that everybody was amazed by." Tony liked Riverfront for that reason alone. "I could stay at work, and I didn't have to worry about nothing," he recalls. "She could get what she needed, and she didn't have to leave her apartment."

And when she felt up to it, Rita could go down to the restaurant or the grocery store and get what she wanted for herself. Over time she became—no surprise—friendly with many of the folks who worked in the tower where she lived. And with a superintendent also on-site, she could get assistance for whatever repairs she needed in her apartment. Plus, she had access to a lovely riverfront promenade and a private courtyard. The Riverfront also had a shuttle bus that picked her up out front and took her where she needed or wanted to go. Between that service and the transit van the city provided, she was able to get to doctors' appointments, go shopping, visit friends, attend Unity Baptist Church—and be dropped back off at home. While it's hard to appreciate today with so many ridesharing and food-delivery services via apps, those amenities were a real help back in the late '90s. They gave Rita a sense of semi-independence.

Her friend Wilma recalls Rita visiting her in Oak Park a few times, brought there by the transit van after leaving a Bible study group in the area. Rita loved studying the Word, and really delving into the Bible's many stories, finding strength in their wisdom. Not long ago, I found more than a dozen pages of notes she'd written on yellow legal-pad paper: "The Book of John, Chapter 11, 38–46. This is the only book which recorded the event of Lazarus. . . . Read I Thessalonians 4:13–18. Paul told them not to sorrow because they would see their love ones again . . . God lives in our souls." And one of Rita's favorite books was *Women of the Bible*, which she said gave those ancient women their rightful due, as much more than mere secondary figures.

One of the biggest bonuses of living at Riverfront for Rita was having neighbors nearby, in the building. Rita made fast friends with a few, including a man named Dre who was confined to a wheelchair. She used to visit him regularly and help him with small things. Basically, she felt safe in that environment—a feeling her limited vision and compromised walking had largely stolen from her. At Riverfront, she felt nurtured, among friends, protected. It was a real community. "This place reminds me of when I was in college at Fisk," she once said to me. I could see that; she never did move off campus while in college, and she loved Riverfront in a similar way.

~

While not to the extent I'd hoped, having made the film did bring me some extra revenue—largely through speaking gigs and freelance writing—that allowed me to help out Rita financially. While she was managing well enough in retirement, she was also living in an expensive high-rise apartment. Her rent was $1,140 a month (more than $2,200 today), so her budget was tight. Sometimes she needed help to make ends meet. She always made it clear that she was just borrowing the money from me, that she'd pay it right back; I respected that as her way of not feeling dependent on her little sister, of maintaining her dignity. She called them loans, and she'd pay on those loans as best she could, and when she needed more money, I'd send it. During that time, she wrote to me on a yellow legal pad, her handwriting much larger than usual, so she could actually see what she was writing. It was the first letter I'd received from her in over three years:

11–8–96

Hey Bridgett,
Just me sending you a payment on my outstanding debt. Thanks for everything. I love you very much.

Love Ya,
Rita

Three months later, she wrote me again on paper from her same yellow legal pad:

Hey Bridgett,
I hope by the time you receive this letter everything will be going well with you.
    I am sending you two more checks, and this will be the last time I will have to pay after the due date for Visa.
    Well, take care and give my love to Rob.

Love Ya
Rita

With the most recent letter, her handwriting had really improved, which suggested that the Cytoxan treatments were helping her vision; she'd been saying her eyesight was improving, despite her ophthalmologist's doubts. It looked as though she was right. That was the thing with Rita's condition: she believed she would get better, and sometimes she did get better, which gave her—and me—so much hope. That's one of the many things that makes lupus so wily; it can and does go into remission.

In keeping with my vow to visit Rita more often, I was with her on August 31, 1997, the day Princess Diana was killed in a car crash. As we watched the nonstop TV coverage together, both stunned, Rita reminded me that I'd worn a "Lady Di" straw hat during my college graduation weekend way back when. I had admired Princess Diana's style like millions of other women, and so had Rita, but what she'd most admired was Diana's ability to leave an unhappy marriage and seek love despite the royal family's pressure, and the media's glare. We sat together in silence for a long time. Clearly, death could chase down anybody, even a young, rich, and beautiful princess. Finally, Rita sighed deeply and said with so much sadness: "Just when she found some happiness, she died." I nodded, feeling a rush of emotion for Rita in that moment, she who kept trying to be happy despite this horrid chronic disease causing her one setback after another.

39

I'd been the lucky one and found some happiness with Rob. We were now engaged, and one of my great joys was seeing how much Rita loved Rob, but more importantly how loving he was toward her. Watching him interact with Rita—his kindness and gentleness and playfulness—made me love him more. When we took her back to the airport after one of her visits, it meant so much to Rita that Rob waited beside her as she sat in the wheelchair until someone arrived to wheel her to the gate. "He was so patient, wasn't in a rush or anything," Rita said to me later. "He didn't just park me to the side like so many people do and move on. He waited with me. I really appreciated that."

She told me she especially liked seeing how he cared for me. "You found a man just like Daddy," she once told me. "He spoils you." Knowing she genuinely adored Rob made our getting married easier for me. I clearly wanted Rita to feel she was gaining another member of the family, was in no way losing her sister to marriage. That helped ease some of my secret guilt, of having found my soulmate when she had yet to find her own special person. I didn't express this feeling to anyone. What I did share with Rita was how taken aback I was by the excitement friends and acquaintances felt when I told them I was getting married. "Why is *that* the most exciting thing about me?" I lamented. "We've been through so much," Rita explained. "People are just happy to share in some good news for a change."

As I planned the wedding, I thought a lot about how to make Rita feel a part of the ceremony, even as I understood that she couldn't do a lot of walking. We chose to get married and have our reception in one location, at the Museum for African Art in SoHo, which had no stairs to climb, and an elevator. I chose my godsister Vatrize to be my maid of honor, so that Rita didn't have to navigate a long walk down the aisle or stand beside me at the altar throughout the ceremony. With Tony accompanying her to New York, he was beside her to tend to her needs. And Rita's dear friend Wilma also came to the wedding, to be with Rita for the weekend, and to be more support. Also, our mother's closest childhood friend, Nanette, came from Nashville, along with her daughter Dee, a nurse. Dee tended to Rita at the hotel, dressing a leg wound she had, and keeping her trained eye on her. That weekend, Rita was surrounded by a penumbra of caretakers, each of whom made sure she was safe. And, feeling safe, Rita had a great time. Re-watching our wedding video recently, I can see that she walks slowly but with purpose to her seat, with the help of a pretty, lace-trimmed cane that complements her outfit; she's dressed in a beautiful cream-colored dress and matching silk jacket she had custom-made for the occasion, and she's smiling. She has her hand slipped through Tony's arm as he holds on to her, guiding her to their front seats, their special bond on display. At the time, I thought Rita was doing so well, but other guests saw what love didn't allow me to see. "It was clear she was struggling, but that she was determined to show up for you," my friend Sharon later said to me.

In that brief span of suspended time during the ceremony, Rita was her old self. At one point, when Rob and I read our vows to one another, I pulled out my little "cheat sheet," and Rita said, "You don't have that memorized? That's a damn shame," and I looked back at her, incredulous. A funny moment. Later, at the next day's wedding brunch, Rita held court at her table, engaging in a lively conversation with my friend Karen's husband, Dale. I remember friends of mine coming over to greet her, kiss her cheek. "She had a great time," Tony confirms. "When we got back home, she couldn't stop talking about it," he says. "I'd hear her on the phone, telling a friend, 'Girl, they had a beautiful sit-down dinner, and they jumped the broom, and her friend Carla sang her butt off. It was really nice!'"

In that Ziploc bag that Rita carried everywhere in her purse, where she kept special photos, one of them was a picture of us at the wedding—a group shot of me and Rob and Rita and Tony and Wilma. Rob has his arms around me and Rita. Her sweet smile dazzles.

My feelings about being the healthy one were ever complicated. But Rita's happiness for me never was. It was pure.

~

I saw her again a couple months after the wedding when Rob and I attended my twentieth high school reunion. One day, during that visit, she and I rode out to Milford, Michigan, forty miles northwest of Detroit, where the sprawling General Motors proving ground is located. She wanted to revisit the place where she once worked as a "light vehicle tester" when she was a twenty-two-year-old young woman, the place where she'd endeared herself to others in the few short months she'd worked there. (One of the many floral arrangements at our father's funeral was signed from "Friends of GM, Proving Ground.")

As we pulled up to the test facility I was awed by its massive size; I hadn't realized that it's situated on thousands of acres. Rita and I went inside the main entrance, and she told the woman at the visitor's desk that she was once a test driver. The woman was impressed, as it was still rare to see women in that job, and she gave us a promotional folder filled with press about the proving ground, including photos that captured cars moving along the simulated highways. Rita really enjoyed her "trip down memory lane," as she called it.

Later, when I'd returned to New York, she wrote me a quick note, letter number twenty-two:

9/7/98

Hey Bridgett,
I'm sending you an article on women test drivers.

Love Ya,
Rita

Her handwriting was its former self, confident and pretty, with flourishes. My heart leapt.

I saw Rita again that fall, when I showed my film at the Detroit & Windsor International Film Festival at St. Andrew's Hall. I got to thank her again from the stage for her role in helping me raise money and lending her support. I hold on to an image of her in my mind from that night: She's coming toward me in the lobby of the venue, her hair in African-style braids that flow down her shoulders; she's looking good, healthy. As she makes her way to me and I take her in, my love for her makes me slightly dizzy, and I have to quickly regain my equilibrium. I'm awash in relief, happiness.

My joy was brief. During Thanksgiving weekend, I opted to go to Cleveland to spend the holiday with Rob and my new in-laws, buoyed by how well Rita was doing. But I got a call that Friday from Tony, who told me that Rita had been hospitalized; I flew to Detroit, Rob beside me. When we arrived at her hospital room, I found Rita sitting on the side of her bed, doctors forming an arc around her. She looked up at me and said, "I had a stroke." Then she started to cry. Never before had I seen her cry over her health—not when she had to take high doses of steroids, nor when she needed to receive chemotherapy, nor when she lost her vision, nor when she had to learn to walk again, nor when she experienced a blood clot in her lung. She'd soldiered through every one of the medical complications the lupus had inflicted upon her.

But the stroke scared Rita. It scared me. Our father had died from a series of strokes when he was fifty-one. She was forty-two.

A CT scan of her brain showed a "left hemispheric stroke in the distribution of the middle cerebral artery." The cause, doctors hypothesized, was either "thrombosis from a hypercoagulable state or possibly vasculitis leading to thrombosis," and definitely lupus-related. In other words, she had another blood clot, this one in the brain, possibly caused by damaged blood vessels. Also, her platelet count was low, a result of her immune system attacking itself. She was treated, once again, with a high dosage of steroids.

Within weeks, her neurologist determined that Rita had "made a nice recovery." She was able to come to New York for Christmas, and other than needing one of her pretty canes to aid with her balance, she had no remaining symptoms of the stroke. And while she'd also been recently diagnosed with hepatitis B and prescribed a new drug to treat that condition, which carried among its side effects "malaise and fatigue and headache," Dr. Indenbaum told her not to worry about that; the hep B was a minor health concern, relatively speaking. And so we celebrated the holidays together, rejoicing in her recovery.

During Rita's visit, I made a miscalculation: Given that we lived in a one-bedroom walk-up, I thought she'd be more comfortable if we put her up in a small hotel in the Village, for a change. But someone stole all the cash out of an envelope she had on her nightstand, taking advantage of her obvious disabilities. I wanted to believe, as she did, that she was always getting better, getting back to her healthier self; I wanted to see her as capable of more than she was, because I wanted her to be. Once again, she'd come so far, and we all wanted to believe the worst was behind her; what else can you believe about someone you love so desperately? I wanted her to be able to stay alone in a New York City hotel as she'd done many times before in her adult life, but she couldn't be left on her own like that anymore. She just couldn't. We promptly checked her out of that place.

I have a treasured photo from that visit, a picture of Rita and Rob. He's bending down, his face close to hers as he holds a glass of red wine and smiles at the camera; Rita smiles too—her hair in those long braids I loved—but her hand is out, as if to say, *Wait!* Yet her face glows, cheeks full, skin smooth, her beauty shining through.

~

In early March 1999, I learned I was pregnant. My ob-gyn advised us not to tell anyone until we'd reached the end of the first trimester, which meant that when Rita came to visit us in April, I didn't tell her. I regretted that after the fact, but at the time I didn't want to have to potentially share bad news with her if I did have a miscarriage. I was almost thirty-nine, and mine considered a geriatric, high-risk pregnancy. When I did tell her, after the twelve-week mark, Rita said that she'd suspected I was pregnant, because she knew *something* was off about me during her visit. "I wish Mama could be here for this," she said. "I'm glad I am," she added. When she said that, I felt it physically, as a kind of double jolt to my heart: my gratitude, and her joy about the baby.

That summer, when JFK Jr.'s plane went missing, and it was later announced on Tony's birthday, July 19, 1999, that fragments of the plane had been found, Rita and I talked through the news coverage together on the phone. When his and his wife's and sister-in-law's bodies were found two days later, I was undone. The Kennedys were writ large in my life for a few reasons: First, John-John and I were the same age; our mother had told me how she and the First Lady were pregnant at the same time. Moreover, the Kennedys were a famous family that had experienced repeated tragedies. As someone whose family had experienced the same, I looked to them as a kind of normative presence, proof that we Davises weren't freaks, or being punished by God. Cumulative losses can happen to *any* family, even the rich, famous, and powerful. This particular public tragedy hit me so hard, and I cried so much that Rita told me, "Listen, you're pregnant. You cannot afford to let this get you so upset. You have to get yourself together for the baby's sake." Again, she was my big sister, worrying about *my* well-being rather than the other way around. It felt good to feel her concern, and it felt good to be on the receiving end, which meant Rita was not in crisis. She was doing fine.

I visited her that summer, a final pregnancy trip before the baby came; we drove around a lot in my rental car, just talking, often about the old days, our family, good memories. She told me that she'd been under the care of a psychiatrist at Henry Ford Hospital, where I was born, and had begun taking an antidepressant, Prozac; as her doctor explained, chronic illness often leads to depression. She said it was really helping to lift her mood, and I was glad she was getting mental health care. We also had a candid conversation about our mother, about what it meant for each of us to inherit some of her strengths, but also some of her flaws. Mama didn't like to ask for help yet felt that others should offer it simply by seeing that she needed it. Rita was the same way. And our mother sometimes lived in denial when it came to the people she loved, not seeing what was painful to see. I was the same way.

I never felt I was doing enough for her, but Rita thanked me often for what I *was* doing, and she made a point of saying how much she appreciated that I never rushed her, always showed her patience. Once, we'd decided to go to our favorite downtown restaurant, Fishbones, and after I parked the car on a slight incline, I found that I couldn't push her so well in the wheelchair that she was now using to help her get around. She apologized, and I told her there was nothing to apologize for as I struggled to get her up the little hill. It was almost comical. Almost. Those days, I'd tell her she was doing so well, given all she was up against. I wanted to encourage her belief that she could get better, even as I didn't give her much room to discuss her fears, or how much effort it took to keep going.

One day while I was with her at the Riverfront apartment, Rita sat in her wheelchair inside her small kitchen, dressed in a sweat suit and eating a sandwich she'd made for herself. I was talking to her about not allowing herself to be stressed, getting enough rest, not trying to do too much. "You can't exert yourself!" I was telling her, probably for the umpteenth time, the way our aunt and our uncle and her friends would relentlessly tell her the same thing, admonish her for overexerting herself. Rita shrugged her shoulders heavily and said, "But I'm not doing anything." And then, her hands trembling (a symptom of her medication), she bit into her sandwich and nibbled a bit. Looking at her sitting there, so vulnerable and alone, I felt devastated. Even now I don't fully understand why seeing her that way on that particular day, hands trembling, caused me so much anguish, why I suddenly felt so deeply sorry for her, or why that brief moment stays so resolutely in my mind, why it still brings tears to my eyes. I guess that was the moment I could no longer deny the brutal truth: Nothing Rita could do would slow the progression of her disease; she *had* done all she could to be treated for it, adjust her life around it, try not to exacerbate it, face it, live with it. But lupus is relentless.

Lupus is also, as I've said, wildly unpredictable. That fall, in the final month of my pregnancy, I wrote in my journal, "Rita's health is good. My job is to stay positive and stay focused!" She sent me a hand-painted card designed by a friend of hers with a gorgeous yellow-and-orange floral design, and the words "I Love You"; inside she wrote, "Bridgett & Rob, thanks for being my 'guardian angels.'

Love Ya, Rita." One month later, on November 8, our son, Tyler, was born. I am writing this on his twenty-fourth birthday, and it awes me to think so much time has passed, how vivid that day nearly a quarter of a century ago remains, as I called Rita to let her know he'd arrived. She missed my call, and so I left a voice message, Tyler's newborn cry caught on tape. She called me right back, and I missed *her* call. But I still remember her voicemail message: "I can hear my little nephew's cries! Tell him his auntie Rita loves him!"

She was managing, with the help of home health-care aides visiting her regularly. Luckily, she was still able to travel, and so Rita came to New York for Christmas '99; Wilma helped her pack and get to the airport and make her way to me. I remember that day, standing at the gate at LaGuardia Airport, watching her walk off the plane, teetering on unsteady legs, dressed in a striped top, her hair flowing, wanting to look good for me. It's another image that lingers. During her visit, I loved watching my sister hold the baby in her arms; she vowed, not for the first time, that *this* nephew was going to call her Auntie Rita. We danced to Smokey Robinson and the Miracles' song "Ooo Baby Baby" (our sister Dianne's favorite) with Tyler in my arms. We talked about how much our mother would've loved and indulged him. We ate Cornish hens for Christmas dinner, Rita's favorite. I took a picture of her holding Tyler, six weeks old and dressed in a red-striped holiday onesie. Rita looks right at the camera, smiling gently; her hair has miraculously grown back despite the chemo, and hangs down to her shoulders, falling over one eye; she's wearing red lipstick and a sparkly gold top. I soon framed the photo and placed it beside Tyler's changing table.

When I took Rita to the airport to return home, I didn't want her to go. I had a feeling. And then I realized I'd made yet another miscalculation by bringing her to the airport on my own, without Rob, who was home with the baby. I hadn't parked the car in short-term parking because I knew that walk was too onerous for her, and we didn't have a wheelchair with us. That meant I had to pull up to the curb, put my flashers on, and get her as far as the airport terminal before returning to my car. I couldn't walk her to the gate. And so I had to hand her off to the airport employee once he arrived with a wheelchair. As he was about to wheel Rita away, I begged him, "Take care of her, okay?" Seeing what he thought was outsize worry in my eyes, he said, "I'll do my best, ma'am." I waved one last time at Rita, she waved back, and he turned the wheelchair around as he pushed my sister through the airport; I stood there, watching until they disappeared.

40

As the year 2000 approached, and the world planned for Y2K and its potential disruption, Rita was *so* excited about entering the twenty-first century. She asked me what I thought was the best phrase: "Happy New Millennium" or "Happy Millennium"? I was touched that she'd asked my advice and told her I thought the first way sounded best, and she agreed. Just as the clock struck midnight on New Year's Eve, I slipped away from the dinner party Rob and I were attending, baby Tyler sleeping nearby, and called her. "Happy New Millennium!" we said to each other. "I'm ready for this new decade!" she declared. "Me too!" I agreed. What neither of us said was that the last two decades of the twentieth century had been, all in all, a real bitch for us.

Funny what memories we hold on to: It's early in the new year and I'm walking to my college office on Park Avenue South from my West Fourteenth Street apartment. It's a thirty-minute walk crosstown, and I love it, a perk of living in Manhattan. I have a brand-new cell phone, my first. I call Rita and leave a message. Excited by this amazing technology, where I'm able to call my sister from a mobile phone I carry in my hand as I walk along the street, I give her my new number— accidentally transposing two of the digits in my excitement—and when I do speak to her later that day, she says she liked the sound of my voice on the recording. "You sound so exuberant," she said. "I played it twice, just to hear that happiness in your voice."

I used to have *her* voice on tape, but I lost it in a basement flood.

As the days moved from winter into spring, Rita's health was good. There'd been one emergency room visit, but the EKG and CAT scan both came back clear. She was coping pretty well with her visual impairment; despite being legally blind, she had a brand-new, more powerful eye appliance that helped her enlarge letters, so she could still manage to read and write. In fact, I found a draft of a lovely letter she'd written to a teacher:

Dear Mrs. Bush,

I am sending $5.00 to two of your 3rd grade students. Jeremy
Joyce and C. Miller displayed such gentlemanly qualities to me.
I met the two students at the AMC Theater. The two young
men assisted me in my wheelchair. Please keep up the good work
with them.

Sincerely,
Rita R. Davis

For Rob's birthday in April, we went to Cleveland to see his parents, so they could see the baby. Rob's father was suffering from ALS,
and his mother felt it important that we come. I remember thinking
that I would've rather seen Rita, but that this was what marriage was
about, taking turns seeing one another's family. I told myself that Rita
was doing well, and it was Rob's eighty-year-old father that we needed
to worry about. I planned to see her soon afterward. Meanwhile, on
April 12, Rita bought four Daily 3 lottery tickets, playing her favorite
three-digit number: 100. (That also happened to be the address of her
Riverfront apartment complex.) She played 100 straight and boxed
(meaning she'd win no matter what order the winning digits came
in); she also played 335 and 900 and 4030. As someone who grew up
around the numbers, and who'd both helped with and then taken over
our mother's business, playing numbers was still very much part of
Rita's everyday life. In fact, her friend Lillian remembers Rita going
to New York to visit me and asking Lillian to play her number, 100,
for her while she was away. Sure enough, the number came out. "I
couldn't wait to tell her when she got back that the Queen had hit the
lottery," says Lillian.

For Easter, she sent Tyler an enormous Easter basket, filled with
everything a five-month-old could want or need—sippy cups, bibs, a
stuffed bunny, teething rings, board books, toys. At the end of April,
Rita turned forty-four. Originally, I'd planned to bring Tyler with me
and visit her for her birthday. She said, "If you're coming alone with
the baby, I will definitely meet you at the airport 'cause you're gonna

need me!" But I ultimately chose not to come, overwhelmed by new mothering and the thought of traveling again so soon with a five-month-old. Instead, I sent her a card that read "For A Special Aunt," and I signed it, "Love, Tyler ☺."

A week later, she visited Beaumont Hospital's "preventative and nutritional medical facility" to receive supplemental drinks meant to help with weight loss. Despite the prednisone's weight-gaining side effect—due to water retention, increased appetite, and wreaking havoc on her metabolism—Rita's internist wanted her to try to lose weight through her diet; this is a never-ending medical bias against fatness: whatever the cause, it's your job to work against the odds to lose weight. Ironically, blood work revealed the next day that her thyroid-stimulating hormone level was abnormally low, i.e., her thyroid was overactive, causing her metabolism to slow down. This was a major strike against her weight-loss efforts, which should not have been her worry in the first place.

With the help of the city's transit van, Rita went to her beloved Unity Baptist Church that first Sunday in May, and afterward she told me how much she enjoyed the service. "Reverend Stotts was really on fire today!" she said. He'd been the pastor of Unity since 1963, and by all accounts was an old-fashioned devoted and humble man of God. Rita absolutely adored him. Wilma says Rita would talk about Reverend Stotts so much that she would tease her and say, "You just go to church to see him!" Says Wilma: "We would laugh about that." On this particular Sunday, Rita said, Reverend Stotts spoke about the church moving toward the twenty-first century "under God's direction."

Days later, on what would've been our mother's seventy-second birthday, Tyler had his six-month pediatric visit; the doctor confirmed that he was hitting all his markers and thriving. Also on that day, Rita went to a doctor's appointment, where from the office she wrote a letter back to her friend Lillian's son, David, who was briefly incarcerated and approaching his release. ("I hope by the time you receive this, all is going fine.") "She was such a sweet, jovial, and warm person who came into my life," David told me recently. "With

Rita, you felt she genuinely cared about you and genuinely liked you. I needed that."

On my first Mother's Day, Rita and I chatted for a long time, mostly about how we wished our mother could've met Tyler, her third grandson, and how ironic that there'd been no granddaughters yet. And later in May, when I turned forty, Rita sent me a beautiful card designed by her artist friend, this one made especially for me. It had three hand-painted balloons in yellow and pink, the number "40" written inside the biggest balloon. Rita wrote in an unsteady hand, "Bridgett, Happy birthday! I want you to know that you are very 'special' to me. Enjoy entering a new decade of your life. Love Ya, Rita."

I placed that card prominently on the altar in my bedroom. In my journal I reflected on turning forty, and my life since our mother's death. "These past eight years since anyone has died have largely been spent watching Rita struggle to stay alive," I wrote.

Rita and I chatted as usual over the phone in the ensuing days. She told me about going back to Beaumont Hospital's weight control center, where she'd been given a box of those special low-calorie drinks. She swore the vanilla flavor was not so bad. I told her that Tyler was teething, and she shared a tip she'd heard: place a washcloth in the freezer, then let him gnaw on that to bring some relief. I told her I'd let her know if that method worked, and we hung up. I had no way of knowing that would be the last normal conversation I'd have with my sister.

When I spoke to Rita next, a day in early June, she told me our cousin Elaine was there in the apartment with her. This surprised me because Elaine lived in Atlanta, and I hadn't heard anything about her visiting Detroit.

"Really?" I asked. "Let me speak to her."

"She can't come to the phone right now," said Rita.

I talked to her a bit longer and asked again to speak to Elaine. I knew if our cousin was there, I'd hear her voice in the background. And she'd definitely want to say hello to me. I suspected she wasn't there, and therefore something with Rita was not okay. Something was wrong. "She was conjuring me in her hour of need," Elaine later says when I tell her about this moment.

Rita also told me Tony was there, but he never came to the phone either. I implored her to go to the hospital, and she promised she would. That entire weekend, I kept calling her, sometimes getting her voicemail, other times getting her talking slightly illogically. With Tony's help, she did finally get herself to the hospital on Monday. She didn't leave for five weeks.

It's known that lupus often attacks the body's organs, and the brain is in fact an organ. Turns out her brain was inflamed, affecting her mental functioning. She received a battery of tests, including EKGs and ECGs, an EEG, a doppler echo exam of her heart, and a 2D cardiac ultrasound, as well as brain MRIs. I spoke to her rheumatologist, Dr. Indenbaum, and told him I was worried about her cognition, that our conversations since she'd been in the hospital had remained "off." But he said not to worry, Rita had had different forms of this before, and he knew the course of treatment needed. A round of Cytoxan and "major amounts" of steroids had begun, he said, and generally did the job, so she should be stabilized soon. Finding myself in the same situation I'd been in six years before, when I went to France to write about the Cannes Film Festival, I told him I was planning to travel to San Francisco with my family for a week, to attend a writers' workshop. Did he think I should come to Detroit instead? He assured me there was no reason to do so, because there'd be nothing I could do if I were there. "We've seen this before," he repeated. "We know how to treat it."

Looking back, I wish I'd trusted my gut. Despite what Dr. Indenbaum was telling me, I knew this was different. Never before had Rita shown any lack of cognition, despite what her body was putting her through. But hope and trust in her doctor overrode my concerns; Tony and I discussed what I should do, and he told me he'd be visiting her at the hospital after work each day, so not to worry. I should go. And so, Rob and I and seven-month-old Tyler flew to San Francisco.

The trip to Northern California and the weeklong workshop with a well-known literary editor was a fortieth birthday gift to myself, as I attempted to jump-start my novel writing again. One of the in-class assignments we were given was to write a brief narrative of a time when you did something that surprised you. I wrote about hitting Rita with that brush after it flew from my hand back when we were teenagers—the first time I'd ever written anything about our relationship as sisters. Also, during the workshop week, we studied the work of Flannery O'Connor, and I learned that this renowned southern gothic writer wrote some of her best work while fighting lupus. O'Connor was diagnosed at age twenty-five. Doctors gave her five years to live, but she lived fourteen more, until age thirty-nine, which I found both moving and frightening. Needless to say, Rita was on my mind the entire week. And then on the sixth day, I got a call on my new cell phone from our uncle John. A doctor had called him—listed as her emergency contact—to say Rita's condition had worsened. I managed to reach Dr. Indenbaum. "Yes," he said, "I think it's best that you get here right away." We took a red-eye to Detroit that night, and so began the ordeal that unfolded across the next four months of Rita's life.

When I arrived at the hospital, she was in a coma, or what they were calling a "semi-coma," caused by her brain's inflammation. I was told by her neurologist that the next few days would be crucial, that it was a wait-and-see situation. Dr. Indenbaum told me that she'd had some seizures, but that was not unusual in lupus patients. So far, he admitted, the steroids weren't reducing the inflammation, but he trusted that the Cytoxan would help. "My hope is that she's not getting worse," he said. "It could take one or two weeks to see improvement." Hearing that, I did what I'd never done with any consistency before: I prayed without ceasing, using my Unity principles to thank God in advance for her recovery. And every day that I sat with Rita and rubbed her face and whispered in her ear, I repeated the same mantra: "Please wake up, Rita. I need you to wake up. Please wake up. I need you to wake up."

Eventually, Rob returned to New York to his job. Still nursing, I took Tyler everywhere with me, in his BabyBjörn and his blue-and-burgundy-plaid Maclaren stroller. Meanwhile, for the first time, I became intimately involved in Rita's health care, becoming her advocate, something she'd done so well for herself over the years (I used to joke that she sounded like a medical student, given her knowledge). I spoke with and got the pager numbers for her neurologist, radiologist, internist, resident, and attending doctor, as well as Dr. Indenbaum; I learned the results of every test—from a CAT scan of her head to more MRIs of her brain, to spinal X-rays, to magnetic images of her chest and abdomen, to a needle biopsy and blood smears; I made sure to be there as a catheter was inserted into her veins, and also when she received a spinal tap; I learned what her blood pressure was on a daily basis, and the names and side effects of all the medications she was taking. I kept track of the names and shifts of her morning and evening and midnight nurses; I became friendly with the nurses' aides. And I got familiar with the rhythms of the hospital's culture. Every day, I got an update on the status of her condition.

Meanwhile, I also stepped in and handled Rita's finances, as well as overseeing her medical-care coverage with insurance companies. It was discombobulating to drop into my forty-four-year-old sister's life in this way, given how independent she'd been. It felt both like spying and trying to read hieroglyphics. I had to figure out the most intimate details of her personal life without her help. Using my pocket calendar/address book that boasted on its cover the words THE MILLENNIUM 2000, I started collecting the telephone numbers of Rita's friends near and far, our relatives in Nashville and elsewhere, as well as her pastor and fellow church members. I collected more than sixty names and numbers, telling myself it was just good to have them. "Rita is facing her biggest lupus challenge to date," is how I expressed it in my journal.

During that time, Elaine actually did come to Detroit—as Rita had earlier hallucinated—and she did visit Rita, at the hospital, with a friend of hers named Janiece. I missed her visit, but she left a note:

Bridgett—
Here this morning, Janiece and Elaine. We anointed with fresh
oil this lovely lady, child of God. We had Prayer and a visit with
our Sister Rita this beautiful day from 7:45–8:30 on our way to
church.

Peace be unto you.

After several days—a lifetime—Rita woke up.

I was so relieved, utterly grateful. She still was not yet her old
self; she couldn't remember what had happened before she came to the
hospital, and she wasn't fully conversant yet. She clearly had suffered
memory loss. But she was alive, and she could speak, and that meant
she could get better. Tyler and I spent the Fourth of July in Rita's
downtown apartment, witnessing the fireworks explode over the Detroit River. I left the next day, after receiving a call from organizers
of a film festival at the New Jersey Performing Arts Center: Was I
still coming to show my film that night? I'd completely forgotten, but
I promised to be at the event. Luckily, Rita was being moved out of
ICU into a regular room. And of course, Tony was there, our bedrock.
After spending eighteen days in Detroit, Tyler and I flew back to New
York. I wish I could say I noticed something amiss at the time with
Tyler's teething process, but my focus was primarily on Rita. Now
that she was out of critical care, the goal was to get her fully walking
again, and back to herself. I lobbied hard with her doctors to get her
to a rehab facility. They complied, and the next step was fighting with
Medicare and Blue Cross Blue Shield to get her back to Heartland's
rehab facility in West Bloomfield. That was the facility where she'd
spent time before, when she'd suffered the partial paralysis, and she'd
done well there, liked the place, and so I was determined to have her
return there. Gratefully, I won that battle, and she was transferred to
Heartland.

Upon discharge, Rita's medical expenses from her thirty-eight-day
stay at Beaumont Hospital—from the semiprivate room to lab work
to medications to tests to therapies to the operating room—totaled

$98,132. In today's dollars, that's close to $178,000. Physicians' charges included an additional $7,982. She was responsible for only $17.47. Medicare and Blue Cross Blue Shield covered the remaining costs. Likewise, the rehab facility was costing $3,589 per week, also covered by her health insurance. That's when I more fully understood what Rita always knew: Had she not pushed herself to work all those years, so many days not feeling well at all, as a Michigan Public School employee, had she not pushed herself to get in ten years of work so she could retire with full benefits, what would've been Rita's options? What quality of care would she have received? What would've become of her?

Microaggressions and implicit bias abounded, I'm sure, in subtle and unquantifiable ways during Rita's sojourn through the medical world's labyrinth. I can imagine what might've happened to her had she been navigating that same medical maze while on Medicaid. Without good insurance, I'm convinced Rita would've been quickly blamed for her own condition, not taken seriously, and essentially doomed from the start. Many studies confirm this. One report published by the Urban Institute in 2022 found that "Patients with Medicaid coverage . . . may encounter providers who have negative perceptions about uninsured and publicly insured people, resulting in providers and their staff shaming, ignoring, or otherwise disrespecting these patients." The report goes on to note that "Providers may also alter their clinical decisions if they perceive, based on the patient's health insurance type or lack of insurance, that a patient may be unable to pay for services."

Even with her "good" insurance, I had to advocate for Rita constantly. For example, one of my priorities was to get a phone in her room at the rehab facility. For some reason, that was a struggle, a service that wasn't automatically provided to patients. But I knew that phones were her lifeline, and a means for me to check up on her regularly; I was desperately looking for ways that Rita's brain could be stimulated to heal; I'd already shared my concerns with both Dr. Indenbaum and Rita's neurologist that she still seemed disoriented, as if hallucinating, unable to remember things; her speech was different, slower, and she often seemed extremely tired, yawning a lot. Her neurologist said the only thing to do was give it time, and so I asked Dr. Indenbaum to help me. The letter he wrote to the rehab facility laid out in clear language what my conversations with her neurologist had not. I was grateful to Dr. Indenbaum, but it was sobering to see it written in black and white:

To Whom It May Concern:

RE: Rita Davis

Ms. Davis is under my care with severe systemic lupus erythematosus. Because of that she has a neurologic problem, which does not allow her to interact with people easily, and she is also blind from the illness.

    For her emotional stability and ability to improve she should have more interaction with people. I have advised that she must absolutely have a telephone, and she should try to be talking to people for hours and hours a day. In addition, I would give authorization to Ms. Davis' sister to turn on the phone.

    I trust this information will be of help.

Sincerely,
Samuel D. Indenbaum, M.D.

"It's scary," I wrote in my journal, about seeing Rita's lupus described as "severe." Yet I also wrote, "My 40th year will be characterized by my growing up and facing much more responsibility for Rita's well-being. It'll be marked by my dealing with all manner of financial matters—hers, mine, ours." I also had another realization: "And this year will also be marked by decisions made about where to live. Will Rita come to New York with me? Will she fully recover (yes, yes, yes!!!)? I am her family, and with that comes responsibility. Full responsibility, I now understand."

41

Twelve days after Rita entered the rehab facility, Tyler and I returned to Detroit. My goal was for us to stay an entire month, leading up to the day I had to return for my fall semester of teaching. I arranged to keep paying Tyler's babysitter the entire time, so as not to lose her. And then I stepped more fully into the role of Rita's primary advocate. Doctors told me they were closely watching inflammation now on her spine and tracking her hemoglobin; I noticed her wincing a lot, and when she said her tummy hurt, I conveyed this to her internist, who had her see a gastroenterologist. Most importantly, I arranged for a meeting with her team at the rehab facility; I brought all her sparkly, sequined baseball caps in an array of colors to her room, so she could wear them and feel a bit more like herself; likewise, I brought a cassette player and a few of her favorite songs on tape—Teena Marie and Rick James, Chaka Khan, Reverend James Cleveland's gospel songs. We got the phone in her room.

Most days, I had Tyler with me, pushing him around in his stroller; I often parked it in Rita's room at the facility. But some days, I took Tyler to our cousin Jewell, whose own son was just two months older than he; I left them playing together on the carpet, Tyler and Joe-Joe, which allowed me to be at the rehab facility more hours, especially during the times Rita received physical therapy. I believed she could get better, using rehab to get back to herself as she'd done before. But when Rita and I met with the team—physical therapist and occupational therapist and social worker and speech therapist and nurse and doctor—the social worker asked Rita what her goals were for improvement, and she couldn't articulate what they were. Her neurological challenges were such that she was unable to express any complex thoughts. That was the difference this time around, and it was a big one.

That's when two thoughts hit me at once: *She may not come back to her former self for a while, and until she does, she may need twenty-four-*

hour-care. I started immediately lobbying for her to stay at Heartland for the maximum one hundred days her insurance would allow—a tricky approval process, but not impossible. I was trying to buy time to set up the next phase of Rita's life. In my little notebook, I wrote what I saw as our options: bring her home and pay a close family friend or two to be her temporary caretaker or find an assisted living facility we could afford; if we couldn't afford any, then sell her house to pay for her care. Meanwhile, Tony and I arranged for his childhood friend who's an attorney to meet me at the facility with the required document so Rita could legally give me power of attorney. Her signature was the shakiest I'd ever seen it.

Somewhere in there, our cousin Ava (our mother's brother's daughter) flew in from Nashville to visit Rita. But Rita wouldn't come out of the bathroom, unwilling for Ava to see her "like this." She adored Ava, and so I just couldn't understand why she wouldn't come out. But Ava, in her loving way, said, "It's okay if she doesn't want to; don't make her."

"I don't remember that at all," Ava recently said to me. "I knew she was getting progressively worse, but . . ." She trails off. "She was my first cousin, and although I was the older cousin, I looked up to her, you know? I remember the good things."

Another time, several family members were in Rita's room visiting, including our uncle John. At one point, Rita looked out the picture window and said, "Look at those big birds flying by; aren't they beautiful?" There were no birds. No one commented on Rita's hallucination, but I will never forget the look on our uncle John's face. In the years since our mother's death, Uncle John and Rita had gotten very close; she often stopped by his house to visit after church, or whenever she was in the area; after her health devolved, Uncle John had stepped in to be a father figure to Rita, taking her to doctors' appointments and wherever else she needed to go. She listened as he spoke about his life, and through him she learned more about our Nashville kin. They really bonded. The worry in his face that day made me see what I hadn't wanted to see.

When I wasn't at the rehab facility, I was handling Rita's finances (paying bills, collecting rent, going to the bank, etc.) and trying to maintain the small details of her life until she could return to it, like going through her mail, returning library books on tape, and canceling her subscription to the *Detroit Free Press*. I spent an inordinate amount of time on the phone with both Blue Cross Blue Shield and Medicare—imploring them to qualify her for the maximum rehab stay. I also located her life insurance policy (I didn't even tell myself what that meant, my looking for it). Meanwhile, having found her telephone book, I called folks each evening to keep them updated on her condition.

What I was *not* doing was paying close attention to Tyler, beyond caring for his immediate needs. That's why when I had him with me at the rehab facility one day, and my oldest and dearest friend Diane met me there, she surprised me when she said jokingly, "Wow, that tooth coming into his mouth has him looking like a little bucktooth thing!" Until then, I simply hadn't noticed anything odd about Tyler's mouth. When I look back at a visual timeline by studying photographs, I see that his face was fine when we arrived in Detroit in mid-June. By late June, in a series of pictures I took of him with Rita's godmother, Lula, the changes to his appearance are slight; you have to look for them. But it stuns me when I look back at photos taken of him in Rita's room at Heartland later in the summer, as he sits beside her friend Wilma, just before Diane made her comment to me. His little face is slightly swollen, creating exaggerated "age" lines under his eyes and too-puffy cheeks. It seems obvious to me now, the slight deformity, but I just didn't see it, until I did.

Nine days after we'd arrived, alarmed by Diane's comment, I abruptly switched plans and decided to fly home immediately, to take Tyler to his pediatrician; I planned to have him treated, if need be, for his teething issue, then return to Detroit. Tyler and I went to the rehab facility en route to the airport, and I gave Rita a big kiss, said, "I love you"; she said back to me, "I love you." I hugged her shoulders, and told her, "I'll see you soon." The date was August 2. I was sure I'd be back in Detroit within a week or two, at the most.

The next day, Tyler's pediatrician, Dr. Senzamici, took one look at his protruding mouth and told me: "You need to go straight to NYU College of Dentistry. Don't go home, just go straight there." She was alarmed without trying to show alarm. I did exactly what she told me to do, walking there from her office. Because it was a dental hospital, I wasn't too worried. Not yet. But when I arrived at NYU, and a dental resident examined Tyler, he told me that my nine-month-old needed immediate surgery to remove a growing tumor in his gum. "I can do the procedure, no problem. We'll operate at Bellevue Hospital," he said, referring to New York City's major public hospital. This new oral surgeon in training was pressing me hard, and it seemed to me he was excited to perform an operation he hadn't yet done. "We need to move quickly!" he said.

I was overwhelmed. First, the words "surgery" and "tumor" terri-fied me. Also, I wanted my son under a specialist's care, not for him to be a guinea pig in a procedure performed by an inexperienced doctor in clinical training. It all felt wrong. I stood there, in the middle of the main floor at NYU College of Dentistry, and burst into tears, Tyler clinging to me in the BabyBjörn carrier on my chest. I hadn't al-lowed myself to cry over anything in the past three months, and now I couldn't stop. Hearing my sobs, an older, kind-faced man stepped out of his office. "What's going on here?" he asked. The resident began to explain, clearly deferential to this man. But he held up his hand to the eager young doctor and asked *me* to explain. Through my sobs, I said, "I'm being told that my son needs surgery, but I want to know exactly what that means, and I want him to have *his own* doctor, and he's only nine months old, and this is so scary and . . ." This kind-faced man held up his hand for me to pause, gently guided me into his office, and invited me to sit down. He told me he completely understood my concern, and he introduced himself. His name was Stuart Super, and he had the right name. "I will be your son's oral surgeon," he told me. "He has some form of maxillofacial tumor, and we'll determine what it is, and from there, we will very cautiously decide what to do next." I thanked him profusely.

I subsequently learned that Dr. Super was revered. An oral surgeon who'd received his Doctor of Dental Medicine degree from Harvard, he had three decades of experience as an oral and maxillofacial specialist and had trained dozens of other oral surgeons; he was also renowned for repairing the cleft palates of children around the world. Had Dr. Super not been there at that precise moment, had he not opened the door to his office to find out what the commotion was all about, everything might've been different for Tyler. What changed for me that day was that my primary focus shifted to Tyler and his needs. I was awash in guilt. How had I missed this? Why wasn't I a better mother? Why had I let myself care for Rita at the exclusion of my vulnerable little baby boy?

Rob and I met with Dr. Super the next day, and he told us his plan: Because of our son's young age, he wanted to be overly cautious, even as he understood the need to move as quickly as possible, because the tumor was growing. Dr. Super said he needed to do a biopsy to determine whether the tumor was cancerous, and then devise a plan for surgery. I couldn't believe what I was hearing—that scary C word— and yet all I cared about was doing what needed to be done for our son to be healthy again. We met with Dr. Super again a few days later, and he carefully examined and x-rayed Tyler's gums. Then he sent us back to the pediatrician for Tyler to get a pre-op exam. It was a Friday. The biopsy procedure was scheduled for the following Wednesday. My dear friend Roz invited us to spend the weekend with her and her husband at their country home in the Catskills, and we took her up on the offer. By now, Tyler's little face was a balloon, causing deep crescents under his eyes and exaggeratedly puffy cheeks. He looked like an old man peeking out from a child's face. Roz later told me that her mother, who was also upstate that weekend, felt her heart crumble when she saw him. But no one made mention of Tyler's face to us that weekend, thank goodness.

Dr. Super saw Tyler once more that Monday; he answered more of our questions, assuring us our baby should be fine going under anesthesia, which terrified me, but all I could do was trust him. I told Dr. Super that Tyler had fallen off our bed one day when Rob had left him there alone, unaware that he could suddenly turn over and crawl. When that happened, I admonished Rob, cradling Tyler in my arms.

I told him, "I cannot bear to lose another person that I love. Do you understand? Do you?!" Now I asked the doctor: Could that fall have caused the tumor in our baby's gum? He assured me it could not have. Meanwhile, the next day Rita was sent by EMS to the hospital, for vital tests her doctor had ordered. I didn't know why.

Tyler's biopsy was performed, and he came home with big black stitches in his gum. Dr. Super told us it was important that the wound heal properly, and that the last thing Tyler needed was to get an infection or be sick in any way. We were super vigilant with him, not taking him outside much, watching the wound. Rita returned to Heartland rehab; meanwhile, we had to wait a full week for the results of Tyler's biopsy, which was torture. Despite my wanting to, I knew there was no way I could return to Detroit in the interim. We were concerned about Tyler traveling on planes and potentially contracting a cold—or worse—leading up to surgery, and there was absolutely no way I was traveling without him. I didn't want to let him out of my sight. Besides, he was still nursing. He needed to be with me.

And so we waited seven interminable days before we got the personal call from Dr. Super on August 23: "The tumor in Tyler's mouth is benign," he said. "There is no malignancy." *Thank God, thank God.*

Two days later, I tried to process it all in my journal:

> I'm exhausted by life right now. My little boy is only 9 months old
> and already we've had this tremendous scare with him—have had
> to deal with the hospital, doctors, nurses, a biopsy. Scary word.
> Wednesday, we got the good news, I thought, life is good. My son
> is going to be fine. Everything else can be worked out.
>
> Today I'm down again. Rita. More doctors, prognoses, and
> decisions for me to make. And so, I've done it. But it has exhausted
> me—figuring out what to do and how to do it. And thinking
> through the decision completely. Can she manage at home? Will
> she be safe?
>
> And most of all, will the disease remain stabilized this time
> long enough for them to lower the steroids? How long can she live
> like this?

Motherhood was enough to thrust me into adulthood. Being responsible for Rita makes me feel like more than an adult. I feel old.

Letting go of the life I thought I would have and living the one I do have is what I'm working on right now. It's a hard thing to do. It's about accepting those things you have no control over and making your life work anyway.

One day, I'll appreciate the journey my life has been. One day, I'll be less self-pitying.

Right now, my faith is erratic. Not good.

Rob and I met with Dr. Super in his office at the end of August, where he explained that the next step would be for him to go in and *enucleate* the tumor from Tyler's front gum. That was the first time I'd ever heard that word, but I used it often subsequently, as I explained to friends and family that the tumor was going to be *enucleated*, or scooped out, of our baby's mouth. Dr. Super arranged for Tyler to have a CT scan, and I had a mild anxiety attack watching his little body go through the machine; on that same day, Rita was sent back to the hospital from the rehab facility via ambulance, where she was given an infusion of electrolytes, and tests that revealed a urinary tract infection. Her discharge date from Heartland was supposed to be the next day, September 1, yet given this latest twenty-four-hour hospitalization, I was able to lobby hard, with her doctor's help, to get that discharge date postponed. But I was told it would only be for a few days, at best. Meanwhile, as we waited for Tyler's date of surgery, I consulted with Rita's team of doctors: Did they think she could live at home?

Dr. Indenbaum, who'd been her rheumatologist for nearly a quarter of a century at this point, was the most optimistic. While her platelet count was low, he told me that could be closely monitored, and if it got too low, he'd make sure her oncologist administered more Cytoxan. "The lupus is under control, and she's improved," he told me. "Her talking is better, even though she's up and down. It's a good sign. She's gotten so much better." He believed her being home was preferable to a nursing home because she'd get more interaction with others.

Dr. Emmer, her neurologist, agreed that she'd come a long way. But he told me that in terms of her brain function, the next four to six months would be critical, and we needed to give it time. When I noted her inability to remember things during a conversation—she'd often repeat the same question over and over—he told me loss of short-term memory was "classic," and not to worry. He'd put her on Provigil, an alternative to Ritalin, as a way to stimulate her brain, and he planned to closely monitor its effects in hopes that her memory would return. He agreed with Dr. Indenbaum that home was best, *if* she had twenty-four-hour care.

Dr. Wehbe, her internist, was the most sobering. He told me that, yes, from a medical standpoint she was "relatively stable": the lupus did seem to be under control, and so they were slowly weaning her off of the forty-five milligrams of prednisone (by five milligrams every two weeks), but her platelet count was indeed still low, so he planned to watch her blood work closely. When I repeated to him that she still seemed a bit confused when I spoke to her, he too told me not to worry about her confusion because steroids can cause that (alongside mood swings, delirium, and memory lapses). At the same time, he'd noticed that in the past when she went below thirty milligrams of prednisone, she had a relapse, so he was careful not to take her down too low. "There's always the potential for relapse," he warned. Again, steroids are a miracle drug *and* a curse. When I asked him the same question about her returning home, he said, "She can be home, but with *intensive assistance.*" He added that he felt she could be left alone for one hour a day, but no more. "The next month or two is critical," he warned.

I again lobbied hard for Rita to receive the maximum allowed one-hundred-day stay at Heartland, but even with her doctors' assessments that she needed twenty-four-hour care, her insurances would *not* approve a longer stay, and so, given her impending discharge, I worked furiously to arrange for as much at-home care for Rita as possible. Basically, I got a crash course in what it means to cobble together long-term care for a loved one in a country that has no safety net or structured system in place. Not unlike what my husband, Rob, and I went through two decades later in trying to finance care for his elderly mother, I was trying to do the same for my middle-aged, chronically ill sister. Her long-term-care insurance had run out the year before. Medicare reps told me she did *not* qualify for twenty-four-hour care, rather "intermittent care" from a home health aide one hour a day, and only that if she was homebound. Blue Cross Blue Shield reps told me that the only way she'd qualify for at-home care was if she needed "skilled care" from a registered nurse or LPN. That care, by the way, would *not* include help with getting in and out of bed, walking, dispensing meds, routine check of her vitals, feeding or preparing food, nor help with her hygiene. If it was determined that her care could be administered by an aide, she wouldn't qualify for BCBS's insured care. With her case pending, either way we'd need to pay for an aide. Heartland's social worker told me all they could offer under Rita's care management was a private-duty nurse, but that was quite expensive, so not an option. A live-in aide would've cost up to $5,500 per month, which we also couldn't afford. Paying for an aide for eight hours per day every day would cost $900 per week, which would've taken every dollar of Rita's income, and then some. It was beyond frustrating and scary. I didn't know *what* to do. Rita's discharge was imminent.

Seeing my desperation, a family friend offered to be with Rita on the days Tony was at his job at Northwest Airlines, where he'd been for less than three years. The plan was for this friend to be with her three days a week for twelve hours, and two days a week for nine hours. For that, I agreed to pay her $250 per week. Another friend offered to stay with Rita several hours throughout each weekend, for free.

As I paid Rita's September rent, and the rest of her bills, chipping in what I could of my own money to cover the gap (sadly, with a new baby, we were living above our means in pricey New York City), I realized that the next step must be to move her into a more affordable apartment at Riverfront. My fingers were crossed that Rita would be allowed to stay at the rehab facility long enough for me to get Tyler's surgery behind us and give him a chance to heal a bit; then he and I would return to Detroit, and I could be there when Rita came home. Meanwhile, I continued to research "care management programs" that Rita might qualify for, even calling the Detroit Area Agency on Aging, and a nonprofit called Project Choice. In both cases, she was too young to qualify for assistance. Somewhere in there, my summer break abruptly ended, and I had to return to work for the fall semester. I was cautiously optimistic, as reflected in my journal:

> Good things happen in my life in the Fall. People don't die in the Fall. School begins and I get a fresh chance to get it right. Tyler was born in the fall . . . it's fall. Good things are due.
>
> Tyler will come through his surgery as he's come through his biopsy and his CT scan—without incident. And Rita will continue to improve. All Good.
>
> And why not? The point of being tested is to be able to enjoy what's good when it comes. I have to believe that, 'cause otherwise those fleeting thoughts I have of jumping off a bridge wouldn't be so fleeting. Otherwise, with no good to look forward to, I'd spend even more time than I already do questioning my choices.
>
> Here's an unspeakable: Given my track record, was it fair to bring Tyler into the world and subject him to this family jinx, this sense that hardship (euphemism) follows my loved ones?
>
> Nobody means more to me than that little sweet boy, and if I've subjected him to any undue suffering, just by being his mother . . .
>
> Then again, there's something vital and inspiring in every situation, right? I don't enjoy this close association with hospitals, and doctors, but I'm learning by force to be less in fear of the whole medical world. And I guess I'm here to face my fears.
>
> And Rita's alive, she's stabilized medically, she has someone willing to live with her. And she has me handling her affairs.
>
> And Ty-boo doesn't have cancer.
>
> I'm grateful. All good.

42

Despite this balancing act I was trying to perform, in a terrible confluence of circumstances, Tyler's surgery date and Rita's discharge date turned out to be the same day: September 11, 2000. I felt some cruel joke being played on me by the Universe, and I remember calling Silent Unity, a prayer line established by Unity Temple, asking that they doubly pray for my son and my sister—as if to get God's attention. I just remember thinking, *This cannot be happening.* But it was happening. I spent the day before Tyler's surgery and Rita's discharge arranging with the various doctors for all of her medications to be prescribed, so Tony could pick them up from a pharmacy, and she'd have them all once she was home. That was much harder than it seemed, given that one doctor prescribed the prednisone, another prescribed the Synthroid for her hypothyroidism, another prescribed the Provigil, and yet another, her psychiatrist, prescribed the Prozac. All total, she was on ten medications, including sucralfate to treat the chemo-induced mouth ulcers, K-Dur for her low potassium, and eighty milligrams of the diuretic Lasix, as well as over-the-counter Extra Strength Tylenol, plus Metamucil and Colace for constipation. It terrified me to think she'd be missing any one medication she desperately needed once back at home. It was down to the wire, but between two different pharmacies, luckily, I got all her prescriptions filled, and Tony picked them up.

In the early morning of September 11, 2000, we took Tyler by taxi to NYU Medical Center, where he was prepped for surgery. Once he entered the operating room, I called Tony to learn how Rita's discharge was going. He was on his way to get her, he said, and it was going to be fine. "Don't worry about Tyler," he said. "He's going to be fine too." I'd come to depend on Tony's positive attitude in ways I was only beginning to understand, and that I'd come to rely on across the decades. Thankfully, Tyler did come through his oral surgery without complication. Because I pleaded, I was allowed to see him immediately, before he was taken to the actual recovery room. He lay there in the OR crying, looking so vulnerable, his mouth covered in bloody bandages. I stood there helpless, not sure I was allowed yet to pick him up. "Go ahead," whispered the nurse. I lifted my baby and pressed him into my chest, blood from his fresh mouth wound seeping into my white shirt. He whimpered, and I cried in relief, covering his little forehead with kisses. I stayed with Tyler that night in the hospital, holding my baby in my arms as he slept.

On that same day, Rita was discharged from Heartland, her diagnosis officially stated on the discharge papers as "lupus cerebritis." Finally, I was given a term for what she'd been going through for the past three months. Defined as "a neuropsychiatric manifestation of Systemic Lupus Erythematosus (SLE)," lupus cerebritis causes all the conditions Rita suffered: acute confused state, an inability to do basic tasks, memory disruption, mood changes, lethargy, seizures, and coma. Little did I know that this type of cognitive disfunction can occur in 20–80 percent of patients with SLE. Rita never knew this either, I'm sure. She was also described on those discharge papers as having hypertension (news to me) and thrombocytopenia—low number of platelets in the blood.

We hired a home health aide from Heartland, paying her $99 per day to come in four days a week for six hours each day to assist my sister; with her insurance, Rita only qualified for a physical therapist's visit three times a week. With the aide, the family friends, and Tony on his days off from work, we'd cobbled together a fragile form of twenty-four-hour care for her that was costing Rita $650 per week.

When I checked in again the next day with Tony, calling him from the taxi that took me and Tyler home from the hospital, asking how things were going with Rita's first day home, he told me, "Everything is fine; no need to hurry here; we've got it under control." But right away, it turned out, it wasn't, and they didn't. First of all, none of us was fully equipped for the level of care Rita actually needed. While she came home with a wheelchair, it took days, for instance, for a hospital bed and hydraulic lift, air mattress, and pressure pad to be ordered and delivered, because we hadn't anticipated the full extent of her needs.

Also, once Rita was home, it became clear to me pretty quickly that coupled with her pricey rent, the cost of medical supplies, prescription costs beyond what her insurance covered, and miscellaneous expenses like groceries, even with her pension, social security, and rental income, as well as Tony's and my modest contribution to the household, Rita could barely afford her own care. (For one thing, one of her tenants on Evergreen, taking advantage of Rita's hospitalization, had stopped paying their rent.) My worries about money grew.

And then the family friend who agreed to be with her on the weekends saw the level of care she needed help with—getting to the bathroom; being fed, bathed, and clothed; given her meds; assisted into and out of her wheelchair with the help of a hydraulic lift; walking with her cane. She helped for a couple days while Tony was at work, but then she bowed out. "I'm sorry, I can't," she said. I understood. Now it was just the aide, the other family friend, and when he wasn't at work, Tony. He recalls that Rita was so apologetic for needing the help, even from him. "I'm so sorry I can't do that myself," she'd say. "I was like, 'We're going to get through this,'" recalls Tony. "You had to get her over that part of feeling bad. I was like, 'Quit tripping. You're sick. I got it.'"

Still, we knew this arrangement wasn't tenable. But what were our options, other than to hope that Rita would get better? Throughout this time, I kept trying to get Rita twenty-four-hour care coverage via Blue Cross Blue Shield. At one point, the "insurance verification specialist" at Heartland wrote a letter to BCBS stating that Rita needed full-time private nursing. I was all but assured that the round-the-clock care was forthcoming. Meanwhile, I continued to call extended family members to keep them updated on Rita's condition. Our aunt Katherine, whose own older sister was gravely ill, called me regularly; I grew irritated by her calls because I had nothing new to tell her, and it took energy to hold it together, to try to not upset her. Her own health was so fragile. "Rita is about the same," I'd tell her. "She's holding on." But Aunt Katherine seemed dissatisfied; I could feel that without articulating it, she really wanted to know why I wasn't in Detroit with Rita. One day during our phone call she said, "I just can't tell whether you care about her that much or not," and I lost it. Despite her being my elder, I screamed at Aunt Katherine at the top of my lungs. "I have lost everybody in my family! One after the other! Not one person has asked me how I'm coping with that fact! You have no idea what that's like, to be facing this thing with Rita given what I've already been through. You have no idea the fear I feel, how terrified I am!" Before I knew it, I was sobbing.

Aunt Katherine was quiet for a moment. And then she said, "That's what I needed to hear. I love you, darling." And she hung up.

Meanwhile, Rita's lupus cerebritis was such that whenever I spoke to her, she systematically asked me where everyone was. "Where's Mama? Where's Dianne? Where's Anthony? Where's Deborah? Where's Daddy?" Each time, I'd have to say, "She died. She died. He died. She died. He died." Her need to repeat herself was so unnerving, I couldn't bear to stay on the phone with her for long. "That really bothered me," says her friend Linda. "Rita prided herself on her sharp mind, and her memory. So, when she got sicker and began to repeat things and so forth . . . that just broke my heart."

Rita also began experiencing nighttime psychosis. "It got bad," admits Tony. "We'd get to the point where I would wake up in the middle of the night and she's yelling into the phone, 'Mama? Mama?' That was a whole episode." Because she remembered our dead mother's telephone number, she was calling her, but new people now had the number, and Tony would have to take the phone from her and apologize to the person on the other end before hanging up. But that would upset Rita. "I was having a conversation with Mama!" she'd yell. "Why are you playing with me?" As Tony puts it, "Her mind couldn't wrap around it." This scenario played out regularly.

And then things got to the point where Rita would get up and try to leave the apartment, calling out for our mother, and inevitably fall, because her walking wasn't good. Getting her up off the floor and back into the bed or a chair was an ordeal. Tony worried doubly about her hurting herself and leaving the apartment. Plus, he wasn't sleeping. "I'm going crazy, got to do something. At no point could I close my eyes," he recalls. Finally, as a last resort: "I had to restrain her," he says. "That gave me sympathy for people whose parents or family members have Alzheimer's." Tony pauses, awash in memory. "I wouldn't wish lupus on a person I hated," he says. "Oh man, it's cruel."

One morning, the family friend—I'll call her Kay—who was helping to care for her demanded to know why Rita had a bruise on her wrist. Tony explained that he had to tie her down at night with restraining straps, because of her wandering. Tony and Kay argued about it. "I cursed her out," he admits, still furious over this so-called friend's accusations that he had in any way hurt his aunt.

I was furious too. Here, this twenty-nine-year-old young man found himself his aunt's primary caregiver every evening—feeding her dinner, giving her her medications, cleaning her up and helping her get around, and calming her down each night when, as he put it, "her energy would swell," making sure she stayed safe even as he lost sleep. This while driving her to doctors' appointments and coordinating aide care in between maintaining his job. I reminded Kay of how much Tony was doing, the stress he was under, when she called me to complain about him; her response was to scream, "Your sister needs *you*! Where are *you*?!"

When I explained that my infant son had just undergone oral surgery and was still under doctors' care, she yelled, "Michigan has doctors too, you know!" Yes, I knew. And I knew that I was being forced to make an impossible choice. I knew.

Needless to say, we let Kay go. Now it was just Tony and the aide navigating Rita's care, and me doing what I could long-distance. Throughout this ordeal, Tony never told me just how bad things were with Rita, or the full extent of what he was going through with her. "Why didn't you tell me?" I implore, twenty-plus years later.

"Why would I add to your stress?" he says. "It was what it was, and you had enough on you with Tyler."

Not that I wasn't aware that we were in a desperate situation. "Rita haunts me," I wrote at the end of September. "What to do if the

24-hour-care isn't, as we'd hoped, forthcoming?" I was also trying to figure out the hardest question of all for me: *When do I get back to be with Rita?*

There was so much to consider: I was told, again, by Dr. Super to try to keep Tyler healthy, and I was terrified of flying with him on the plane; what if he caught a bad cold, or a virus? My fear wasn't completely rational, I knew, but with Tony saying he had everything under control, I opted to wait a bit longer for Tyler to completely heal from his surgery wound. I recently looked at a photo taken of him during those days and was stunned. I'd forgotten how swollen his face remained even three weeks after surgery. Dark lines slash across his protruding cheeks, making him look like a child suffering from deep fatigue.

Also, there was an uglier reality for me: "Of course, a huge part of me doesn't want to go be in Detroit where bad things happen," I wrote candidly in my journal. "Where I'd have to see her like that, where I was when I should've been paying attention to my son's growing gums."

I was immobilized by a sister's fear and a mother's guilt.

~

With Tyler's wound healing, I did finally decide on a return date to Detroit—October 12, the day after Tyler's one-month postsurgery checkup. Dr. Super wanted to make sure he'd scooped out all of the tumor; he felt he had, as he'd been "aggressive" in his enucleating. (We later learned that he'd removed the buds for three of Tyler's permanent teeth, which he'd be missing until he got implants as a young adult.) Dr. Super was waiting for Tyler's mouth to heal before putting him under sedation again for an X-ray. Given his young age, eleven months, he couldn't sit still for an X-ray without sedation. There'd be another CAT scan too later in the month, for which we'd have to fly back to New York. All unnerving.

And yet I'd made the decision to bring Tyler with me to Detroit. Even that was a hard one, but my attempts to wean him so I could leave him in New York with Rob and our babysitter hadn't worked. He was clingier than ever, nursing hungrily and often. I told myself that had a lot to do with the surgery. Successful or not, that ordeal of going under anesthesia and the knife had to be traumatizing for a baby. Being honest with myself, I admitted I also needed to continue breastfeeding Tyler; the bonding soothed me.

Somewhere in there, we learned that BCBS had rejected our request for twenty-four-hour care for Rita. Now all we had was the aide from Heartland for a few hours a few days a week and Tony when he wasn't at work. That clarified for me that I needed to prepare for being in Detroit at least a few weeks, which likely meant taking a family leave of absence from my job. Tony was also looking into family leave, and whether caring for an aunt qualified. In his optimism, Tony felt Rita was getting better, slowly getting back to her old self, having more and more lucid moments. I could see too that her memory was somewhat better, or rather that she'd resigned herself to what she couldn't remember, and when she asked me about our loved ones and I had to tell her they were gone, she now just said, "Oh, okay." She was accepting things.

Beyond advocating for Rita, I started focusing on selling her house, so as to use the proceeds toward her care. I understood that eventually Rita would need to qualify for Medicaid once she'd exhausted all her assets. Medicaid, as a federal-state program, only covers long-term care for the poor. I'd spoken with an asset-protection attorney, but he confirmed that it was too late to put her house in a trust, so we had to sell it. Given the costs of home health-care aides and assisted-living facilities, it wouldn't take long for us to spend down her money before she was in fact poor. At that point in the future, Rita could expect to receive state-funded care for twelve hours a day. But I'd already been warned by a social worker that given Michigan's byzantine Medicaid rules, the cost of overnight care would still be the family's responsibility. Only if Rita was placed in a nursing home would she be covered for twenty-four-hour care.

I also planned to use that time to deal with the tenants in Rita's house who weren't paying their rent, and by November 1, when a place would become available, we needed to move Rita into a smaller, more affordable apartment at Riverfront Towers. Most urgently, we had to find a new aide ASAP that we could somehow afford to pay, allowing Tony to keep his job at Northwest Airlines and me to keep mine at Baruch College in New York. We had a big to-do list.

43

On October 10, the day before Tyler's follow-up appointment, and two days before our planned arrival, Rita had a seizure in front of her home health-care aide, who promptly called 911. Because the aide didn't call the private EMS service we'd used in the past, the ambulance workers took Rita to the closest hospital, which was the public one, Detroit Receiving. As soon as I heard what happened, I managed to get her ER doctor on the phone. He told me that she'd lost consciousness briefly because her electrolytes were off, and her sodium levels too high, which can cause seizures, but he was relatively certain that intravenous fluids would bring her levels back down to normal. And then he told me, this doctor who was just a fellow in ER: "She should lose some weight and keep her lupus under better control." This arrogance, insensitivity, and all-out gall is once again what so-called implicit bias looks like in real time.

My response to his callous comment was to insist he speak to Dr. Indenbaum in order to learn about her medical history. And when I talked to Dr. Indenbaum myself, I implored him to help me get Rita out of that damn hospital, and transferred to Beaumont Hospital, where he was on staff. But he advised me to wait, given that she was already headed to ICU at Receiving; in fact, he said that Receiving was possibly the better place for her in this instance. He assured me he'd be in close communication with the doctors there, and it should be okay, and I shouldn't be alarmed—no need to rush to her bedside. Given all Rita had been through, high sodium levels, he said, weren't that serious, treated easily enough. I agreed grudgingly and did what I knew to do, getting the beeper numbers of her doctors at Receiving, as well as her ICU nurses' names and shift schedules, recording it all in my little notebook. Rita was placed on floor 4N, in bed 4A.

I've revisited this moment and my decision many, many times, turning it over in my mind: Rob specifically asked me that day: "Do you want to go to Detroit right now?" I paused for a long time, and then said, "No."

Within that pause, before I answered Rob, I turned everything over in my head: I was, first and foremost, exhausted. Also, I was uncomfortable with the idea of leaving my eleven-month-old for long hours with family or friends in Detroit, but also concerned about bringing him into a hospital filled with sick patients—his mouth still full of stitches; unfortunately, Rob had already reached his maximum time off at his job at an advertising firm, so his traveling with us wasn't a viable option; Dr. Indenbaum *had* told me he wasn't too concerned, didn't think Rita was in danger. Also—and this is the hardest to admit, even now—I was suddenly and overwhelmingly afraid of flying, a spontaneous yet real phobia (and a condition I still suffer from). I'd been on planes due to crises four separate times in recent years, including the red-eye from San Francisco to Rita's hospital bed that summer, as well as that interminable flight from New York to Detroit on my birthday, when I didn't know by the time the plane landed whether our mother would be dead or alive—two of the worst hours of my life. In my return to magical thinking, if I wasn't flying into Detroit because of an urgency, a crisis, then everything was still okay. Rita was still okay. And if I did fly home immediately, would the plane fall from the sky, killing me and my little boy? After all, bad things happened to those I loved. And if the plane didn't crash, what horror would I find waiting for me once I landed?

I didn't know in real time that I was going through an anxiety attack. I didn't know that fear was fueling my denial, spurred by all the successive losses in my young life, and what I couldn't bear to face. That understanding would come much, much later, after years of therapy. In the moment, I only knew that when I spoke to Tony, in his infinite grace he simply said, "Stay put. I got this."

He and I decided Rita's latest hospital stay gave us a reprieve—especially Tony. For a few days at least, he'd have a break from the caregiving, and we'd have a chance to breathe, regroup, and think through long-term care solutions. Together, we decided that a better use of my time in Detroit would be later, once Rita was back home from the hospital; I ran this by Dr. Indenbaum, and he agreed, and so I rearranged my plans to travel there upon her discharge from Receiving, and after Tyler's scheduled CAT scan. We set a new date: October 22, with my added goal of weaning Tyler by then. Meanwhile, Rita was getting the care she needed from medical professionals; Tony would visit her regularly, as would her close friends and our uncle John, as proxies; and from New York I'd talk to her on the phone every day while handling as much as I could to prepare for what was next, all while staying in communication with her various doctors and the hospital's social worker. We also hoped to get her back to Heartland for more rehab after this latest hospital stay—again, trying to buy much-needed time. That was our plan. In hindsight, I can see the role denial played. Years later, a therapist helped me see that denial isn't a choice, that the psyche refuses to see what may be, to others, obvious. My current therapist has told me that denial in my case was a healthy and needed response to both a history of family loss and the very real possibility of what might happen in the present. In other words, my reasoned mind knew better, but my heart never allowed that knowledge in.

On an episode of *The Pulse* podcast the narrator, Justin Kramon, shares how his mother had "the talk" with him about her own end of life, which made him deeply sad and mourning her even before she died. He poses the question: *Is talking about death with a loved one who's gravely ill better than just pretending death isn't there as a possibility?* Ultimately, he concludes that, "There's not a right way to do this. A major illness forces you onto this weird little island where the rules of living don't apply. You have to figure out your own way to cope."

On my little island, I believed in Rita's ability to bounce back. She'd done so many times. With proper treatment, why couldn't she do so again?

~

Rob and I took Tyler to his postsurgical appointment, where we learned that Dr. Super felt he had indeed removed the entire tumor, to be confirmed after the pending CAT scan. There *was* the possibility of a recurrence, and that would require the doctor examining him closely every year. Dr. Super never told me just how rare that particular gum tumor was, but when I asked him, "One in a million?" he didn't correct me. I do know Tyler became a case study in his classrooms, and I was told that somewhere his case is in a dental textbook.

That ordeal largely behind us, I switched my focus to arranging for Rita to move to New York to live with us; I knew I had a massive number of details to put into place to make that happen and began learning all I could about assisted-living facilities in Brooklyn. And then, on Friday the thirteenth, our eighty-three-year-old aunt Bea died in Nashville. She'd been our father's big sister, and like a mother to Rita during her time at Fisk University. She and Aunt Bea had remained close through the years. I had to decide whether to attend our aunt's funeral; ultimately, I knew I wasn't ready to purchase another emergency ticket, board another plane toward a lost loved one. Instead, I went with my small family to Long Island for the weekend, to be by the beach, staying in a friend's house on Sag Harbor. Tyler's surgeon had been optimistic, and I needed to be. "We should celebrate our good fortune," I told Rob. But really, I just wanted an escape. I was emotionally shattered, and desperately grasping at a semblance of normalcy. I believed Rita was out of danger, knew Tony was checking on her, knew I'd see her by month's end, and felt some assurance by talking to her on the phone every day. But when I spoke to her friend Wilma and told her where we were, how we'd chosen to "get away" for a couple days, Wilma was speechless; and I knew then how bad it looked, how wrong it must have appeared to be "on a vacation" in Long Island at that moment, and not on my way to either Nashville or Detroit. At one point during the weekend, Rob took a photo of me and Tyler on the beach; both Tyler and I have our eyes closed as I hold him in my arms. Rob later told me he couldn't bear to look at that picture. "You were so sad about your aunt, so worried about Rita," he said. "And I felt so helpless." But I later found myself drawn to the same image, the only document that captures on my face what I was feeling at that time, that confirms my torment. In its strange way, that photo assuaged my subsequent guilt.

Nine more days went by as Rita remained in the hospital. I was told by doctors that she was "stable," but that all of her vitals were not yet where they needed to be. During that time, I kept researching options for assisted-living facilities in New York City where Rita could potentially stay. I narrowed it down to three. I knew I had to jump several hurdles before a big move could happen, and I ran over the steps like a litany in my head: *sell her house, apply for Medicaid, get her back in Heartland for rehab, move her into a cheaper Riverfront apartment.* As scheduled, Tyler had his CAT scan, which came back clean, thank God. I was now all set to head to Detroit over the weekend.

Meanwhile, I talked to Rita every day. But on that ninth day, for a reason I couldn't get an answer to, she was transferred off floor 4N, bed 4A, to the fifth floor, to a different ICU, to a new set of nurses whose names I didn't know, nurses who had not been monitoring her for nine days. Throughout that same day, a Thursday, I couldn't reach her by phone or through the nurses' station. And as fate would have it, even though he was off from work, Tony didn't visit her that day, planning to visit her the next day. That was *also* the day of our beloved aunt Bea's funeral. I'd had to explain to her sister, our father's remaining sibling Aunt Katherine, how sorry I was not to be there, but that "too much" was going on with both Rita and Tyler. "I understand, darling," she said to me. I talked to Dr. Indenbaum yet again that same day, revisiting the idea of having her transferred to the hospital where he was on staff. And again, he told me he didn't think that was necessary. He told me to contact him when it was time for her discharge, so he could recommend that she return to the rehab facility. I said I would.

"I always felt Rita put too much trust in Dr. Indenbaum," her friend Linda later confessed to me. "I wanted her to maybe consider a new doctor."

On the tenth day of Rita's hospital stay, October 20, a Friday, a doctor I'd never spoken to before at Detroit Receiving called mid-morning to say that she'd lost consciousness, that sometime during the previous night her blood pressure had dropped precipitously, and they couldn't get it back up. She wasn't expected to survive. What were my wishes as her medical proxy? I was stunned by this news and begged him to please do all he could to keep my sister alive as I made my way to her. "Okay," he said. That's all he said. "Okay." I hung up and called Tony at work. Next, I called Linda, who I knew was closer to the hospital, and asked her to rush there. I then called our aunt Florence, telling our mother's sister that Rita was not expected to make it through the day; could she please go to the hospital to be with her? She agreed. And then I did the very thing I'd been so afraid of doing, the thing I'd been trying so hard to avoid: I jumped on the first plane I could get, with Tyler, and flew to Detroit, praying the plane wouldn't drop from the sky, and not knowing what news was waiting for me when we landed. I hadn't seen my sister in nearly three months.

I arrived in Detroit at nighttime, and purposely didn't call Tony because I needed the presence of mind to drive to the hospital, and I was terrified of what he might tell me. I have this memory of struggling to get Tyler's car seat installed in the rental car, so frustrated I broke down in tears, my son's little face filled with confusion. Once on our way, I called Rita's godmother, Lula, and asked her to please not tell me anything, just talk to me. She agreed. But at one point, when I said, "Now all my family is gone," she didn't deny it. She was quiet. And so I knew.

Sure enough, when I arrived at the hospital, Rita was already gone.

Linda met me, anguish written across her face. "I insisted they keep her here until you arrived," she said, and then she held Tyler in her arms as I went in to see my sister. She lay atop a metal table, thin sheet covering her. "Oh, Rita, I'm sorry!" I cried out. "I'm sorry, Rita. I'm sorry."

I was sorry for so much. Sorry I hadn't come sooner, when she entered the hospital ten days before and I let fear coupled with my son's tumor distract me; sorry I hadn't come the day before, when I couldn't reach her on the phone and felt something was wrong; sorry I hadn't prayed long and hard enough, as I'd done when she was in a coma and woke up. I was sorry too for wrong choices I'd made in the last four years of her life: not coming to celebrate her fortieth birthday, nor her forty-fourth; not meeting her in Nashville as we'd planned one summer in between those milestone birthdays; and not spending New Year's Day 2000 with her.

Mostly I was sorry that I couldn't give her a last wish. She'd found our mother's passing so beautiful—surrounded by her loved ones, me holding Mama's hand as she took her last breath. That's what Rita would've wanted too. Not another sudden death. But I got there an hour too late. She died alone.

~

"I just feel like there was more I could've done," I said to Dr. Indenbaum, when I told him Rita hadn't made it, that she'd died.

"There was nothing you could've done," he assured me, his voice low and sad.

I thought, *Could you have done more?* But I just thanked Rita's longtime doctor whom she'd trusted and adored, and then I hung up, never again speaking to Dr. Indenbaum. (He died four years later, at the age of seventy-two.)

The document that came later from Medicare showing procedures she was given on the last day of her life included an echo exam of Rita's heart, the insertion of a catheter into her artery and her vein, a chest X-ray, and ninety minutes of "critical care." So perhaps what the doctor I spoke to briefly that night said, as my sister lay beside us lifeless, was true: *We did all we could to save her.* But I wasn't convinced. Why had her pressure dropped, why had she been moved to another ICU room, why hadn't I been notified the day before? I chose to have an autopsy done. Based on the results, the death certificate lists Rita's immediate cause of death as "possible septic shock due to or as a consequence of systemic lupus erythematosus." Other "significant conditions" listed were seizure D2, lupus cerebritis, and hypernatremia (too high concentration of sodium in the blood—what her doctor had told me not to worry about).

Both my sister Deborah and my sister Rita likely died from sepsis while patients at Detroit Receiving Hospital. Both cases pointed, in my mind, to negligence, and this time I wanted to do something about it. I just *knew* this issue was rampant, and after some research at the library, I found a report published by the Institute of Medicine in 1998 showing that based on studies, at least forty-four thousand and perhaps as many as ninety-eight thousand Americans died in hospitals each year as a result of medical errors. Yet when I spoke with a medical-negligence attorney, he told me that Rita's twenty-four-year history with lupus, and all the years of taking steroids and, later, chemo—both known to compromise the body, making it vulnerable to infection—would make my claim a tough one to prove. Honestly, I realized I didn't have the heart for it anyway, and so I let it go.

But what I haven't let go of are the questions that still haunt me to this day: Had I been there, would I have seen signs of her pressure dropping, or caught her seizure in time to do something? Would I have demanded despite her doctor's advice that she be transferred to Beaumont, the private hospital in the suburbs, rather than the county hospital in the heart of Detroit? Would she have avoided sepsis had she been discharged sooner? Would I have insisted her doctors take her condition more seriously? Did Dr. Indenbaum underestimate how serious things were until it was too late? Did we all?

Would she have died from lupus anyway?

Several factors conspired against Rita and me in those last four months of her life: no longer having our immediate family to rely on; her being without a life partner or spouse; my living in New York tied to work and family obligations; Tony being a twentysomething young man, both valiant yet often overwhelmed by the responsibility of caretaking; my having an infant son facing his own health scare; this latest bout causing cognitive loss so she couldn't advocate for herself; the financial drain that made it harder to care for her; and finally, Rita having a disease that was utterly relentless. As Tony said, "People have no idea about lupus. The disease attacks some part of you, you recover from that, and then it comes back and attacks another part. It's a lot of different diseases."

And it's hard to fight a lot of different diseases.

"Hers were like dog years—each one the aging equivalent of seven. And only now do I see that," I wrote in my little notebook days after.

Did she even stand a chance?

I'd never acknowledged to anyone, including myself, that Rita might die from lupus, my mind trying hard not to absorb that knowledge, but I'd been in secret terror all the time that she would. That was a terrible way to live, my constantly trying to stake out a life amidst Rita's progressive illness, feeling guilt, always working against some imaginary, or not-so-imaginary, clock, being ever distracted so that I could never fully devote myself to what I was doing—caring for her, or trying to create the resources that would make it easier to care for her. As I'd scribbled on a notepad in my office one day: "I'm impatient. I've got to get things done, make it big, so I can really help her."

A horrible catch-22.

Now I know that my secret fear was anything but irrational: lupus is a top-ten cause of death in Black women ages fifteen to forty-four, and Black women with lupus die up to thirteen years earlier than non-Hispanic white women with lupus, according to the Lupus Foundation of America. And in a stinging revelation, Rita's friend Lillian recently told me that a doctor once told Rita she had very little time left, and when she showed up to see him a year later, he was stunned. "Yes, it's Rita Davis, and I'm still here," she told the doctor.

One more thing I now know for sure: No matter how hard you try—and I really tried—you cannot advocate from afar for a loved one in a hospital setting. And especially not if your loved one is a Black woman. I'll never have that closure, that satisfaction of knowing that I cared for my sister in her final days, at her bedside.

"Well, so much for my thinking people I love don't die in the fall," I wrote in my journal. "People I love die in every season: Winter (Daddy, Anthony, Deborah), Spring (Mama), Summer (Selena Dianne, baby Brandon), and Fall (Rita)."

It just didn't seem possible that she, someone so full of life, could die.

44

In the little notebook where I'd kept all the notes on her care, I placed a small check mark by each of the sixty names I'd collected of people in Rita's life, as I called them one by one to share the bad news. I was determined to hold it together during this process, but I lost it when I spoke to Zachary, the love of Rita's life, bursting into tears at the sound of his voice. By far the hardest call to make, though, was to our beloved chosen cousin Elaine, who'd first met Rita when she was a two-year-old sitting on her porch, and Elaine told her grandmother she'd "found a baby" and wanted to keep her. Elaine, who'd taught Rita how to handle her monthly periods; Elaine, who'd taken Rita to Fisk to begin her college life at sixteen. I sobbed, while Elaine kept saying, "Our beautiful Rita, oh God, our beautiful Rita . . ." After that call, I lay on the carpeted floor of Rita's apartment and cried out in anguish, weak with the weight of regret. I kept saying, "I failed her. I failed her. I failed her."

Tony knelt beside me and put his hand on my back. His touch was firm, comforting. For the last eight years, her home had been his. As I looked up into my nephew's face, tears streaming down mine, he said: "Listen to me. You did not give Rita lupus."

Those words got me up onto my feet, and through the next week of planning my sister's service—the first funeral I'd ever been solely responsible for.

In the same little notebook, where the day before her passing I'd written, "Dr. I. thinks she should stay at Receiving until discharge," I now wrote the phone number for Flowers By Deb in Hamtramck, and made a note that "We need three cars, seating 4–5 people each"; I scribbled figures for funeral and burial costs, and details for wiring money from my New York bank account. "Get her a spot near Mama at Grand Lawn Cemetery," I wrote. And in another note: "Bring her clothes & wig & red lipstick, undergarments."

I chose to bury Rita in the pretty satin cream-colored dress she'd worn to my wedding.

Tasked yet again with the job of writing a family member's obituary, of summarizing a loved one's life in a brief narrative, for her I wrote:

> *Rita was unforgettable. She embraced life, proving with her own that quality of years matters more than quantity. Throughout her adulthood, she battled a chronic illness, yet refused to complain or let it stop her from doing all the things she loved—traveling, attending her beloved Unity Baptist Church, socializing with friends, being there for others and keeping her faith in God . . .*
>
> *She was a dynamic personality and people were naturally drawn to Rita. She could have you laughing just in the way she turned a phrase or told a story. And she could light up a room when she walked into it—sure to be dressed in beautiful, vibrant clothes, matching high heels and dazzling earrings. And then there was that gorgeous smile.*
>
> *Rita was a woman with a big heart. She inherited from her mother a generosity and compassion that found her constantly giving to others in need. In fact, she had a way of taking time with those in society whom others often ignored. Hers was a net cast wide, including people of all ages and walks of life. People often turned to her for counsel, and she offered her guidance and support freely.*
>
> *Not surprisingly, many claimed Rita as their best friend. But to no one was she a better friend and cheerleader and model of inspiration than to her baby sister, Bridgett.*

For the program, I chose the words "A SERVICE OF MEMORY FOR CELEBRATING THE LIFE OF RITA RENEE DAVIS," and below that a stunning photo of Rita smiling, and wearing her favorite royal-blue-and-black sequined dress. The Bible verse I selected was one of her favorites, and mine: "I am the resurrection, and the life: he that believeth in me, though he were dead, yet shall he live: and whosoever liveth and believeth in me shall never die." I asked that donations be sent in her memory to the Michigan Lupus Foundation, the first time a request like that had been made for a loved one in our family.

I didn't wear a colorful outfit to her service, despite Rita's love of colorful clothes, and this new practice of folks wearing bright colors to funerals. I wore a black skirt suit; it matched my somber mood. Unity Baptist Church was overflowing with people who'd come to pay their respects. Over two hundred people signed the guestbook. Our step-father, Burt, in a nursing home suffering from Alzheimer's, would've been the only other immediate family member there, besides Tony, but he was in no condition to attend. I'd asked three people to speak at the service: Elaine, Linda, and Andrea, a dear church friend of Rita's who, blind from diabetes, had found solace in Rita's deep kindness. (Andrea would die from complications caused by her disease just a year later.) I did not speak; others got up spontaneously to share their reflections. Rita's dear pastor and friend Reverend Stotts delivered the eulogy. Flowers and plants were abundant, coming from not just family and friends ("You were blessed to have the Queen," Linda wrote on her floral card) but also classmates from Fisk University. The service was, I'm told, beautiful; I'd like to believe it celebrated Rita's life, but I remember almost none of it—words said, music played, songs sung—only that I was grateful to see each and every one of those dozens and dozens of people who came up to greet me. My friend Diane chose not to attend, and instead babysat Tyler, so my little boy didn't have to be at a funeral too. Throughout the service, I couldn't help thinking how I'd wanted so desperately to care for Rita financially, to be her safety net, alleviate her money woes. Ironically, when I finally did spend thousands of dollars on her, it was to bury her.

I did manage to get a plot for Rita relatively near our mother. For her headstone, because she loved angels, I chose a design with an angel carved into the stone. It simply reads:

BELOVED SISTER AND AUNT
RITA R. DAVIS
APRIL 29, 1956–OCT. 20, 2000

Miraculously, Rita lived eight more years after our mother died. I know for sure now that was in fact a miracle. And just as she'd said about our mother after her passing, I told myself the same about Rita: *She's not gone, she's just moved on.*

Tyler celebrated his first birthday three weeks after Rita died. We had a small party for him in our six-hundred-square-foot Manhattan apartment; I placed the photo of him and Rita, taken over the previous Christmas holiday, alongside his birthday cake with its sole candle. That photo has remained in Tyler's various bedrooms ever since, displayed prominently, so that he's grown up seeing that image of his infant self being held by the aunt he never got to know. Auntie Rita.

In the weeks that followed her passing, many people said to me, "I'm so glad you have Tyler." I knew they meant well. Even my husband Rob told me, "I know I wasn't enough to keep you here after losing Rita; I know it was Tyler who gave you a reason to live." He was right. I didn't have the option of grief-laced suicide because I had a child depending on me. I was so grateful for him, loved him so much, my little boy. But I didn't like the implication that having my son was a consolation for losing my sister. Yet, even I wrote in my journal: "Has he replaced her in my life?"

Of course, my fear notwithstanding, such a thing was impossible. I couldn't replace Rita. As soon as she took her last breath, life felt emptier, the richness she carried into every room with her gone alongside her smile, her mannerisms, her voice. Rita knew me before I knew myself, loved me no matter what. She was my best friend. We have secrets between us that are buried with her, secrets that will be buried with me. And she was the one person left on this earth who confirmed that we'd been a family *before* the onslaught of tragedy. She and I went through so much together. That bond was irreplaceable.

And it still is.

~

Across the course of our forty-year relationship as sisters, I cherished each of the twenty-two letters Rita wrote to me. I wish I'd been able to find the ones I wrote to her. In the year after her passing, I wrote four new letters to Rita—as a way to process a grief hardly contained within five stages. Famed psychotherapist Francis Weller has a special term for grief. He calls it "the wild edge of sorrow"; that's where I was, barely hanging on to that edge. Writing to Rita kept me from letting go.

On the last day of the first year of the new decade, I wrote letter number one:

12/31/00

Dear Rita,
It's such a beautiful, snowy morning, and I can feel you, at peace.
    What a journey it was! Thank you. You deepened me.
Enlarged my heart. Taught me how to pay attention, to honor family, to stay connected.
    What we had was so beautiful and fragile and unique. I miss having someone to love that way.

Your baby sister,
Bridgett

Throughout that first year, I had several harsh crying spells, racked with sadness and regret and a lack of closure. I was desperately trying to understand my new reality: *Who am I if I'm not someone's sister?* I shared with my friend Jane that no one seemed to understand my sorrow, and she said that people aren't used to siblings remaining so close into adulthood, which is why others might be surprised by how hard I was taking Rita's death. When she told me that, all I could think was, *That's pathetic.*

I was so lonely. And alone. Who could understand what Rita had been to me? That my child and my husband and Tony notwithstanding, *she* was my origin family, now taken from me? As the days and weeks passed, I captured some of my fears in the pages of my journal. "I'm afraid of forgetting details," I wrote. "She was the family griot, now what?" And: "How do I immortalize her, too?" On the first day of spring, I wrote:

> Rita has been dead for months. Since the fall. Three seasons ago. Putting the words "Rita" and "dead" together looks so odd, so bizarre. Mama is dead, Daddy is dead, et al., but not Rita. She's too alive in my head. Too immediate and recent and right there with me in this phase of my life . . . All the huge stuff of my life that my mother, father, and other siblings missed? Rita was there. And now she's gone, too. Hard to believe.

On what would've been Rita's forty-fifth birthday, I nursed Tyler for the last time. He was seventeen months old and would've happily kept going. But I decided it was time to wean him, move on. That evening, I wrote letter number two:

April 29, 2001

Happy Birthday Rita. Happy Birthday.
Losing you now feels inevitable. It feels that way because of how you were talking once you came through the coma that summer. You talked about the past, and you wanted to know where people had gone. And it seemed ludicrous to your impaired mind that none of them were here. And it was ludicrous. It hurt me so each time I had to tell you that Mama was dead, and Daddy was dead, and Dianne was dead, and Anthony was dead, and Deborah was dead. It is ludicrous. And now you too. It's like you were destined to join them. Because I was little comfort for you. You had more family on the other side than this one, and I had my own little family, and so where did that leave you? I'm so sad about that.

There are a lot of things I'm happy about too . . . I'm happy that we worked on our relationship, and we got to enjoy the benefits of that work. We were close, weren't we? All our trips together—to London, to Mexico, to New York, to

Disneyworld . . . we had fun. I'm happy too that I helped you whenever you asked, and that I visited every summer, and we spent every Christmas together. I'm happy that we knew how much one loved the other, and that we had long stopped arguing. I'm happy that I was a positive influence and that you admired me and that I admired you and I told you so.

I'm happy that when you were feeling low or depressed about something someone said, you'd call me and we'd talk, and you'd say, "I feel better now that I've talked to you."

I'm happy that you came to the wedding and enjoyed it so much. And I'm so happy that you met Tyler, was there to experience it all—my pregnancy, his birth. I am grateful to you for holding on as long as you did.

I'll always hold on to the memories Rita. Growing up we knew each other was there. And we made Mama proud, could bask in the glow of that knowledge. We were good girls, who went forth and got our educations and made something of our lives. She was so proud of you, of me. As young women, we leaned on each other through the losses, and as we went through your illness together. Being a comfort to one another.

Today, I'm going to call each of your good friends. To say hi. To say thank you. Tonight, for dinner we're going to have Cornish hens. In your honor. 'Cause you loved them, and we always ate them on the holiday. And this is a holiday. Forty-five years ago, Mama pushed you out, and you changed the lives of people you touched. You really did. Everybody has a Rita story. But I'm the luckiest one of all, 'cause I knew you the best and the longest. I'm the one who can smile the most.

So, I'm going to try not to dwell on what didn't work out. I want to let that go and hold on tight to what did.

If love could've kept you here, you'd be here.

All my love,

Your sister,
Bridgett

On the anniversary of the date that I lost her as I'd always known her, I wrote letter number three:

June 3, 2001

Dear Rita:
It was on this day, a Saturday, one year ago, that you first began to slide into the lupus bout that would take your life.

One year ago.

And in that year, of course, my life has been slapped around, and I've been forced, repeatedly, to prove my will to live. Prove it! That inner voice keeps telling me. Prove death wouldn't be easier, sweeter, a whole lot quieter. No more memories, no more tears, no more pain, no more regrets, no more loneliness, no more sadness, no more self-pity, no more struggle to climb out of this abyss and fly once more. Just pure, luscious silence . . .

It's so difficult to live without you. I am not who I was one year ago, and my life is not in the place it was one year ago, and I do not have the plans for my future that I had one year ago. So begins my new life, beyond your transition: this is it. It's going to be like nothing else I've lived, and something I can't even imagine.

Help me through this, Rita.

Love,
Bridgett

~

On the one-year anniversary of Rita's death, I was told by Audrey, my therapist: "You couldn't predict the future, as much as your own hindsight tries to tell you that you should've known." And then she added: "What I've gotten to know about you in this past year makes me absolutely certain that if you'd known or been told, you would've been there."

Feeling somewhat freed by my therapist's words, that night I wrote letter number four:

October 20, 2001

Dear Rita,

I miss you. I have missed you every day in these past 365 days. Missed you in ways I haven't fully allowed myself to admit— your voice, your support, your love. I miss your bravery and your honesty and your compassion. I miss your life, which was so different from mine. It's a hole so big that I admit I've had many days when I didn't want to go on. You know that, don't you? That I have fought with myself to go on. Tyler, who you loved so much and were so happy about, is your gift to me. His presence is my inspiration. And you know what? He has your spirit. He's a fighter. Like Mama said, you came into this world fighting. And the truth is, you went out of it the same way. You fought for a long time against a horrendous battle, and you kept your faith, and you didn't give up. And now, one year later, I am prepared to do something huge:

I'm going to let you go, Rita. It's for the best. It's not what I would've wanted, but it's for the best.

I don't believe we're meant to die young. It's just that life is supposed to be worth living for as long as you can. And that's what you did. You lived the best and the longest you could. I realize now that you were tired. And I can admit this too: that last bout had taken you away from yourself, and I wouldn't want you to live like that. Because I know you wouldn't have wanted to. Your mind was what distinguished you; it was what kept you separate from those who were just sick. You had a condition, it's true, but you were vibrantly alive thanks to your mind. God gave you a sharp, quick-witted one. Lupus could take away your mobility and you could survive that. But not your ability to think and reason.

Death, I now see, is not the worst thing that can happen to a person.

Does this sound strange? What I mean is that I'm happy for you, that you aren't struggling anymore. I think you did a lot of holding on for me. I know you did. That had to be hard, and I thank you so much. Thank you. If you'd left me sooner, I just don't know . . .

I do wish now that I had had the foresight to spend more time with you in those last few years, just hanging out, being together. But of course, that same foresight would've made me fatalistic, believing that you weren't going to get better. And you and I both needed to believe otherwise. We never lost faith. Even right before the last bout, we both believed you'd be okay. And if in those final days you had your doubts, you didn't tell me. You let me go on. You always encouraged me to go on. Thank you for that, for that gift of freedom.

We didn't talk about your own death, but I do know that you had some of Daddy in you. You didn't want to live just any old way. You wanted some quality of life, and you didn't want to be a burden to anyone. I remember how you felt about Curtis Mayfield's paralysis. I tried to convince you that his was an extraordinary spirit to be able to still record music. But you knew better. You were closer to it than I, and you refused to be convinced. And you often quoted Mama's words: *If you can't get better, death is a relief.*

You left me in June, and you gave me a few extra months to deal with it before your body stopped. You showed me that you weren't the same and that way, it would be easier to say good-bye. And it was. Except for the guilt.

I am, on this first anniversary of your death, going to let go of the guilt. I can't carry it anymore, and like your darling friend Linda said, you wouldn't want me to do that. You knew I wasn't perfect. But you also knew I loved you and didn't want any harm to come to you. That's all that matters now. I finally realize that. Because I simply can't go on this way, and be what you wanted for me: healthy, happy, whole.

I love you so much, Rita. Forever. And I'm not afraid for you. Your body is at rest and your soul is free, and that's the way it should be. . . . I don't know what's on the other side, but I believe that whatever you've transitioned into, you are certainly not in pain, not worried about anything, and not lonely. You're a presence around me. And from this day forward, I'm going to try to be happy about what I do have—that presence and my memories and the knowledge that love lives on.

Life is eternal. I promise to honor yours. You.

Love,

Your sister,
Bridgett

EPILOGUE

Rita would've loved living in the twenty-first century. She was so excited for the new millennium, as if she knew the digital age would suit her. I *know* it would've made her life easier.

She would've benefited greatly from the evolution of phone calls. Rita loved talking on the phone every day, sometimes for hours at a time, as a way of connecting with friends and family. It was her lifeline. "It's how I do my visiting," she often said; making and receiving calls anywhere, anytime, thanks to cheap unlimited long-distance plans—especially to and from our cousins in Nashville—would've thrilled her. And along with a landline, she would've enjoyed having a mobile phone, never having to miss a call, or even be at home to make one. Skype, and later the smartphone's FaceTime, would've been a dream come true for her, she who once said to me, "There should be a way for people to see each other when they talk on the phone, like in *The Jetsons*." She would've used the technology the way my daughter, Abbie, does; she's 750 miles away at college and sometimes likes to be on FaceTime with me while she packs for a trip, or eats her lunch in the campus cafeteria, or fills out important forms. Seeing someone's face brings them closer to you.

Speaking of connectivity, Rita would've enjoyed attending church virtually on the Sundays she needed to rest, streaming the weekly service into her bedroom as she sat propped up with pillows, pleased to see those in attendance, being shouted out as one of the "sick and shut-in," hearing the pastor's sermon in real time. She would've definitely owned an iPad, using it to listen to her collection of books on tape, FaceTime friends, watch new movies as well as her favorite old ones (*Do the Right Thing*, *The Wiz*, *Beaches*) and the plethora of TV shows now available via streaming. I'm certain she would have been a fan of the myriad talk shows that came in the wake of Oprah's, but also of some reality TV—maybe the *Real Housewives* series or the

Bravo stories of people often shunned by society, or the finding-your-mate-on-an-island shows.

Google searches would've been Rita's friend. She enjoyed investigating, finding out things that others couldn't, "helping people out of crazy situations," as Linda put it. "I used to tell her she should start a business called 'Ask Rita,'" says Linda. Imagine her having the entire internet at her disposal. Learning new things mattered to Rita, and when I donate to Wikipedia it's in memory of her thirst for knowledge, her love of facts and figures and dates.

The letter writing that we did with one another would've turned into emails. Social media, in particular Facebook, would've connected Rita to folks scattered across the country (and, if you count her grad-school friend George Bassey in Nigeria, around the world). Rita would've used FB for the ways it operates at its best—building community, thwarting isolation. She would've been FB friends with her Mumford High and Fisk and Atlanta University classmates; our Nashville clan; church friends; Riverfront Towers community; ex-boyfriends and childhood friends; and her massive Detroit network. I can imagine all the FB groups she would've joined. She might've been a fan of YouTube, perhaps mostly for the funny videos, less for the "news." She liked getting her news from reliable sources, and I suspect she would've watched MSNBC or CNN as well as the local news (to catch the day's winning lottery numbers!). I think she would've been on Instagram mainly to follow accounts like that of actress Viola Davis. She would've enjoyed how Davis uses her platform to share inspiring messages, feel-good content, and laugh-out-loud funny posts with her millions of followers—all meant to uplift the spirit.

~

Most of all, the twenty-first century would've given Rita a community of fellow lupus sufferers, who could've helped her feel less alone. From early-aughts chatrooms to FB groups, she could've discussed her flare-ups and fatigue with others who'd understand, who'd validate her experiences in a safe space where they'd support one another through the journey. As Jennifer Brea, who suffered for years from chronic fatigue syndrome, said during a TED Talk: "Had I gotten sick before the internet . . . I might've killed myself." Today celebrities talk publicly about their lupus journeys, most notably actress Selena Gomez and singer Toni Braxton (whom Rita adored and who reminds me of her). Gomez told *Elle* magazine in 2021, "My lupus, my kidney transplant, chemotherapy, having a mental illness . . . these were all things that honestly should have taken me down." But knowing she could help others by example kept her going. In a livestream on TikTok, Gomez addressed relentless negative comments about her body by explaining that she tends "to hold a lot of water weight" caused by the medication she takes to combat the lupus. Also on TikTok, she explained to millions of fans after some commented on her hand movements that the tremors were a side effect of her medication. In 2023, Toni Braxton told *Essence* magazine, "I'm comfortable being vulnerable now about the disease, but before I wasn't. I was told not to tell anyone I had lupus. I was shamed. People told me you'll never work again." She added that once she embraced her diagnosis, she felt empowered and decided to advocate for herself and others. That same year, she posted on her Instagram account to her millions of followers: "I know I'm not the only person who's put off doctor appointments before. But for people living with lupus . . . skipping a visit can be serious." Two days later, she posted about a lupus charity walk she'd be participating in. These celebrities' testimonies—especially coming from women of color—would've been so validating and affirming for Rita, and might've caused others to be more sympathetic, understand her condition more. Maybe then people wouldn't have said to her: "You just need to rest, stop doing so much!"

I'm pretty sure Rita would've listened to podcasts, like *The Lupus Living Podcast,* hosted by Gwen Alexander, a Black woman lupus survivor; she could've had reference guidebooks in her personal library like *The Girlfriend's Guide to Lupus,* which covers everything from how to eat an anti-inflammatory diet to how to maintain a sex life. And although *The Lupus Book: A Guide for Patients and Their Families* first came out in 1995, neither I nor Rita had heard of it. Today, Amazon lists a plethora of such books, including memoirs as well as "lupus awareness" daily journals. And of course, there's now an app for that. The leading one is called LupusMinder, designed by and for lupus patients, and allows users to track their symptoms and share them with their doctors, and list medications and track side effects. Virtual roundtables on managing lupus are hosted regularly by the Lupus Foundation of America (LFA). And there are now "chronic disease self-management programs" designed to help Black women with SLE manage both their symptoms and treatment and communicate better with their health-care providers.

Imagine if Rita could've simply typed the word "lupus" into a search engine.

We now have a lupus awareness month, which is May. World Lupus Day is May 10 and comes with an online lupus awareness tool kit. Nearly sixty cities participate in the "Walk to End Lupus Now" that Braxton promoted. And yet the LFA, founded the year after Rita was diagnosed, *just* launched a rebranded campaign in 2023 to connect specifically with Black and Latina women—even though women of color disproportionately suffer earlier, longer, and more severely with the disease. This is why one of Rita's friends from college could say to me recently, "I never thought lupus was anything that serious. I thought it was something that you could manage." And that's why her friend from graduate school, Sam, has tried to learn more about lupus and what sufferers are up against. "Because of Rita," he told me. "When she passed, I was in shock more than anything else." He had no idea about the apparent severity of the disease that he'd underestimated, hadn't really understood.

And that's why Rita's ex, Zachary, has encouraged his grandson, a scientist, to research the disease in hopes of one day finding a cure.

If Rita were still here, she'd surely be deeply involved with Lupus Detroit, a local group begun by one woman, Sharon Harris, who suffers from both discoid lupus and SLE. The organization's slogan is "Lupus warriors working for lupus warriors," and she launched the effort in 2009 mainly to give emergency grants to those living with the disease and needing financial help. Lupus Detroit also offers monthly support-group meetings and holds fundraisers, including its own walkathon. "Lupus Detroit shows me love, compassion, and empathy," says Kamai Sanders, an active member. "I feel like I finally belong to something!" I would've loved that for Rita.

I'm glad that today's lupus sufferers—who tend to be 90 percent women—are referred to not only as "lupus warriors" but "lupus survivors," terms I don't remember hearing back in Rita's day. That may be in part because only in recent years have two new drugs been introduced to treat lupus; unlike the older treatments that focused on suppressing the entire immune system, these new drugs target specific molecules to impede inflammation, allowing sufferers to be in remission for longer. The prognosis for living with lupus is apparently better than ever before, according to the LFA, whose website boasts: "With close follow-up treatment, 80–90% of people with lupus can expect to live a normal life span." The org does provide caveats: "Medical science has not yet developed a method for curing lupus, and some people do die from the disease . . . [and] for people who have a severe flare-up, there is a greater chance that their lupus may be life-threatening."

~

If she had lived, if her own life span had been normal, I would've had Rita in my life on 9/11. It would've been my sister I called first to share my fears on that day, as I was living in Lower Manhattan and alone with our toddler son, my husband nearly three thousand miles away in Seattle. She would've been terribly concerned about us, just as I would've been terribly concerned about her and her compromised health during the first wave of Covid-19 pandemic cases. Rita would've been vigilantly wearing her mask, washing her hands, and socially isolating and distancing. She would've gotten her vaccines. She might've been affected by the shortage of hydroxychloroquine, a drug that helps control inflammation and lower the risk of lupus flare-ups, and that Rita would've surely been taking.

She would've been the first person I talked to about Michael Jackson's death. She was there, helping me get ready for my first-ever concert to see the Jackson 5 at Detroit's Olympia Stadium back in 1971; she loaned me her gladiator sandals that laced up the legs, to go with my hot pants. We would've watched Whitney Houston's and Aretha Franklin's televised funerals together. Both Luther Vandross dying alone from a stroke and *Soul Train*'s Don Cornelius dying by his own hand (after many years of suffering seizures) would've really saddened her. And because we both thought she reminded us of our mother, I know she would've felt the same sadness I did when Coretta Scott King died from ovarian cancer.

Performing artist Lizzo, plus-size models, and the fat positivity movement would've all been a good thing to Rita. She did not subscribe to fat-shaming and fought against it, especially the idea that fatness equaled unattractiveness. She once said to me, "They always want you to feel *less than* about your weight. But every big woman I know has had a man in her life." Would she have tried Ozempic or Wegovy as weight-loss drugs, given her compromised health? I don't know.

About the deep-sea submersible, Titan, that imploded in 2023, she'd likely be outraged that this über-rich man took his young son with him on such a risky voyage. About Harvard's first Black woman president being forced to resign, I can hear her now: "It's a damn shame how they do us." She would've rooted for Meghan Markle. I think she might've tried CBD and even cannabis to help with her symptoms, and her mental well-being. The overturning of Roe v. Wade would've angered her. I have no idea what she would think of AI, or driverless cars, but I know she liked progress, was forward-thinking. When we were teens, Rita said to me, "We should be able to see a song as well as listen to it," anticipating music videos.

And, oh, how I wish we'd gotten to experience Barack Obama's presidency together! She would've loved the excitement and hope and historic spectacle of his ascension, and she would've loved him, but especially his wife, Michelle. Everything that Michelle came to mean to brown-skinned Black women, Rita would've embraced. She'd have understood Michelle. "Oh, my goodness, we would've been on the phone talking about her for hours!" says Linda. I'm sorry they missed that opportunity. And I'm sorry I missed the chance to have Rita to discuss politics with during the last three contentious presidential elections. She would've had so many thoughts. I know she would've admired Stacey Abrams, voted for Hillary Clinton, and been excited by Kamala Harris's historic presidential run.

I'm pretty certain she purposely would have avoided watching any videos of police killing Black men. She would've cried over George Floyd's murder.

Here's what hurts the most: That Rita never got to see Tyler, her nephew, grow up and launch his career as an actor. That she never even got to meet my daughter, who now attends the college Rita introduced me to, and who reminds me often of her. She would've appreciated Abbie's long, colorful, and hand-designed nails, her fabulous African-style braid extensions, and her love of some sparkle. I'm imagining her at Abbie's Sweet Sixteen party, looking diva fabulous. For a long time, Abbie favored the color blue, as did Rita. That's why I keep her pair of royal-blue spike-heeled sequined pumps on Abbie's bedroom shelf—a talisman evoking the auntie her niece never got to know.

And then there's Tony: I wish she could've witnessed the impressive man our nephew has become, how her influence has landed on his life; how he has a great work ethic as a valued employee for the same company he was working for when he lived with her—Northwest Airlines–cum–Delta Air Lines; how he's in a strong long-term marriage, is an engaged and joyful father of two, and has a deep faith in God; and how he remains a devoted and helpful son to his mother, visiting her almost daily. Rita would be so proud of Tony, and she'd be bragging about him to everyone.

As I write this, I'm sixty-four, the age my mother was when she died. Rita would be sixty-eight. She and I thought we'd grow old together like the Delany sisters, Sadie and Bessie, who lived to be 104 and 109 respectively, and whose lives spawned a book, *Having Our Say*, that Rita owned and loved, as well as a play and TV movie. Or we thought we'd be like our own aunt Bea and aunt Katherine, our father's sisters, who didn't live as long but were deeply close, calling each other not by their first names but rather "sister." I recently heard an episode of the *Death, Sex & Money* podcast in which two sisters, Jessica and Betsy, call themselves "soulmates." They weren't always close, but as middle-aged adults they're each other's last call of the day—even though they live in two different time zones. Rita and I would've been soulmates like that.

It's so strange to me that Rita's friends are all alive and seemingly thriving, when she's not. Her contemporaries are in their late sixties, some entering their seventies. It's as it should be in a society where life expectancy as of 2022 was, despite the pandemic and opioid epidemic and rise in suicides, inching back up to where it had been two decades ago—77.5 years, according to a CDC report. And those with material means are expected to live much longer. Based on a 2016 Harvard University study, the wealthiest men in America can expect to live fifteen years longer than the poorest; for women, the difference between rich and poor lifespans is a decade.

But let's be real. Black people—rich and poor—can expect to live shorter lives. Life expectancy for us as of 2022 was 72.8 years, a lower number than whites in part due to perinatal deaths. For Black men in particular, it's bleaker. When journalist Danyel Smith wrote for the *New York Times Magazine* about hip-hop's fiftieth anniversary, she noted that death was as much its legacy as virtuosic MCs. She purposely stopped counting after her spreadsheet listed sixty-three people, almost all of them Black men, who'd died before their time. "So much of Black journalism is obituary," wrote Smith.

Just thinking about the well-known Black men who've died in their forties and fifties and sixties since 2020, I can easily name twenty—a couple I knew personally; I list them because I believe in the power of naming names: record executive Andre Harrell, fifty-nine, congestive heart failure; actor Andre Braugher, sixty-one, lung cancer; actor Ron Cephas Jones, sixty-six, pulmonary disease; DJ Casper, fifty-eight, cancer; cultural critic Greg Tate, sixty-four, cardiac arrest; author Randall Kenan, fifty-seven, likely from heart-related complications;

actor Lance Reddick, sixty, heart disease; hip-hop artist David Joli-coeur, aka Trugoy the Dove, fifty-four, congestive heart failure; Earth, Wind & Fire drummer Fred White, sixty-seven, undisclosed cause; rapper Coolio, fifty-nine, heart attack from a drug overdose; fashion designer Virgil Abloh, forty-one, cancer; actor Chadwick Boseman, forty-three, colon cancer; controversial YouTube star Kevin Samuels, fifty-three, hypertension; actor Michael K. Williams, fifty-four, drug overdose; DJ/dancer Stephen "tWitch" Boss, forty, suicide; civil rights activist Dexter King, sixty-two, prostate cancer; rapper DMX, fifty, drug-induced heart attack; Broadway dancer Hinton Battle, sixty-seven, undisclosed cause; author Eric Jerome Dickey, fifty-nine, cancer; rapper Biz Markie, fifty-seven, diabetes.

Contrary to myth, drug overdoses on this list are the exception, not the rule. Most died from chronic diseases that we now know are stress-induced, i.e., these men died from weathering. As Dustin J. Seibert wrote in a guest column for HuffPost, "Black men don't need statistics to know that we need a heightened sense of awareness just to exist; that interminable feeling of stress is the connective tissue to many of our other maladies."

Meanwhile, Black women die before our time having to worry not only about police violence and chronic diseases, but also domestic abuse and maternal mortality. To name just four well-known Black women we've lost since 2020, as examples: EMS worker Breonna Taylor, twenty-six, police killing; author bell hooks, sixty-nine, kidney failure; Olympic athlete Tori Bowie, thirty-two, complications from childbirth; restaurateur B. Smith, seventy, early-onset Alzheimer's disease, diagnosed at age sixty-four.

Exactly why did Rita die? Not how, but why?

Author Louis Bury writes in his memoir, *The Way Things Go*, that his sister was diagnosed with severe pediatric lupus erythematosus at age sixteen and told she could expect to live until age thirty. His sister not only lived past that prognosis; she gave birth to twins at age thirty-one, a high-risk medical procedure for any woman but especially a lupus sufferer. His sister also became a heroin addict in her twenties. She survived the lupus, childbirth, and opioid addiction, and is now in her forties. Rita, on the other hand, also was diagnosed accurately and early, remained under the close care of a renowned rheumatologist, took her medications faithfully, adjusted her lifestyle to her condition, never engaged in drug or alcohol use, opted against childbirth, had a strong support system, as well as good health insurance, and still died at age forty-four. Why? Bury's sister is white; Rita was Black. An unfair comparison, perhaps, and maybe my question is unanswerable. But isn't it similar to the question of why tennis star Serena Williams—rich, famous, and physically fit—almost died in childbirth from life-threatening blood clots she had to fight to have taken seriously? Dr. Geronimus reminds us what likely led to those blood clots in the first place: Serena was a pioneering Black woman in a virtually all-white country-club sport treated with hostility and subjected to gendered and racist stereotyping throughout her highly visible career. "Serena was trapped . . . in a body that had been weathered, which trumped all of her other advantages," writes Dr. Geronimus.

Rita weathered her own difficult breach birth at a county hospital; microaggressions by her teachers in elementary school; a near abduction by a man on the street as a teen; an abusive and mentally ill college boyfriend; colleagues cheering the Ku Klux Klan in front of her; a racist home seller who tried to snatch back her house; successive familial losses; two-plus decades of navigating a medical world known to carry myriad racial biases as she fought a chronic disease; and daily movement in her Black-woman skin through an often hostile society. She is one real-life, flesh-and-blood example of what systemic injustice means in actuality—the literal embodiment of it. Those injustices landed hard on Rita's body, and her immune system fought back, yes, attacking itself in the process, and eventually she died, leaving those of us who loved her behind to cope with the massive loss to our own lives. Rita's was one such body among millions of Black bodies that weathered and weathered, and then gave out.

As poet Claudia Rankine has said, "We are a mourning people."

What I have today that I didn't have in 2000 are more resources for my grief, just as there are more resources for lupus survivors. Griefthemed books and podcasts and TV shows and films and even grief counselors abound. Certainly, since the pandemic and the deaths of over one million Americans and counting from Covid-19, people are finding language to speak about collective and personal grief. But back when we were losing loved ones, Rita and I felt like freaks, and after she left me, I felt like a singular freak. I was alone in my grief, often hiding it, carrying it around as a sad secret. That secrecy kept me grieving. I now know it didn't have to be that way. As the psychotherapist Weller explains on Anderson Cooper's podcast, *All There Is*: "Grief, when we're really in it, we are in the commons of the soul. Anytime you walk down the street, any pair of eyes you look into, they will know loss; no one's been excluded from that club. One of the most if not the most common human experience is one of loss. But when you're in a grief-phobic culture, that language, those commons, don't get to be visited."

I was in many ways like the poet Natasha Trethewey, whose mother was killed by her ex-husband when Trethewey was nineteen. During a book talk for the poignant and beautiful memoir she wrote decades later, *Memorial Drive*, Trethewey said: "The grief is something I carry with me. It doesn't go away. It's actually, I think, what made me who I am. I like who I am. Who I am is someone who carries the grief." Trethewey likened the experience to palliative care for an unhealing wound. "You live with it," she said. "That is all I can do with the wound that I have."

That was me for many, many years—living with it. The passage of time has finally helped me understand author Jamie Anderson's insightful description: "Grief is just love with no place to go."

I've poured my love for Rita into this book, grateful that it finally has someplace to go.

~

The good news is that Rita's legacy is cemented. It's glimpsed in the people she had the most influence over: Fannie, because her birth motivated our mother to find a way out of no way, launching her numbers business when Rita was just two years old; me, because of the myriad ways that having her as my sister influenced my life; Elaine, because Rita brought her into our family, where Fannie became her godmother and shaped her life as much as loving Rita did. And perhaps most of all Tony, because he grew up and into a young man under her watch, married a wonderful woman whose style and confidence remind us of Rita, and now brings his compassion and understanding of chronic illness to an extended family member with MS, as well as women on his job who suffer from similar chronic conditions. Add to the list the girlfriends and male friends and boyfriends and others whose lives were changed by knowing Rita—all confirming this fact when I spoke to them.

"I'll never find another friend like Rita," says Linda, a sentiment that all of Rita's close friends echo. Annie told me that talking about Rita, after nearly twenty-five years, has been a form of therapy for her. "It has helped me," she said. "Because we were very close, and after that happened, I really never . . . I put it in the back of my mind . . . but every five or six years, I go through my pictures of us—it puts a smile on my face because she has such a smile on her face—and I'll read her obituary . . . then that's put away for the next five or six years . . . I miss her." I sensed the same from all of Rita's friends, a yearning to finally talk about her. "Rita was just a lovely person," says Lillian. "I always called her queen. Queen Rita."

A life touches so many people; that's its beauty and its mystery. From the moment Rita was born—she whose name means *child of light*—everything changed. Her presence shifted the molecules in the air, and that which didn't exist before came into being. This will never be undone: The people she encountered, the places she found herself, the situations she lent herself to, all help tell the greater story of her life, yes, but also the moment in history she lived. Rita's life mattered, and it keeps mattering.

And my own? I return to the questions I posed to myself when she died: Who am I if I'm no longer someone's sister? Now I know that I will always be Rita's sister. But who am I when the person I defined myself against is gone? I still have no clear answer to that one; the closest I've come is in a letter written by Rainer Maria Rilke, the German lyric poet:

> *The great secret of death, and perhaps its deepest connection with us, is this: that, in taking from us a being we have loved and venerated, death does not wound us without, at the same time, lifting us toward a more perfect understanding of this being and of ourselves.*

Through telling her story, I have loved being in an active, intimate relationship with Rita again. And just as Rilke proclaimed, I do feel I know her better, in her absence. I know myself better too.

As Rita would say, "Girl, that's a win-win."

ACKNOWLEDGMENTS

Writing about a loved one is not new to me, and yet it remains, each time, newly illuminating. This is due in large part to all the people who open their hearts and share their memories, expanding my understanding of a person so dear to me. This time is no exception.

I'm indebted to my sister's community of friends, among them Linda Fegins, Jill Armenteros, Wilma Glenn, Annie and Sam Foster, Lillian Simpson, Jennifer Pierce, Pierre Luttrell, and Elijah Troupe. Thank you all for sharing your love of Rita with me.

Special thanks to the alumni of Fisk University who helped me understand its significance in 1970s Black history. And to Sonny Hill, my Spelman sister, who helped me find Rita's Atlanta University classmates.

This story could not be told without my nephew Tony, my remaining family member who was there for so much of it; I am ever grateful for the memories you and I uniquely share.

Nor could this story be told without my dear cousin-friend Elaine, who had a special relationship with each of my sisters—especially Rita. You bore witness, and your insights have been invaluable. My gratitude is immense.

To my wise and nurturing agent, Anjali Singh, who believed in this book right away: thank you for championing me and my work throughout the years.

I owe much to my brilliant editor, Adenike Olanrewaju, who understood viscerally this tale of two sisters, and who guided me both expertly and gently through the challenging terrain of what turned out to be the toughest book I've ever written.

More thanks to the entire HarperCollins team, including marketing coordinator Zaynah Ahmed, publicity director Stephanie Mendoza, and assistant editor Liz Velez. From the beautiful cover to the copyediting and fact-checking, it takes a village to produce one book, and I'm grateful for my publishing village.

Big hug to my dear friend Eisa Ulen Richardson, for reading early chapters and offering incisive feedback, alongside sister-girl support. And to my friend Linda Villarosa, whose brave reporting and writing on how racism ages and sickens Black people gave me the framework and inspiration to tackle my own family's experience with that injustice.

To my children, Abbie and Tyler: you inspire me, and you remind me anew why I do this in the first place—so you may know your rich familial inheritance.

And to Rob: your unwavering support and steady love provide the perfect antidote to loss, filling me each day with a sense of abundance and possibility.

ABOUT THE AUTHOR

Bʀɪᴅɢᴇᴛᴛ M. Dᴀᴠɪs is the author of the memoir *The World According to Fannie Davis: My Mother's Life in the Detroit Numbers*, a *New York Times* Editors' Choice, named a Best Book of 2019 by *Kirkus Reviews*, and featured as a clue on *Jeopardy!* She is the author of two novels, *Into the Go-Slow* and *Shifting Through Neutral.* She is also the writer/director of the award-winning feature film *Naked Acts*, which was recently rereleased to critical acclaim. She is professor emerita at the City University of New York's Baruch College and the CUNY Graduate Center, where she taught creative, narrative, and film writing. Her essays have appeared in the *New York Times*, the *Washington Post*, and the *Los Angeles Times*, among other publications. A graduate of Spelman College and Columbia Journalism School, she lives in Brooklyn with her family.